Affirmation

Affirmation

The AIDS Odyssey of Dr. Peter

DANIEL GAWTHROP

New Star Books
Vancouver
1994

Cover design by Kris Klaasen/Working Design
Cover photograph by David Gray. Photo used by permission of the CBC *Evening News*, Vancouver
Author photograph by Judson Young
Printed and bound in Canada by Best Gagné Book Manufacturers
1 2 3 4 5   98 97 96 95 94
First printing, June 1994

In recognition of Peter Jepson-Young's desire to provide comfort care for people living with HIV/AIDS,
a portion of the royalties from this book will be to the Dr. Peter AIDS Foundation. This money, in turn,
will go directly to the Dr. Peter Day Centre, a daycare facility for PWAs. For more information write:

The Dr. Peter AIDS Foundation
Box 63635, Capilano P.O.
North Vancouver, B.C. V7P 1S3

Publication of this book is made possible by grants from the Canada Council, the Department of
Heritage Book Publishing Industry Development Program, and the Cultural Services Branch, Province
of British Columbia

New Star Books Ltd.
2504 York Avenue
Vancouver, B.C.
V6K 1E3

Canadian Cataloguing in Publication Data
Gawthrop Daniel, 1963 –
  Affirmation

  Includes index.
  ISBN 0-921586-35-3

  1. Jepson-Young, Peter — Health.   2. AIDS (Disease) — Patients — British Columbia
— Vancouver — Biography. I. Title.
RC607.A26G39 1994   362.1'969792'0092   C94-910280-6

For Paul & Jeanine

Contents

Politics And Power

Crossroads

Foreword

by David Paperny

People in the news business are a cynical bunch. We think we've seen it all. We crank out a lot of stories and peek into a lot of people's lives. And we're always moving on. So I didn't expect much to come from my assignment back in July 1990 to check out some local doctor who had AIDS and wanted to talk about it on TV.

I first met Peter over lunch. I didn't know it at the time, but he had only a bit of vision left, and he was having trouble establishing eye contact with me. I found it disconcerting. In fact, I perceived him as a rather awkward character and we left the restaurant unsure if we would go ahead with any story at all.

But we did. First five daily diaries. Then weekly for over two years. By the end, Dr. Peter was known by Canadians across the country, and his diaries have since been seen around the world. Peter's candour won over the hearts of millions of viewers, and their acceptance of Peter taught both of us an inspiring lesson: that we *are* a compassionate and a tolerant society. So much for newsroom cynicism.

Peter's diaries would probably never have worked if we had planned them out, if we had known exactly where they were heading. Maybe that's one of the good things about our society's dislike of dealing with death; we don't get too caught up in considering how things are going to end. Instead, we try to concentrate on living. That's exactly what Peter did, and that's what viewers found so captivating about his story. Despite the awful attacks that AIDS inflicted on his poor body, Peter always remained a vital, optimistic individual.

I experienced Peter's tremendous *joie de vivre* best when we travelled to Dublin, Ireland, together in the summer of 1991. We were invited to present the AIDS diaries to an international festival of public broadcasters. The responsibility I felt, travelling overseas with a blind person with AIDS, scared me half to death. But Peter was a great travelling companion. In fact, he was the life of the party. The theatre, the pubs, long touring days, even screenings of subtitled foreign films — he was game to do it all. Actually, after a few days I began to rely on him, because Peter had an uncanny sense of direction and I was constantly getting lost.

Over the two years that we worked together, we broadcast 111 diaries, several hours of programming. What viewers saw was a young man become an old man. The fact that we recorded these major changes in Peter's final years on videotape is quite remarkable. Yet despite the intimacy of Peter's diaries, there was so much more that we didn't capture on tape. And I regret that there was little of Peter's life before AIDS that was revealed to me, let alone the camera. Daniel's book helps fill in a lot of the gaps, and when Peter's pre-diary years are laid out as a backdrop, one gets a true sense of the phenomenal development that Peter went through. The book underlines how he was, in many ways, a very normal individual with all the usual imperfections. But he rose to the challenges of AIDS with remarkable inner strength and courage. Daniel's book shows us the three-dimensional person that Peter was, not a media-created hero.

Without the CBC project, Peter's life, and death, would have passed like the lives of too many people with AIDS: much too quickly and unnoticed. So I'd like to emphasize how thankful I am to my colleagues at the Canadian Broadcasting Corporation who gave me the chance to produce the diaries, and supported me as the series went along, in particular the bosses who had the courage and commitment to start and sustain the series: Graham Ritchie, executive producer at the time, senior producer Sue Ridout, and director of CBC British Columbia, John Kennedy. Thanks to editor Paul Hartley and reporter Ian Gill. And thanks most of all to the newsroom cameramen: John Collins, Rick Warren, Pat Bell, Ted Huang, Mike Johnston, Doug Kerr, Doug MacCormack, Rick Smalley, and Al Stewart, and Don Waterston. They all treated Peter with great respect and made him feel comfortable in front of their cameras. They formed a rare bond with Peter (perhaps it was their mutual obsession with telling dirty jokes).

When CBC International Sales hunted for a larger audience for Peter's story, they discovered a powerful and empathetic gang at Home Box Office in New York City. Led by Sheila Nevins, HBO introduced Peter to America. From there, the world was his oyster.

I would like to thank Peter's parents, Bob and Shirley Young, and his sister Nancy and her family. Over time they grew to trust me and eventually welcomed me into their homes. Thanks also to Peter's devoted partner, Andy Hiscox, who put up with me and endless intrusions by what must have seemed like a surveillance camera. And I am forever grateful to Dr. Jay Wortman, who had the foresight to bring Peter to the CBC.

On a personal note, thanks to my wife Audrey Mehler and our adorable kids. Many of my happiest memories of Peter are of the times that he'd drop by the house to play with the family. I'll never forget the time the kids patiently escorted him down our steep hill to the beach. Then, in their excitement, they completely forgot that he was blind and demanded that he play tag with them. Of course he was "it." And of course Peter played along.

My parents taught me the importance of taking on social responsibilities. I credit them for my becoming a TV current affairs producer. It's a great privilege. I have always been sensitive to the tremendous potential of television to educate, to inspire, to influence. The medium rarely lives up to its potential, but the AIDS Diary project did, in large part because of its simplicity, because Peter spoke *directly* into the camera and directly into people's hearts. It's no wonder that he made this the most fulfilling project of my career.

Reality as I know it was completely overturned on February 9, 1994, the day that *The Broadcast Tapes of Dr. Peter* was nominated for an Oscar. What began as a small news story was now going to the Academy Awards! Unbelievable. How Peter would have relished that fantastic weekend. I was so proud to carry his story into that international spotlight. And although Peter had died almost a year and a half earlier, it felt as if he was right by my side, sharing in the glory of our project. We didn't win the Oscar, and I didn't get the chance to thank Peter — in style! Fortunately I have that chance now. Thank you, Peter, for adding so much to my life.

Affirmation

Introduction

S eptember 10, 1990
Halfway into the CBC's six o'clock television newscast,
anchorman Kevin Evans returned from a commercial break
and introduced a new feature to that evening's 150,000 viewers in
British Columbia. "AIDS is an extraordinary disease," he explained,
"and that's why this week on the evening news we're venturing into
something extraordinary: an AIDS Diary — an intimately close
portrait of life with AIDS."

The newscast cut to the story and viewers caught their first glimpse
of a handsome young man in a pale blue dress shirt, walking slowly
toward the camera on a busy sidewalk. "Hi, I'm Peter," he began ear-
nestly. "I'm a physician here in Vancouver, and I'm going to be talking to you about a disease which is affecting more and more
Canadians on a daily basis. The disease is AIDS." He continued his
monologue as he approached the camera:

Perhaps you feel there's enough information about AIDS in the popular
press, but we're going to be approaching this from a different point of view.
I'm going to be introducing you to someone with AIDS to help provide a
name, a face, and an identity to this disease. The person I'm going to

introduce you to is myself. I'm a doctor, but I'm also a patient — a patient with AIDS.

In the second and final scene, Peter was shown sitting in a quiet living room. He spoke in a softer, confiding tone, with his dark brown eyes focussed on the camera.

My personal experience with AIDS began in September of 1986. As a gay male I knew I was a member of a high risk group but there was no indication that anything was wrong. Toward the end of that month, over about a ten-day period, I went from being able to climb the Lions[1] to not being able to climb a flight of stairs without stopping for breath. On September the 28th I was admitted to St. Paul's emergency with a very high fever and very short of breath. I spent the worst night of my life hoping against hope the pneumonia was a common virus, but unfortunately the next morning the diagnosis was made. It was AIDS.

I spent the following three weeks in hospital. In spite of being on a hundred percent oxygen, even lying flat in bed, I wasn't able to breathe enough to provide my body with what it needed. So it was necessary for me to be on a mechanical ventilator for four days. Following this I developed a toxicity from the medication which caused my heart to beat in a very irregular fashion and eventually led to several cardiac arrests.

During those three weeks, I had a lot of time to think, and a lot of things to think about. At one point, out of a morbid sense of curiosity, I spoke to my G.P. about what my life expectancy might be. I seem to recall the numbers nine to fourteen months. All I could think about was that wasn't going to be me. From the first day I was in hospital I was determined to beat this thing. It's now four years later. I've had the four best years of my life and I want a lot more.

With those two opening scenes on the CBC *Evening News*, Peter Jepson-Young made the final transition from private individual to "Dr. Peter," public citizen. It was just one step in his long journey with AIDS, but for Peter the decision to go on television was cathartic. The diaries offered him a chance to continue practising medicine despite AIDS-related blindness, by educating the public; to criticize homophobic prejudice wherever it occurred; and to share aspects of his private life he had never even discussed with his parents.

The success of the five-part TV news series in September 1990 exceeded even Peter's expectations. By the end of that first week, in which he addressed five different topics related to his illness, the diaries had proved so popular that senior producers decided to continue the series on a weekly basis. Over the next two years, Dr. Peter became a household name in British Columbia.

I n recent years it has become a sore point with many people living with AIDS (PWAs) that their illness is described in the media with the militaristic imagery of war. While it is true that they often face a series of battles — the "combat" with opportunistic infections, the "fight" against societal and governmental indifference and homophobia — many PWAs have sought alternatives to the perpetual confrontation that such jargon implies. Peter was one of those who found an alternative.

From the earliest episodes of AIDS Diary, he demonstrated that his life with this illness was more of an odyssey than a war. He used AIDS as an opportunity to take full control of his life and set priorities in a way he would never have done when healthy. Within weeks of his diagnosis with AIDS in the fall of 1986, Peter was back at work practising medicine, travelling, meeting new people, and pursuing the parties and excitement he had enjoyed before he got sick. Life didn't end with AIDS — it just got more interesting. Even as a doctor, his illness was an occasion for constant discovery about the body and its immune system. AIDS, said Peter on many occasions, "is fascinating medicine."

Even in 1990, as Kaposi's sarcoma crept into his life and another infection robbed him of his vision, Peter was able to redirect the focus of his life. With the onset of blindness, he was forced to face the fact that his time on earth was limited, and that his relationships with friends, lovers, and his family would have to become much more meaningful. When he went public with his illness, Peter's critics in the gay community saw his failure to discuss his earlier hedonism as a fundamental flaw in the diaries. But Peter never let this bother him. Instead of using "AIDS Diary" as a personal confessional in which to atone for previous sins, he simply repeated the common sense arguments he had often ignored while he was healthy; by arguing that viewers should "Do as I say, not as I have done," he hoped to ensure that none of them would make the same mistakes he had.

By the fall of 1990, the act of coming out of the closet was easier for the average North American gay man than it had been in more repressive times. In Vancouver, the existence of gay media, the visibility of *queer culture* during the Gay Games in August, the variety of social groups designed for gay men and lesbians, and the presence of openly gay politicians, were only a few examples of the changing climate. For a man about to come out on television, the timing couldn't have been better.

But it hadn't been easy for Peter Jepson-Young. The product of a comfortable, middle-class upbringing, he had grown up to believe that doors would always open for him and that by applying his skills to the world of medicine he would achieve an honoured place in society. The fact that he was gay never caused any problems while he was healthy; for most of his life he was able to enjoy the benefits of both straight and gay worlds without having to make an issue of his sexuality. It was only when AIDS forced him to come out to his parents that Peter felt the shame and fear that so many gay men experience simply because of who they are. By deciding to go public four years later — against the wishes of Bob and Shirley Young — he was able to confront that shame and rise above it, once and for all.

The AIDS odyssey of Peter Jepson-Young is a story of affirmation: for his parents, Bob and Shirley Young, who never really knew a significant part of their son's life until he became ill; for Andy Hiscox, Peter's partner, who was finally able to come to terms with being gay through Peter's influence; for the viewers of AIDS Diary — particularly those suffering from terminal illness — who found inspiration and courage from Peter's message; for people with AIDS and the gay community, who saw in Peter an out-of-the-closet media symbol who could represent their experience with pride and confidence; and, most importantly, for Peter himself. The overwhelming response to the diaries by family, friends and strangers he met on the street was the final affirmation in this odyssey.

In the information overload of today's television market, with its hundreds of satellite channels and flavour-of-the-month celebrities, Dr. Peter was truly an anomaly: he managed to hold a local news audience for more than two years simply by describing himself, his illness, and the world he lived in. After his death, the meditation Peter had conceived in the spring of 1987 as a way to maintain his strength and courage remained an inspiring message of hope for thousands of viewers — gay or straight, healthy or ill:

> *I accept and absorb all the strength of the earth to keep my body hard and strong;*
> *I accept and absorb all the energy of the sun to keep my mind sharp and bright;*
> *I accept and absorb all the life force of the ocean to cleanse my body and bring*
>   *me life;*
> *I accept and absorb all the power of the wind to cleanse my spirit and bring*
>   *me strength of purpose;*
> *I accept and absorb all the mystery of the heavens, for I am a part of the*
>   *vast unknown.*
> *I believe God to be all these elements, and the force that unites them.*
> *And from these elements I have come and to these elements I shall return.*
> *But the energy that is me will not be lost.*

The impact of this diary — and many of the other 110 that Peter produced with the CBC's David Paperny — will be felt for years to come. Indeed, after broadcasts in several countries around the world, an Oscar nomination, and plans for the first AIDS daycare centre in Canada, it's clear that Peter's prediction — "the energy that is me will not be lost" — was a prophetic understatement.

Here then, is how it all came together.

PART 1

Coming Out Alive

I didn't feel that I could discuss my sexuality with my parents. For me, I'd been gay since I could remember. It was just a normal part of who I was, but I knew they wouldn't take that view. They're a product of their generation and the cultural stereotypes they'd been fed. It was a large part of my life I couldn't share with them and I got to be 29 years old and had never dated women, and they didn't ask. I wouldn't have lied if they had. Unfortunately, they found out in the worst way possible when I became sick with AIDS.

AIDS DIARY 3, SEPTEMBER 12, 1990

1

Small Town Boy

July 8, 1986

The man by the water fountain was, as Peter used to say, a "total hunkosaurus." Tall, tanned, and muscular, he wore thin, high-cut track shorts and smiled at Peter when he caught sight of him riding by on his bicycle. The two were alone in a secluded area of an Ottawa park near Peter's apartment on a hot summer afternoon. Peter returned the man's smile, got off his bike, and walked toward him.

As he approached, the stranger knelt down beside the fountain, picked up a steel manhole cover with one hand, and began doing arm curls with it. Still smiling, he continued his iron-pumping while stepping backwards, and Peter followed. When the man put down the cover and raised his eyebrow, as if to challenge his new acquaintance, Peter was intrigued. "No problem," he grinned, picking up the cover and lifting it over his head with both hands.

But the lid was heavier than expected. He had to move backwards to regain his balance. Suddenly he stepped directly in the manhole and fell into the opening, still clutching the steel cover. With his right elbow landing on the edge of the hole, he had no time to prevent the cover from falling on his arm, fracturing it in two places. Horrified, the stranger helped Peter to his feet and escorted him to Ottawa General Hospital before fleeing the scene, never to be heard from again.

The accident couldn't have happened at a worse time. Peter Jepson-Young, 29, had just completed his one-year internship as a doctor in training at Ottawa General and was due to return home to North Vancouver at the end of the month to begin his career in medicine. Instead he found himself a patient in an elaborate operation; the skin and muscle of his arm had to be pierced, the bone exposed and then put into place and joined by clamps that held a plate across the damaged bone. "How the hell did this happen?" one of the doctors asked him. Peter thought for a moment and told him exactly what he would tell his parents when he phoned them later that day: "I took a bad turn and fell off my ten-speed."

If not for the fact his accident was the result of a bungled gay seduction, Peter would have loved to tell his parents what really happened that day. His spectacular crash was so typically clumsy that they might actually have laughed, despite the severity of the injury. It would have reminded them of so many other incidents in his life where Peter, trying to show off, had fallen flat on his face. There was the swimming class when he was eleven, where he grabbed a ring buoy off a lifeguard's chair and ran toward the pool, not realizing the buoy rope was tied to the chair. With his mother and dozens of others watching, Peter was yanked off his feet when the rope ran out. Then there were his early days in medical school, when his eagerness to learn resulted in some red-faced moments. The first time he put on his surgical gown he was baffled by a foot cover he kept trying to fit on his head; the first time he tried to measure someone's blood pressure, he placed the cuff inside out. Like many an amateur bodybuilder who prided himself on his physique, Peter's occasional clumsiness was a source of amusement in the family.

But this time it wasn't funny. The truth would have destroyed the illusion he had so carefully cultivated to satisfy his parents: that he was an orthodox heterosexual man who would continue the family name by getting married and having children. Despite his own private acceptance of his sexuality, his parents' expectation of grandchildren hung over him, silent but persistent, like the 1853 portrait of William

Jepson-Young they displayed proudly in the hallway of their North Vancouver home.

T he portrait of William shows a handsome 23-year-old Irish immigrant shortly after his arrival in the colonies. William Jepson, the illegitimate son of a minister's daughter, was adopted by a wealthy woman named Young. He emigrated to Canada as William Jepson-Young and became a building contractor in Toronto. His descendants gradually moved west and by the time Robert Douglas Young was born in Vancouver early in the Depression, the family no longer used "Jepson" in its surname.

Bob and Shirley Young's only son, Peter William, was born at Royal Columbian Hospital in New Westminster on June 8, 1957, two years after his sister Nancy. Bob, an accountant for the Royal Bank of Canada, was transferred often and the family seldom remained in one community for very long. By 1964 the Youngs had lived in Port Moody, east Vancouver, and then Burnaby, before moving to the small Vancouver Island town of Duncan. Two years later Bob, now a branch manager, was transferred to Nanaimo where the family remained until 1972.

Peter Young was a happy, middle-class child of the sixties. A favourite of his teachers and popular in the neighbourhood, he was constantly occupied with swimming, camping, and other outdoor activities. He was an expressive boy with a vivid imagination, and Shirley Young recognized this when she gave her eight-year-old son a personal diary for Christmas in 1965. Just as she had always taught her children the importance of positive thinking, Shirley constantly reminded Peter that keeping a diary was a valuable outlet for self-expression.

Aside from recording the Cub meetings, marbles, and Monopoly games that most boys his age took part in, the diary reveals that eight-year-old Peter had a critic's eye for Rogers and Hammerstein musicals (*The Sound of Music* was "better than *Mary Poppins*," he wrote, following a screening in Victoria), a natural sensitivity toward other boys ("When we were coming home from school Greg began to feel sick so

I fanned him with my fan"), and a sense of curiosity that would later serve him well as a doctor ("Michel and I looked through his mirgrisope [sic]. We looked at hair, spit, rain, dust, a scab and blood").

He also displayed a creative if somewhat mischievous sense of humour. One winter, Shirley was leaving the house with Peter's sister Nancy when the two were startled by a rat running across the breezeway connecting the house to the garage. When they returned later in the day, Shirley parked the car outside and told Nancy to run to the front door. As they approached the house, a huge cloud of snow flew up in front of them and a large, furry blob ran across the lawn. Their shrieks of fright were soon replaced by the sound of laughter from Peter's upstairs bedroom; the young prankster had wired together two old tennis balls, buried them in the snow, and yanked on them with fishing line from inside his window. On his parents' sixteenth wedding anniversary, Peter set an arbutus tree on fire after stuffing firecrackers into its holes in an attempt to blow up the woodbugs. Bob Young had to rush out in his suit and tie to chop away at the tree and extinguish the fire. Peter, terrified by what he had done, was not punished.

There were few signs of overt sexual expression at this time, but Peter was already aware of his attraction to other boys, and much later in his life friends and relatives would speculate about his innocent episodes of cross dressing. There was the time he wore his mother's high heel shoes and wrapped a towel around his head while he played on the swing set, pretending he was Princess Grace of Monaco, and the times he dug into his sister's clothes trunk to try on a dress. Once it was a beaded, 1920s flapper-style dress draped over his body, another time a 1950s prom gown. As an adult, Peter amused his friends by telling how he was trying on the prom gown in the bathroom when his mother knocked on the door. Hurriedly taking off the dress and stuffing it under his housecoat, Peter came out of the bathroom as if nothing had happened — but the dress disappeared from Nancy's closet shortly afterward.

It wasn't until he was fourteen, when Shirley gave him a copy of the standard self-help manual for sixties adolescents, *Ann Landers Talks to Teenagers About Sex*, that Peter realized the full implications of his feelings. He took the book to his bedroom, flipping through it randomly until he came to a chapter that immediately caught his eye: "What You Should Know about Homosexuality."

By the early 1990s Ms Landers was known for her compassionate, tolerant view of gays and lesbians, but the well-known advice columnist was promoting quite a different view in 1963. Instead of encouraging her teenaged correspondents to love themselves for who they were, she supported the claim of "experts" that "homosexuality is a gross symptom of a serious psychological disturbance" which "can lead to profound anxiety, possible blackmail and long-term entanglements with undesirable people." Landers concluded that "most homosexuals yearn to be normal. Twisted and sick, through no fault of their own, they want desperately to be 'like everyone else'." The only salvation for anyone gay was to seek professional help in one's early teens and be "willing and able (and financially capable) to undertake intensive therapy." The final section read:

> To those of you who are reading this chapter for information only, and not because you are seeking help yourselves ... be thankful you have been blessed with healthy, normal sex drives, and remember that not all boys and girls are so fortunate. When you encounter people who are "different," remember that their lives are probably unbelievably difficult and that they are faced with the enormous problem of adjustment. You can help by understanding.[1]

Shirley Young, who had never heard the word "homosexual" before she got married, had no idea the topic would be covered in Ann Landers' book. She thought she was being helpful and understanding by giving it to her son; like most parents of gay teens during the late 1960s, she had no way of knowing how hurtful such information could be. To an impressionable young Peter, however, Ann Landers' book was a devastating indictment of his most intimate thoughts; either stay in the closet, she advised, or suffer the rightful damnation of society at large. If he didn't want to be shunned, Peter would have to bury his true feelings or project an image that gave no direct clue of his sexuality. Like other gay teens, he would struggle through high school with this issue.

Sitting in front of the television set with his father, Peter would wince whenever the flamboyant performer Liberace came on screen. "You see that, Peter?" Bob would say, "that's what *those* people are like." He didn't explain what he meant by "those people," but Peter got the message. Loud and clear.

Shortly after Peter began Grade 10 in the fall of 1972, the family left Nanaimo and moved back to the Lower Mainland where Peter attended Delbrook High School in North Vancouver. At sixteen he was working as a lifeguard at the Vancouver Aquatic Centre — a popular meeting place for gay men — when he was invited out to lunch one day by a man who swam frequently at the pool. Peter politely declined. Later, when he described the incident to his straight high school buddy, Al Dodimead, he made it sound as though he was disgusted by the offer.

"I think this guy was really interested in me," he told his friend.

"That's pretty gross, Peter. So what did you do?"

"Oh, I just left."

Secretly, however, Peter hoped that any number of other, more desirable men would make a similar offer. Years later Dodimead suggested that Peter may have been trying to gauge his reaction, to see if it was safe to come out of the closet.

Like many gay teens, Peter found it frustrating to be surrounded by so many straight boys openly indulging and rejoicing in their own sexuality without the slightest fear of ostracism. The pursuit of sex among straight males was encouraged from an early age. But Peter received no encouragement in movies, television, or advertising for his gay feelings. Instead, his efforts to appear like one of the boys were doomed to failure.

In the spring of 1975, just before his high-school graduation, he joined Dodimead and three older straight friends on a trip to Hawaii, the object of which was to meet women. Peter's admission that he was a virgin only made his good-natured friends encourage him all the more. "If you can't meet a lady in Hawaii," they joked, "you're not going to meet one at all." One day at their resort in Maui, a group of attractive young women showed up at their building to use the swimming pool. Peter had gone down to the pool by himself moments earlier, and was already in the water when the women arrived wearing nothing but bathrobes. The women took off their robes, jumped into the pool, and rubbed their bodies against his.

"Yeah? Yeah? So what happened?!" his friends asked when he recounted the incident.

"Well," Peter sighed, "I got so excited I had to leave."

Peter continued to engage in macho bonding rituals even after he had entered the University of British Columbia as an undergraduate and had gone to New York's Fire Island for gay holiday retreats. After several rounds of beer at UBC one night, he and his high school buddies were driving back to North Vancouver when they decided to take a detour along Davie Street in the heart of Vancouver's downtown gay district. By this time Peter had picked up several men in the neighbourhood's bars, but on this night, in the presence of his straight friends, he couldn't resist shouting a few catcalls as the car passed a female prostitute on the street. Dodimead later recalled that Peter's drunken machismo was the most exaggerated of the group.

It wasn't long before Peter discovered the positive gay role model he was seeking. David Kopay, a ten-year professional in the National Football League, had come out of the closet in the fall of 1975 after reading a Washington *Post* series on homosexuality in sport that included several interviews with closeted athletes. Shortly after his autobiography was published in 1977, he appeared on all the big U.S. talk shows to promote his message of self-esteem and tolerance. Kopay's suggestion that being a masculine, robust athlete with conservative values somehow made him a better homosexual because he was more acceptable to the mainstream makes for fairly dated reading in the 1990s. But his message in 1977 was exactly the confidence boost that Peter required. Finally, being gay didn't mean having to be like Liberace.[2]

❖

August 1977

John McKinstry, a rugged 30-year-old landscaper in jeans and a T-shirt, was sitting at a table in front of the dance floor at the Gandydancer when a young man came up to him, grabbed him by the shirt, and said "Let's dance!" He turned around to face the stranger, a handsome jock of about twenty. With deep brown eyes and a charming smile, he was irresistible. "Sure!" McKinstry replied.

Within ten minutes on the dance floor, Peter Young was asking McKinstry to take him home. Overwhelmed but intrigued by his aggressive manner, McKinstry consented. Driving his mother's Volkswagen closely behind, Peter followed the older man to his home about three miles south of the downtown nightclub.

Peter was going into his third year of a cell biology major at UBC, he told McKinstry. He had just started going out to gay clubs and didn't know anybody. Would John introduce him to people? McKinstry was charmed by Peter's eagerness and his ambition to be a doctor. And Peter didn't seem to have the hangups about sex and intimacy that so many other men had. "Tell me what your fantasies are. I want to know what you're into," he told an aroused McKinstry.

After several hot hours of frolicking, Peter got up to get dressed. "Why don't you spend the night?" McKinstry asked.

"I can't," said Peter. "I've got to get back home. I live with my parents."

"So ... ?"

"They don't know I'm gay. I don't want them to ask questions."

When he finally did spend the night with McKinstry, on New Year's Eve, he woke up the next morning to call Shirley and let his mother know he was alright. "Sssshhh!" he told his lover, lying beside him. "Don't make a sound." For the year that the two men saw each other, Peter would finish making love by getting into his car and taking the half-hour drive back to Bob and Shirley Young's home in North Vancouver. Peter invited John to his parents' home several times while they were away, but Bob and Shirley never did meet their son's first boyfriend.

While John gave Peter a guiding hand into the gay community, Peter offered his older boyfriend a playful sense of spontaneity. In the middle of a winter afternoon it wasn't unusual for Peter to end his day at UBC by dropping in on McKinstry and coaxing him away for Spanish coffees at a downtown lounge. He was generous, and was constantly buying John clothes — once he returned from a trip with three button-down, Oxford cloth shirts.

It was an affectionate, though in many ways unrealistic, partnership. McKinstry was an experienced, working-class gay man who was out of the closet and wanted to settle down with one lover; Peter was a young, inexperienced yuppie who was eager to explore. He often asked John to introduce him to his friends, but would then be surprised by John's indignation when he ended up in bed with one of them. When confronted about it he would shrug with his bashful, charming grin, "I'm still with you, aren't I?"

Before long Peter was well acquainted with dozens of men in the Vancouver gay scene, and his presence was felt immediately when he walked into a bar. "Who the hell does *she* think she is?" one skeptic remarked at the Gandy, within earshot of McKinstry. Watching his young boyfriend cruise his way through the crowded nightclub, McKinstry was resigned to the inevitable "He's hot, that's who he is." Peter carried himself with the certainty of someone who always gets what he wants. He was attractive, well-dressed, and charming — a combination which attracted more men than it repelled. He fit right in at the Gandy, a place referred to in the gay community as a "stand and model" (S&M) bar.

"When I was your age and was first coming out," McKinstry told Peter, knowing what he was about to unleash, "I went to San Francisco. That was in '67. You should go there now — it would really open your eyes."

That was an understatement. By spring 1978 the Castro district was enjoying its well-established reputation as the Shangri-La of North American gay culture. With hundreds of men in the streets holding hands and kissing openly, dozens of bars and pubs with a strictly gay clientele, parties and festivals galore, and America's first openly gay elected official, Harvey Milk, making big changes at City Hall, San Francisco was the place to be. The halcyon days of the Castro would be interrupted by Milk's assassination the following November, and by the discovery of an epidemic three years later, but for a young suburban undergrad from Canada with active hormones and a great body, the sense of freedom inspired by San Francisco that spring was intoxicating. Peter had finally found the perfect travel destination, the equivalent of Hawaii for his straight pals. Like so many others in the 1970s — gay and straight — Peter joined the sexual revolution that had swept North America since the late sixties.

But his relationship with McKinstry was doomed. Within a year of their first meeting the older man had grown tired of Peter's sexual wandering. When he walked into the Gandy one night and found his boyfriend with his arm around another man, McKinstry decided to break off the relationship.

At the same time, Bob and Shirley Young were optimistic about their son's chances for marriage; they saw Peter spending more time with Flora Hillier, a glamourous, cosmopolitan young woman he had met in a painting class at UBC. Like many of the women who were drawn to him, Flora didn't know Peter was gay when they first met. One night after class she drove him to his Twelfth Avenue home. "Oh, look at that beautiful apartment," she said, peering into a window. "A couple of poofters must live in there." Peter smiled bashfully as he got out of the car. It was his apartment.

Although Peter's interest in Flora was limited to her intellectual savvy and taste for elegant dining, fashion, and sports cars, Bob and Shirley never completely abandoned hope that the two might get married. Whenever Flora drove up in her MG for a visit, they would invite her for dinner, holidays, or other family occasions. But Peter always nudged her from behind while telling them, "No, no, she can't make it."

According to Flora it was Bob and Shirley Young's traditional ways that prevented them from realizing their own son might be gay. "Bob and Shirl had middle-class assumptions about everything, including sex," Flora explained later. "You know — 'Michelangelo couldn't possibly have been gay, he was Italian.' " Flora, for her part, was mystified by Bob and Shirley's denial. She wondered what made them assume she was romantically involved with Peter, since she had spoken often of her boyfriends and had even introduced one of them when Bob and Shirley met her on a ferry one day.

Peter did occasionally drop hints about his sexuality, but nothing short of a complete admission would have got through to his parents. "You know Dad, I haven't met *any* girl that I could marry," he told Bob.

"Don't worry," Bob replied, laughing. "You're only twenty."

When Peter brought home a flamboyant young man for dinner one night, Bob was too distracted by the man's obnoxious manners and seeming contempt for the Youngs' lifestyle to realize what Peter may have had in common with him. "Jesus, Peter," Bob sighed, once the man had left. "Don't bring anyone like that home again. You want people to think you're like him — you know, a homosexual?"

"Come on, Dad," Peter responded, flustered. "Don't be ridiculous."[3]

M ay 26, 1981
He later described it as the happiest day of his life: after his third attempt in more than a year, Peter was finally accepted by the School of Medicine at UBC. He thought he had made it after his second attempt when he had a strong interview and the exam didn't seem as difficult as he had expected. But when the results came back and he had scored a single mark below first class, he was devastated. Now he was set for life.

One decision from his undergrad days caused a significant change in Peter's image once he began medical school. When he received his Bachelor of Science in the spring of 1979, his diploma read Peter William Jepson Young, his full name as he had dutifully signed it when he first registered at UBC. Now, as a medical student, Peter saw the advantages in using this full name. First, it would quickly distinguish him from other doctors named "Young" in the phone book. Secondly, there was something Ivy League about the Anglo-Saxon, double-barrelled "Jepson-Young" that made people notice. A third, more subtle reason may be that Peter was declaring his independence from Bob and Shirley Young, becoming the person he wanted to be instead of following his parents' expectation. "Peter was just reinventing himself," Flora Hillier reasoned. "People do it all the time."

Although it took him three tries to get into medical school, once he got there he seemed more relaxed than most of his classmates. While roommates Debbie Money and Stacey Elliot tore their hair out over assignments, Peter would turn on the classical music and brew a cup of tea while he worked. His studying was helped by a near-photographic memory that allowed him far greater recall than many classmates who crammed for days before an exam. During one exercise, Peter was asked to identify a peculiar-looking organ. The professor was stunned when he correctly identified it as a cat's heart — that particular organ had only shown up once among hundreds of presentations.

He was also one of the more enthusiastic participants in the medical school skit nights organized by Elliot. From "The First Annual Cadaver Awards" of 1981-82, to the final skit night in 1985, Peter displayed a consistently campy sense of humour, and a talent for mimicking famous comedians and televangelists. It was clear he knew how to play to an audience.

In fourth year, Peter divided his time between studies and practicum work at St. Paul's Hospital. Located in the heart of the West End, home of Vancouver's most visible gay population, St. Paul's was the only health care facility in British Columbia that was willing and able to treat people with AIDS when the first patients began dying in 1983. The sheer volume of cases soon led to the establishment of an AIDS care team, a group of doctors which met regularly to discuss treatment issues and coordinate various levels of care for AIDS patients. By 1985 St. Paul's was considered one of the leading hospitals for AIDS care in Canada.

One of the patients, among the first to be diagnosed in Vancouver, was an ex-boyfriend of Peter's. Given the hospital's reputation, Peter was surprised and disturbed by some of the stories his friend told about his treatment at St. Paul's. Nurses were still wearing gowns, gloves, and masks before entering his room. When his food arrived, the tray and everything on it was disposable, and the people who brought the food would leave it outside the door to be taken in by a nurse or a visitor. Peter couldn't help wondering how he would respond to such treatment if he had AIDS himself.

Peter's internship at Ottawa General Hospital was a rude awakening to the realities of medical practice. A 100-hour work week was not unusual, as he explained to his mother in a letter. "I spent this past weekend completely at the hospital — from 9:00 a.m. Sat to 5:00 p.m. Monday. I thought I'd go nuts," Peter wrote Shirley on January 22, 1986. "Saturday was a zoo as I was on call for the surgical floor and emergency. Emerg was nuts — saw everything from a collapsed lung from a toboganning accident to some guy who lost a finger in a squash game. At 3:00 a.m. I was busy trying to put a drunken biker's hand in a splint (he'd cut two tendons in his R hand cause he'd fallen with a beer bottle ...) He was busy trying to grab every nurse that went by — and the floor paged me to tell me that two patients upstairs were experiencing severe chest pain and shortness of breath. There I am with wet casting plaster all over me and the biker has the gall to ask why everyone is so bitchy." Despite this hectic pace, Peter excelled in all twelve categories of his emergency rotation and in one report was said to show "excellent skills and judgment far exceeding level of training."

On April 5 Shirley described how saddened she was by news that Peter was "feeling less than perfect emotionally." She suggested that perhaps this was because he was "in a state of uncertainty job-wise" and that, "having no real focus," he should set some goals for himself. Shirley never hesitated to act on her son's behalf. A week later she had contacted the British Columbia College of Physicians and Surgeons, and asked the College to put Peter on a mailing list to receive information about B.C. locums. Working a locum, a short-term contract for another doctor's practice, is a common way for new doctors to start out. Shirley's efforts cleared the way for Peter to return to the west coast that summer.

During his year in Ottawa, Shirley wrote her son almost weekly to offer encouragement and support. She also reminded him how much she was looking forward to his life after school. "So many people I work with (really nice, kind people) have had so much heartache with their children," she wrote on January 23. "There is no such thing as the 'perfect' parent — most just do their best but not everyone is as fortunate as we have been. You and Nancy have made our lives meaningful and now that we see the grandchildren that really is the frosting on the cake. Hopefully one day we will see your progeny and they will be just as wonderful (more wonderful is not possible!)."

Peter's letters to Shirley were filled with descriptions of his hospital work and anecdotes about life in Ottawa. But he said very little about his extracurricular life. What he could not mention in his letters was that he was seeing a twenty-year-old Lebanese man named Sam whom he had met through a group of gay friends that he also didn't mention. The only person in his family who met Sam was Nancy, who came out to visit Peter at the end of March.

Peter and Nancy had always been close. Nancy was his confidante, but Peter had told her nothing about his feelings for other men. One weekend night in 1979 Nancy was watching the late TV news when she saw a group of men dressed in drag outside a screening of *The Rocky Horror Picture Show*, a film that was fast becoming a cult classic. One of the men being interviewed, wearing a wig and a black garter, was Peter. "He phoned me up to tell me he was on the news and I said, 'I *thought* I recognized you'," she recalled. She wondered then if Peter was giving clues about his sexuality, but only now, as they spoke in his Ottawa apartment, did Peter finally tell her that he was gay.

"He was so happy that he told me, it was like this big relief," she recalled. "And then in one breath he said, 'And I want you to meet the person I'm in a relationship with, his name's Sam and he's coming over for dinner tomorrow.' I lay there in a flood of emotion, pissed off, wondering why he'd waited so long to tell me." Nancy said nothing to Bob and Shirley when she returned to the west coast, but she was so angry she decided she didn't want Peter to be the guardian of her children any more.

"I was really hurt. I was livid. It was like 'I'm gonna punish you for this.' I said, 'I don't know if I want you to be the guardian.' Then I got it off my chest and sat down with Lionel [Nancy's husband] and told him [Peter was gay] and he said, 'I don't have a problem with anything you're telling me.' " But Nancy still felt betrayed by her brother. "You know, 'I trusted you, we had a friendship.' It was really immature." Eventually she got over her anger and changed her mind about the guardianship issue.

While Peter had difficulty coming out to his family, he had no hesitation being explicit with medical school colleagues. The UBC School of Medicine yearbook for his graduating year includes a picture of a suntanned Peter during a summer 1984 medical residency in New York. The photo, taken at Fire Island, the popular gay resort, shows Peter lying on an inflatable mattress in a swimming pool with his hand on another man's mattress. The caption reads: "Peter Jepson-Young finds family practice on Fire Island much more comfortable on his back." On another occasion he shocked fellow students by bringing his male lover to a weekend retreat for couples. By the time he finished medical school and left for his internship in Ottawa it seemed as though everyone knew Peter was gay except for his family.

L ate in the spring, several of Peter's friends began to notice that his habit of clearing his throat had gradually developed into a persistent cough. Patrick Johnston, who had met Peter through a mutual friend who was interning at Ottawa General, pointed it out to Peter but he refused to have it checked. "A number of us suspected that he was sick because for about six months before Peter went back to Vancouver, he had this awful cough. And it just never went away," recalled Johnston. "I remember asking about it once, and he said 'Oh, it's just this allergy.' But I mean, I'd had allergies and I wondered what effect it had. And I remember talking to friends and speculating whether Peter was in fact sick. [But] he's a doctor and we didn't want to second guess. But I do remember one time I tried to probe a bit, because this [cough] had gone on for four months at this point. But he just kind of shut down right away and he clearly didn't want to get into it."

On July 29, 1986, Peter met his parents at Vancouver International Airport with his right arm in a cast. He would never tell Bob and Shirley what really happened on the day he broke his arm in Ottawa, but the incident soon became insignificant. Within two months he would have a far more serious health problem to contend with.

2

Lifting the Mask

Once Peter was back in Vancouver, the cast on his arm was replaced and his orthopedic surgeon instructed him not to practise medicine or participate in sports for six to eight weeks. But Peter, ever his own worst patient, ignored this advice and carried through with a locum on Saltspring Island and began another in Victoria.

On Labour Day weekend he was windsurfing with medical school chum Richard Bebb on Elk Lake, just outside Victoria. At one point, when he had sailed far into the middle of the lake, his mast fell down after a turn and he bent down to lift it up again. Lifting a windsurfing sail is a strenuous task under normal circumstances, but Peter became exhausted very quickly and was gasping for breath. Eventually an elderly man in a power boat came by and asked if he needed help. Embarrassed, Peter agreed to be dragged back to shore.

By this point, Peter was beginning to worry. Strongly suspecting that his symptoms might be HIV-related, he finally decided to have some tests done. His own doctor, Michael Maynard, had repeatedly advised him to be tested long before he went to Ottawa, but Peter had refused. How could he face Maynard now if it turned out he had AIDS?

After the long weekend trip to Elk Lake, Peter arranged an appointment with a new doctor, Phil Sestak, one of the few AIDS specialists in the city. In recent weeks, he told Sestak at their first appointment, his cough had grown progressively worse, and the fatigue he had noticed on Elk Lake kept returning whenever he exerted himself. He also told Sestak he was suffering from a bad, recurring sinus infection. Eleven days later Sestak noticed a rash that turned out to be an allergic reaction to the antibiotics he had prescribed for the sinus infection. Peter also had several enlarged lymph nodes that Sestak had noticed with many of his patients who were HIV positive. The tests he had taken at Peter's previous appointment showed immunological changes that were consistent with the presence of the human immunodeficiency virus, but these did not confirm a positive diagnosis.

The next day, September 16, Peter and his North Vancouver high school chum Marc Tessler went on a hiking trip to the Lions, a mountain peak north of Vancouver. Photos taken that day show Peter posing triumphantly at the top of the trail. There isn't a trace of concern on his face. But within days of the trip his fatigue intensified, his breathing grew heavier, and he began to feel fever symptoms.

Meanwhile, Sestak consulted Michael Maynard, who three years earlier had encouraged Peter to participate in a lymphadenopathy study of gay men with enlarged lymph nodes. Vancouver dermatologist Dr. Alastair MacLeod had been disturbed by the number of gay male patients complaining of swollen lymph nodes, diarrhea, and weight loss, and with a group of St. Paul's Hospital physicians began a confidential lymphadenopathy study of 770 gay men in B.C.[1] The study was to determine whether the enlarged lymph nodes were indicative of some form of cancer, or whether they were related to a mysterious new disease called Gay Related Immune Deficiency (GRID) which had been spreading in the last two years. Peter reluctantly agreed to enter the survey on the advice of Maynard, but because he never willingly tested for HIV, no physician actually had access to information about his status.

Sestak and Maynard did have access to other immunological studies that were done at the time, such as white blood cell count, Immunoglobulin A and Immunoglobulin G levels, and other studies that examined various aspects of each patient's immune system. By comparing Peter's recent test results with those tracked down from 1983 and 1984, Sestak and Maynard were able to determine the likelihood that Peter was HIV positive. In fact, Peter's Immunoglobulin A had also been rising in February 1984. "I think we should talk about HIV," Sestak concluded.

On September 22, Sestak told Peter he had seen the results of the test and that one of the immunological studies had changed quite significantly; the results were compatible with, but not necessarily indicative of, HIV-positive status. 1986 was still early enough in the epidemic that the exact significance of such an immunological marker was not fully understood without further tests. But Sestak wasn't about to lie to Peter. While he may have tended to guard this kind of information from other patients, Peter's status as a fellow doctor made it impossible to avoid giving him the facts in the clearest possible terms. Peter was anxious but he tried to be optimistic. "Well, I guess we'll see how it goes, won't we?"

On September 24, Peter told Sestak he was suffering from fevers and muscle pains. Sestak asked if it could have been a reaction to a vaccine for hepatitis he'd given him earlier, but Peter said he had previously received two shots for hepatitis and had never had a reaction. Now, for the first time, he began to fear for his life. At first he had thought his symptoms meant nothing more than a common flu, but within ten days of a hiking trip in which he had managed to scale the Lions, the robust 29-year-old could barely walk up a staircase without losing his breath.

Despite the pain he was feeling, Peter took a trip to Nanaimo to see Nancy and her family. By Saturday September 27, his coughing was so bad he was feeling nauseous. He could no longer hide his condition from Nancy. "If I find it any harder to breathe," he told her, "I want you to take me to the hospital." Nancy was confused; her brother looked healthy but he seemed badly out of shape, and there was something ominous in his words. Later the next day he returned to Vancouver after spending most of the morning lying on the couch.

"He called when he came back from the Island, and he came to see us. He really didn't look well and he was coughing very badly," Shirley Young recalled later. "And I was concerned because he had taken a hepatitis B booster shot the week before. We said, 'Well, let us know after you talk to the doctor.' " Peter called Phil Sestak to say he'd had five days of very high fevers and an irritating cough that had made him vomit the day before.

Sestak arranged to meet him at his office immediately. When Peter arrived just after 6, he was short of breath and completely distressed. His vital signs were elevated, he had a yeast infection in his mouth, an increased respiratory rate, and high fever. Sestak called emergency at St. Paul's Hospital and advised that Peter be admitted immediately as he was experiencing symptoms consistent with viral pneumonia. Peter walked the half block from Sestak's office to St. Paul's, where he was admitted just after 7 p.m. The specialist who'd be treating him, Dr. Lindsay Lawson, was stunned when she saw Peter, the same bright young medical student who had worked beside her while doing practicums for UBC medical school. As she prepared for Peter's bronchoscopy test, it occurred to her that this was the first time St. Paul's Hospital staff had dealt with a colleague who appeared to have AIDS.

Peter phoned Bob and Shirley. "I'm in the hospital," he said. "And the doctor's going to keep me in overnight because he suspects I've got pneumonia." He would later refer to it as the worst night of his life; only two months after finishing the final preparation for his medical career, he was now a patient in St. Paul's emergency, waiting to find out if he had AIDS. Looking at the worried faces of his colleagues, Peter knew what the answer would be. As a student he had seen dozens of men check into this ward with similar symptoms. Some of them never left. When Lawson finished the examination, Peter was taken to his room where he spent the night gasping for breath.

The next morning, September 29, the test result showed a positive reading for *Pneumocystis carinii* pneumonia (PCP), an AIDS-related infection of the lungs. After Lawson ordered daily infusions of the antibiotic pentamidine to reverse the pneumonia, Phil Sestak walked into Peter's room and gave him the bad news. Peter immediately called Shirley at work. "I'd like to see you and Dad," he said, his voice breaking. Shirley was worried by Peter's tone. She knew he had spent the night under observation for fever symptoms but had no idea how

serious it was. Now he sounded weaker than the previous day —
more urgent, emotional. When his parents arrived late in the afternoon, Sestak greeted them at the door.

"What's the matter, Phil? What's wrong with Peter?" they asked.

"He's very sick with a kind of pneumonia. It's quite a bad disease
and he's very ill. He's really going to need your support."

Bob and Shirley were confused. Sestak wasn't telling them everything. He escorted them into Peter's room and they saw their son lying
in bed, hooked up to an intravenous tube, his face pale and sweating.
"Peter, dear," Shirley pleaded. "What is it, honey? What's happening
to you?"

"It's *Pneumocystis carinii* pneumonia," he said, struggling for his
breath. "PCP is a rare and bizarre form of pneumonia that only certain illnesses allow ... " He looked up at Sestak, and then back at his
parents.

"Oh God, mom," he said. "I've got AIDS ... and I'm gay." While
his parents stood speechless before his bed, he shook his head and
began to sob, "I'm so ashamed." After all those years of silence, to
dump the news of his sexuality on his parents this way was more than
he could bear.

Bob stepped up to his bedside and hugged him. "Now listen son,
you don't have to be ashamed of anything."

But the Youngs were stunned. Although AIDS had been in the
news for at least five years, they had never thought about it very
much. AIDS was something that happened to other people's families,
not theirs. The realization their son could be dying pushed aside all
thoughts of sexuality for the moment, and Shirley tried to be optimistic. "He's going to survive, he's going to do well," she told Sestak
hopefully. "He'll just be in the hospital for a few days, this isn't so terrible. The prognosis for AIDS patients is getting better and better.
He'll do okay, won't he?"

Later that week, after visiting Peter at St. Paul's, Shirley stopped by
the AIDS Vancouver office seeking support. She seated herself across
from a counsellor and immediately broke into tears. "My son's in the
hospital with AIDS," she cried, "and he's a physician."

The woman stopped her suddenly. "Oh, that explains it."

"Pardon me?" Shirley froze.

"That explains why a reporter stopped me this morning and said 'Is it true that there's a doctor in St. Paul's with AIDS?'"

Shirley Young's depression immediately turned into panic. She could read the headlines already; Peter's promising career in medicine would be over before it had even begun. As it turned out, Peter's identity was never revealed to the press.

It was two days after Peter told them he had AIDS before Bob phoned Nancy to tell her of her brother's condition.

"Is Lionel there?" Bob asked when he called on Wednesday evening.

"No, he's at work. Why?"

"Your brother's not doing well."

"What do you mean?" Nancy was puzzled. She knew her father was holding back information.

"He's ill and he's in the hospital."

"We'll be on the first ferry tomorrow morning."

Nancy slept poorly that night, knowing it could be AIDS. The next morning, however, Shirley called and told her not to bother coming until Friday after work — Peter had pneumonia, but he was doing better. It wasn't until Nancy and Lionel arrived at Bob and Shirley's home on Friday that her parents finally broke the news that Peter had AIDS. But Nancy could feel no emotion, not even when she walked into her brother's hospital room and he burst into tears.

"You don't have to worry about the kids," he told her. "They can't get it from hugging or kissing me."

"I know, Peter. I know."

Only when Phil Sestak took her aside to explain the effects of AIDS-related pneumonia did the reality finally sink in. "I didn't stop crying for eleven days," she said later.

❖

octors were not optimistic about Peter's chances for survival. When Phil Sestak saw him on September 30, Peter was in worse condition than the previous day and his breathing rate had increased drastically with the reduction of air space in his lungs. The X-ray did not look promising. Usually the slide turns out black in the lung area to denote air space, but Peter's X-ray was a complete "white-out" — there was virtually no room for air to enter either lung, they were too crammed with PCP organisms. "We really didn't expect him to make it," Sestak said later. "You couldn't see very much air space left. It was quite dramatic, he had an extremely aggressive form of PCP." Sestak had Peter moved into the intensive care unit (ICU) for an overnight stay on October 1.

Pneumocystis carinii, one of the most common AIDS infections, occurs most often in people whose immune systems have completely blown apart, and usually patients have had some advance warning that they are at risk for PCP — either the AIDS diagnosis has already been made or they have been treated for other infections before the PCP occurs. What was extraordinary about Peter's case was that he was able to survive such advanced symptoms even though he'd had no treatment before he was hospitalized. For the first three weeks of October he hovered near death as his body reacted violently to a host of previously untreated infections. During this time he was like a human yo-yo, transferred from one acute care unit to the next as doctors responded to his latest crises.

On October 4 Peter was rushed back to the ICU, struggling for breath. "We got into the elevator and the oxygen tank ran out," he recalled in an interview, "so we had to go from the eighth floor of one wing into another wing in the hospital and it was a pretty panicky trip." When he arrived at ICU, tubes were inserted in his throat and nose — an experience he later described as "like having a garden hose shoved in your nose, you can feel cartilage cracking and stuff like that."[2]

He spent the next four days on a ventilator. Alert and oriented for some of this time, Peter slipped in and out of consciousness. When he suddenly developed multiple infections of bacterial pneumonia, doctors added two intravenous antibiotics — cefazolin and gentamicin — to the pentamidine treatment. He was transferred back to the ward October 10 with improving lung function and respiration, but three days later suffered a violent response to his medication — a rare, malignant arrhythmia of the heart called *torsa des points* — and had to be rushed to the coronary care unit.[3]

After suffering two cardiac arrests, Peter was put on an isoproterenol drip to keep his heart rate at about 80 to 85 beats a minute. For the next few days his progress was monitored carefully, and his doctors — recognizing that the cardiac arrests may have been caused by a reaction to the pentamidine — changed his medication to co-trimoxazole for the remainder of his antibiotic course.

"He was a bit confused, a bit inappropriate — having a hard time holding his bowels," recalled Sestak. "Those kinds of things were difficult for him because they were so undignified and people saw how sick he was and that his bodily functions were breaking down." During this time it was the support of his family and friends that kept him going. Nancy, who wasn't working at the time, split shifts with Bob, Shirley, and Ross Murray, often spending the entire night in the hospital room by his side. Marc Tessler, Flora Hillier, and others came by regularly.

At the same time, Peter was finding ways to lift *their* spirits. He managed to maintain his sense of humour and release much of the tension surrounding him. Flora Hillier recalled an incident in which Peter — hooked up to so many tubes and machines that he couldn't talk — shared a joke with a friend by writing on a pad. "They were writing on a piece of paper, like the Woody Allen joke when he's robbing the bank in *Take the Money and Run* — 'I have a gub' instead of 'I have a gun.' Marc [Tessler] wrote this and Peter started to laugh, setting off all the machines and getting the nurses to come running in to stabilize his heart rhythms. Peter laughed his guts out about a lot of things."

On October 17 he was transferred back to the ward from the coronary care unit, and weaned off the isoproterenol. He no longer required oxygen by mask and was able to get up out of bed and walk on his own. On October 20, less than three weeks after he nearly died in hospital, he was released with instructions to consult Sestak for follow up. He was to take regular doses of co-trimoxazole, the anti-viral drug acyclovir, and the anti-depressant amitriptyline. As much as possible, Peter maintained ultimate control of his own treatment. "We would offer suggestions or tell him what we recommended," Phil Sestak recalled, "and he invariably went along with our recommendations. He was really in control, particularly when he wanted us to step back."

Peter still had difficulty walking when he first came home to his parents' house. He was very weak and for the first couple of weeks suffered from night sweats that required a change of bedsheets once or twice a night. But he was determined to get back into shape. "I remember Bob and I sitting one evening watching TV with him and there was a ski show on," Shirley recalled, "And he said 'That's my goal, it's to get strong enough and well enough to ski again,' which of course he did."

As Peter regained his strength and his health became less of a day-to-day concern, Bob and Shirley began to consider the implications of their son's gayness. In the several weeks after Peter was released from hospital, Shirley would ask him why he had made the "choice" to be gay; Peter always told her he was born that way. Shirley wondered why she was having so much trouble believing this until she read a book called *Mother, I Have Something to Tell You*. It said that a parent's discovery of her child's homosexuality is often accompanied by a grieving process, and that parents need to mourn the loss of their hopes and dreams for the child. "He would have been such a super dad," Shirley said later. "You wouldn't be normal if you didn't have these hopes and dreams — especially if it's your only son."

They were concerned about how Peter's gayness could affect them socially. They didn't want anyone to know they had a gay son, much less one who had AIDS. They were also afraid that if their son's illness was common knowledge, he wouldn't be able to practise medicine. So they decided to tell only Peter's godparents, Don and Sally Gilchrist.

Shirley's fear and shame about her son's illness was exacerbated by outside events. She was haunted by news stories of the Ray family in Georgia, who had their house burned down when it was reported that three of their hemophiliac boys had AIDS. Shirley thought, "If neighbours can do this in the case of innocent children, how are they going to react to a young man who's gay and is a physician? They might say that's all the more reason why he shouldn't have come in contact with the virus." The fact that she still used the word "innocent" to distinguish the Ray children from her own son revealed much about Shirley's continuing struggle with the gay issue, but her shame was hard to abandon when she was constantly surrounded by the homophobia of friends and colleagues. Shortly after Peter was released from hospital, Shirley was on a coffee break at the North Vancouver school board office when someone said that AIDS was God's revenge for unacceptable lifestyles. (She could hardly have been reassured by another person's argument: "Well, hardly. I don't think God would let children and elderly people and others have the illness as well if it was strictly a revenge illness.") Even the most well-intentioned people didn't bother keeping informed about AIDS unless they knew someone who had it. If they didn't have to know, why bother learning? Shortly after Liberace's death from AIDS in 1987, one of Shirley's friends who didn't know Peter was ill commented on how tragic it was that the showman "did so much good in the world, and yet he'll only be remembered because he died of AIDS?" Horrified, Shirley believed her friend was right and that AIDS would be all that people remembered about her own son.

Bob, meanwhile, remained silent. He could never hear "fag" jokes the same way again, but the revelation of his son's gayness was like a rude joke in itself. He was trying to come to grips with it — one night after leaving the hospital he had told his wife, "You know what's sad is that he doesn't have a partner to help him through this" — but both he and Shirley thought Peter was pushing the sexuality issue a bit far. They found the gold-banded earring Peter bought shortly after leaving hospital a rather excessive political statement, a "flaunting" of his sexuality. The earring, according to Bob, immediately signified gayness. Regular guys from North Vancouver simply didn't wear them unless they were part of a psychedelic rock band. He didn't understand why Peter should be so visible about his sexuality.

Peter didn't think it was excessive at all. Following the initial shame and emotional breakdown he experienced when he came out to his parents in the hospital, he began to reexamine his entire life, particularly the way he separated his gay friends from straight ones. After he left hospital he was determined to spend time only with those people who truly cared about him, gay or straight.

But Peter was barely home long enough to discuss any of these issues with his parents. Within three weeks of leaving hospital he was working again. On November 1, Phil Sestak called from a vacation in Kansas to say he had broken his ankle and fallen ill. He would be off work for November, December, and part of January and would need someone to take up his practice. Peter, anxious to get back to work, immediately offered to fill in. From the second week of November he alternated with another doctor and worked two or three days a week to cover Phil's patient load until he recovered. It was the least he could do for the man who had helped him through his own crisis the previous month.

On November 7 he wrote to a friend in New York, describing his illness in full detail and apologizing for an earlier phone call.

> Generally the whole ordeal left me weak as a chicken. It's over with now, I am home. I'm eating like a pig, exercising, etc. I start on an AZT trial in two weeks. I'm going to beat this thing. I will be around when the cure is discovered. My family and friends have provided such unbelievable love and support and strength I can't even begin to describe. I go back to work next Wednesday to replace the GP who took such good care of me.
>
> Corky, I'm sorry I lied to you over the phone about everything being okay. I just found it too much of a bomb to drop when the other person has no time to compose themselves ...

On December 18, 1986, Peter became one of the first four people with AIDS in British Columbia to begin treatments of azidothymidine, known most commonly by its trade name, AZT. He was eligible to go on the drug at no cost to himself because he had been diagnosed with an opportunistic infection in the last six months (ironically, his failure to be tested in 1985 had turned out to be a stroke of good fortune.) Because he was a doctor, Peter was much more aware of the latest developments in treatment than the average patient, and his membership in the medical fraternity guaranteed that his name would be near the top of the list for new drugs. AZT initially proved useful in maintaining his strength and appetite as he returned to a semi-regular pace of work.

Sestak, returning to Vancouver from his trip to Kansas, was stunned by Peter's progress. "Most people take about six to eight weeks to recover [from PCP] enough to go back to work, but Peter was back at full-time work less than three weeks later," Sestak recalled. "His pneumonia was very severe, and it's rare that you see someone who has to be ventilated recover so quickly. It was remarkable."

Within three months of leaving hospital, Peter had gained 25 pounds and was exercising regularly. His doctors had given him nine to fourteen months to live, but for the next three years he would have few health problems.

3

Freelancing

For Peter, the opportunity to continue working after his AIDS diagnosis meant a lot more than simply repaying a debt to his doctor; it was a chance to regain his health, his confidence, and the lifestyle he had enjoyed before his illness. Working for Phil Sestak meant he would have daily contact with other people who were HIV positive or had AIDS — an ideal situation both for doctor and patient as he could empathize more than the average MD, even if he didn't inform patients of his own HIV status. The situation was "like a gift," Shirley Young explained later, "because he was going into a practice where the nurse knew of his situation [and] a lot of patients were HIV positive. And it happened to coincide with AZT becoming available." In January 1987, Peter moved out on his own again, into an apartment downtown.

Shortly after his work for Sestak ended, Peter learned that he had secured a locum at a practice in Mill Bay on southern Vancouver Island. His joy was cut short, however, when one of the doctors at the practice learned that Peter had AIDS and decided to withdraw the locum. Phil Sestak wrote to Dr. Robert Chan, the chairperson of the B.C. Medical Association's (BCMA) Infectious Disease Committee, requesting that the committee meet to formulate guidelines for physicians with HIV/

AIDS who still wished to work. "I am hopeful these guidelines will follow those recently released by the [Centers for Disease Control] in Atlanta, in which it is suggested that there be no limitation of work so long as the individual in question is mentally fit, and does not expose his or her bodily fluids to others," Sestak wrote in a letter to Chan on May 29, 1987.[1]

At the same time, Peter's efforts to find meaningful employment in his home province were being stymied by provincial politics. B.C.'s Social Credit government had recently set a cap on the number of new physicians who could set up practices in the province. (This was justified as a cost-cutting measure designed to reduce the number of medical services billed for.) Once the cap was set there were only three choices available to young doctors who had completed family training: do locums, leave British Columbia, or buy a practice at enormous expense and thereby acquire the necessary billing number.

For Peter the choices were not so clear. Since he had already been denied work in Mill Bay because he had AIDS, he would have to be even more careful about what information he disclosed to colleagues. For the next year and a half he worked without a billing number, taking on locums in the Lower Mainland and Ontario, and briefly attempted to settle in New York City. There were many times during this period that Peter was more worried about his future career prospects than his health. Indeed, in a daily journal he kept from spring 1987 till spring 1989, the word "AIDS" is not mentioned once, and only once does Peter make any direct reference to his condition.

After a trip to Europe with his best friend, Ross Murray, Peter spent an easy summer working in the geriatric division of Vancouver's Riverview Hospital, a mental care facility, for $342 per day (it was "like a paid holiday," Peter wrote in his journal). In early fall he decided to spend several weeks in New York, visiting friends and looking for work. At the end of October he fell in love with an interior designer he met at a New York nightclub, returned home briefly and introduced his boyfriend to everyone, then packed all his belongings and moved to New York on November 20. His plan was to write some qualifying medical exams that would allow him to practise in the U.S. He couldn't write them until June, so he spent the winter working at odd jobs, doing apartment renovations, and running errands for neighbours.

By late February 1988 his relationship had ended, so he returned to southwestern Ontario where he secured a locum in a small rural community near Lake Huron. This full-time job as an emergency doctor exposed Peter to the harder edge of life: among his patients were a 26-year-old prostitute from Toronto who got into a drunken argument at a convenience store and trashed the place before drinking a bottle of windshield wiper fluid in the police cruiser, and a 60-year-old schizophrenic who arrived in a coma after drinking a bottle of wood alcohol. "We're gearing up for another long weekend which for us means absolute craziness," he wrote his godparents Don and Sally Gilchrist in the summer. "I'm going to make up a sign that says 'sunburns don't constitute an emergency' and put it in our waiting room. Oh well, if they're willing to wait 3 hours — sometimes I have trouble dealing with people who are that stupid. I am my father's son."

Peter finally received some good news in August 1988 when the restriction on billing numbers was lifted by the B.C. courts. He could now practise anywhere in B.C.

He had good reason to return home: the Ontario physician who had hired him for a locum was suing him for what he claimed were unpaid royalties. Most agreements signed between a locum doctor and a physician with a practice call for a 60-40 split in which the locum doctor pays 40 percent of his income from the practice to the other doctor. But Peter, without considering the agreement carefully, signed a contract that called for him to pay the other doctor an additional portion for any work that he obtained outside of his practice.

"Peter didn't have a lot of street smarts," Bob Young said later. "He signed over a large chunk of his income to that doctor. He was silly to sign it in the first place, but he needed the work so he signed it." The Ontario doctor felt he was perfectly within his rights to sue for unpaid royalties, but Peter believed he should not have to pay royalties for work he had found outside of that doctor's practice. The doctor was so relentless in this action over the next four years that Phil Sestak was eventually compelled to write a letter to Peter's Ontario attorney — Flora Hillier's sister — saying his patient "could tolerate neither the physical nor the mental rigor of a court appearance."[2] (The doctor continued his pursuit of royalties even after Peter's death, sending letters to the CBC.)

On September 20 Peter returned home and did locums in Chilliwack and Vancouver. The following spring he was hired for a provincial government job with Government Employee Health Services that was to start in June. While waiting for that job to begin, Peter spent two months at Simon Fraser University in Vancouver, working as a physician for students and staff.

He also began to acquire furnishings, mostly from auctions, for his apartment on Fourteenth and Fir, in the south Granville district of Vancouver. Peter had baronial tastes bordering on kitsch that gay men jokingly refer to as "baroque faggot." He had a penchant for oak furniture and tapestries that one wouldn't normally expect in a man in his early 30s, and he loved to brag about the great bargains he found at the local auctions. "I was after a light fixture, Bruce was after a rug and Joan wanted this pair of chairs that have since been described as the Gabor sisters, Eva and Zsa Zsa," he wrote Flora Hillier, describing one outing.

> The kindest thing that can be said about my taste is that it is eclectic. The light fixture I bought is a ceiling one for my dining room. I really couldn't have imagined anything more perfect. It's empire style; a bronze bowl with brass appliques of Romanesque style women holding garlands above their heads. The bottom is a brass acorn, the top a brass ring from which protrudes eight eagles heads on top of which sit stylized flame cups originally to hold candles but had been wired. The whole thing is suspended from the ceiling by four chains made to look like grape vines. I dewired the eagles heads to again hold candles and rewired the bowl to hold two light bulbs so that there's a choice.[3]

In March 1989, Peter decided on a whim to take a trip on his own to Costa Rica. It was a dull excursion, not like his trips with friends. During the two-week holiday he discovered a small, dark bump on his scrotum — a thrombotic vein that had grown considerably in size since it was last examined by Sestak. There was another bump just above it and he suspected the two might be manifestations of Kaposi's sarcoma. Although KS, an AIDS-related skin cancer, had proven to be one of the most debilitating HIV infections, Peter responded with a dose of creative visualization. "I don't know what to say," Peter wrote in his journal. "There's no reason to get in a stew about this but at the same time positive action is necessary. I'm visualizing the bumps being attacked by proton flashes of energy from the sun from the outside and from my body. They are surrounded by antagonistic, electrical-like flashes that are killing them cell-by-cell."[4]

When he returned to Vancouver and a biopsy of the lumps showed KS, Peter's wish to have them surgically removed prompted a friendly argument with Phil Sestak. Peter's response was comical: "Phil thought I wanted them to be removed for cosmetic reasons — really! If someone else was interested in pawing around down there this might be a consideration but presently it's not," he wrote. "I told Phil that this was, after all, my scrotum and therefore rather elephantic at the best of times. He felt it was better to leave them alone as any trauma may induce greater growth after removal. So I live with them and try to get them to go away on my own."[5]

Sestak recalled, "He wanted [the KS lesions] removed because the two of them he thought were primary cancers, and he wanted to prevent the spread of primary cancers. I, on the other hand, thought he understood that KS is a bit unique in the sense that because of immunodeficiency, lesions arise in one or several different places at varying times and it really has nothing to do with it spreading from one location to another. And I didn't realize that Peter didn't understand that until he asked me this question. I thought well, the reason we actually remove them from other parts of the body is cosmetic reasons." It was Peter's first AIDS-related infection since the fall of 1986 so he wasn't about to press the panic button. Positive thinking continued to be the rule.

Ma*y 9, 1989*
The death of Vancouver AIDS activist Kevin Brown after a much-publicized four-year illness was noted by the press with glowing obituaries unprecedented in most mainstream local AIDS reportage. Brown, one of three founders of the Vancouver Persons With AIDS Coalition (later B.C. PWA Society), was one of the first people with AIDS in British Columbia to go public with his illness and lobby governments on behalf of other PWAs. The former teacher and one-time employee of the UBC Bookstore "was the face of AIDS," said the Vancouver *Sun* obituary. "He made the city of Vancouver and the country care about the individuals AIDS affected." The article cited Brown's efforts in lobbying the provincial and federal governments for increased support, research, and drugs for PWAs. He was instrumental in getting AZT released for study in B.C. in late 1986 — just in time for Peter Jepson-Young to use it. The *Sun* also quoted one of Brown's doctors on his contribution. "At a time when very few people had the courage to do it, he had the guts to go public," said Lindsay Lawson, who a year later would witness the transformation of another one of her patients, Peter Jepson-Young, into the next "human face" of AIDS. By that time, Kevin Brown's name would be erased from the general public's memory — to be replaced by a physician known only as "Dr. Peter."

4

Going Blind

On June 12, 1989, Peter began his job as an occupational health doctor for the provincial Government Employee Health Services. While his main duty was to assess government employees in Vancouver to see if they were fit to return to work, he was also called upon to provide counselling for alcohol abuse, job stress, and other areas. Tim McNamara, a correctional officer at Oakalla Prison during this period, recalled that Peter was "extremely pleasant to deal with."

> He was one of the few people that actually listened to us. He was a gentle listener — he could really make you feel comfortable, like you were the only person in the room ... He was just very good at allowing you to express your emotions, and for a lot of heterosexual men that's really difficult. I think that gay men have a great deal to give in diffusing the anger and a lot of the odd frustrations that are in heterosexual men, and Peter did that. He saved my marriage.

Peter's health remained stable for the first three months on his new job. The only problem was an occasional minor skin problem that required Sestak to remove a number of small viral growths from his face. By September, however, Peter began to notice a blurriness in the vision of his right eye. A visit to Sestak on September 7 revealed "significant peripheral changes" in his vision. The next day he saw his ophthalmologist, Dr. Peter Nash, who confirmed that he had developed cytomegalovirus retinitis. Cytomegalovirus, a herpes virus that has been linked to cancer, is another common AIDS infection. CMV retinitis refers to the strain of CMV that disintegrates the retina, causing blindness.

By September 28 the vision in Peter's right eye was becoming increasingly clouded. Nash reassured him that his left eye was doing well, but by December 6 he agreed that Peter should begin daily intravenous treatments of ganciclovir. On December 13 he began the treatment but soon experienced problems combining this drug with AZT. Certain components of his white blood cell count began falling, placing Peter at increased risk for bacterial infections. Sestak and Peter decreased his AZT rate and put him on a new drug to boost his white blood cells.

Throughout the fall of 1989, Peter suffered several bouts of panic, anxiety, and depression for which he saw a psychiatrist. He was also experiencing occasional irregular heart rhythms which Sestak thought might be related to the earlier heart problem from his 1986 hospital stay, and they decided to conduct regular electrocardiograms.

He was beginning to feel the weight of the many losses piling up around him: failing eyesight, the spread of KS lesions, and dwindling sex drive. ("I tried to drum up a fantasy the other day, and all I got was a test pattern," he wrote to Flora Hillier on October 31.) He was frustrated by the sexual and emotional barriers he was encountering with his new lover, Brian. At the same time, he was being subpoenaed by an Ontario court in the case of the doctor who was suing him.

"Generally, until I was diagnosed [with] CMV retinitis, my overall mood and psychological state was pretty healthy," he recalled in a later interview. "I tried to maintain as well as I could a sense of optimism — and perhaps a denial, if you want, that AIDS is a fatal illness. You know, 'Nothing in medicine is a hundred percent.' And I was determined from the time I was in hospital that, if need be, I was going to be that one who wasn't going to succumb.'"[1] In early 1990, however, he felt his optimism was running out.

On January 22 he received a further loss; he got a phone call telling him that Sam — his Lebanese boyfriend from Ottawa — had just died of AIDS after developing PCP, the same illness that had struck Peter three years earlier. He was despondent and "acutely stressed out" when he spoke to Phil Sestak the following day.

In February, he had a plastic intravenous dome inserted under the skin in his chest to make it easier to hook him up for intravenous treatment. He continued to suffer bouts of fever, problems with the peripheral vision in his left eye, and by March he was looking increasingly ill — aging, with his hair falling out. "He's having great emotional difficulty," Sestak wrote in his log book on March 15. On April 3, still suffering from fevers, Peter learned that the dome was infected with bacterial organisms and had to be removed. Two days later he was admitted to hospital for the first time in three-and-a-half years with fevers, severe joint pain, and a bad rash. Doctors inserted a second dome which would remain for the rest of his life.

"I think Peter's finally losing the battle," Sestak told Bob and Shirley over the phone. "I'd like to promise that he has another year, but I don't think that'll happen." After his six-day hospital stay, Peter was tired and disoriented, not responding well to medication, and on April 13 he was back in hospital with serious dehydration. Along with a blood transfusion, he received intravenous fluids.

His release from hospital that month was less triumphant than his return to practice in 1986. His supervisor at Government Employee Health Services told Peter he was withdrawing his contract extension because Peter had shown a patient his own chart. The supervisor argued that this was a breach of policy, but Peter disagreed. The real reason for his dismissal, he suggested later, was that his boss had long suspected he had AIDS. Their working relationship had gradually worsened until his contract was terminated. He launched a complaint with the B.C. Council of Human Rights, charging that he was discriminated against because he had AIDS. Peter demanded compensation for the amount he would have earned had his contract been extended, and a lengthy campaign for disability benefits ensued. (The case was finally settled weeks before Peter's death when B.C. Health Minister Elizabeth Cull intervened on his behalf, awarding his estate an undisclosed amount of money.)

Peter's frustration with this fight, along with his anxiety about the loss of his vision, was dominating his life at the very moment that gay Vancouver was preparing for a giant celebration. In the last days of July, while Peter dealt quietly with his own personal struggles, staff and volunteers for Celebration 90 were in the final weeks of a countdown to the third Gay Games and Cultural Festival — the Vancouver gay and lesbian community's biggest showcase of pride since the beginning of the AIDS epidemic. With an estimated 20,000 participants and visitors from around the globe, the Gay Games were the world's largest international sporting and cultural event in 1990. The event featured a full schedule of competitive sports, artistic exhibitions, and performances — not to mention all-night carousing and a carnival atmosphere that promised to transform the downtown core into a seven-day Mardi Gras of gay and lesbian culture. During this period, straight people in the West End would have the experience of being the sexual minority.

For Peter the celebration was a mixed blessing. He had eagerly anticipated his involvement as a volunteer doctor for the swimming events, but now he could barely see the pylons he was stepping into at poolside. He had always been a people watcher; now he had to endure the most stunning assortment of gay athletes with hardly any vision remaining in his one good eye. At the Vancouver Aquatic Centre — where he had worked as a lifeguard in his teens — he attended to swimmers and offered assistance wherever he could, but with only part of his left eye still useful, Peter found the frantic pace around him disorienting and he was continually bumping into people. Some of his friends thought he was being stubborn and unrealistic about his involvement. "I didn't think he should be working at all," Michael Simmonds said later. "He wasn't really a danger to anyone else, but he was bumping into things and could have hurt himself."

Unlike his friends on the English Bay water polo team, who looked forward to winning medals, Peter had nothing to prepare for but total blindness. Over the summer he had an instructor from the Canadian National Institute for the Blind train him with lessons in mobility. CNIB instructor Jay Wadsworth was amazed by Peter's power of retention. In twenty years of mobility training he had never seen a newly blind person adapt so quickly. Simply by pacing his apartment, Peter was able to memorize every corner of his home to the point that he could pick out any compact disc in his music collection. On August 23, the same day he received his white cane, he managed to put together a three-course meal for his father's birthday despite having only a speck of vision left. He amused Bob and Shirley by telling them how, while out shopping for the food, he had stopped by his favourite delicatessen on Granville Street and struggled to open the door — only to learn from a passing woman that the store had gone out of business.

This period was often frustrating. One night after having dinner at Ross Murray's apartment a few blocks away from his own, Peter insisted on walking home alone even though it was dark. When he banged his head on a signpost and began bleeding profusely, he spun around and — having lost his sense of direction — began violently thrashing the sign with his cane. The same thing happened while he was with Jay Wadsworth and accidentally wrapped himself around a newspaper box on Granville Street. He spent several minutes thrashing the box with his cane, screaming at it. He knew where he wanted to go, but couldn't get there fast enough. "I've got to get a dog!" he told Wadsworth, who shook his head sadly. Many blind people applied for guide dogs, but few of the newly blind had the mental or physical agility to work with one.

For Peter, the final indignity was his loss of control over his own medical treatment. When he was first diagnosed with CMV retinitis he had assumed that, since he was a doctor, he would have no problem getting approval to take the required medication at home. But it took two months of bureaucratic wrangling before the treatment was finally approved. "Once the decision was made they said, 'Well, you can do it at home, but if you do it you're going to have to pay for all the supplies yourself,' " Peter recalled later. "Well figure that one out! For most other people, it means going to hospital for about three hours every day. This is very difficult if you're trying to carry on with a job, or if you're weak or feverish. And in many cases, the cost-benefit analysis seems to be, 'You're going to go blind in all likelihood, so perhaps you should just hang on to your health, hang on to your mental well being, and prepare yourself for the eventuality of losing your vision.' "[2]

And they were right; as Peter watched the last days of summer slip away, his world was darkening by the minute. "How are you today?" his medical school roommate Debbie Bebb asked him over the phone. "Well, I can see that TV set out there in front of me, but I can't see the picture," he replied. The next day he couldn't see the TV set. By Sunday morning of Labour Day weekend, he could see nothing at all. Two weeks after that he would be the subject of a CBC television news feature — and he would never see a single frame of it.

5

Going Public

The series of events that led Peter to the Canadian Broadcasting Corporation began four months earlier, in his final few weeks with Government Employee Health Services.

With his career options limited by increasing blindness, Peter turned to a colleague for advice. Jay Wortman, an articulate young doctor he had known casually for about three years, was associate director of the provincial Sexually Transmittable Disease Control program. When Peter moved into an office down the hall from his in June 1989, all Wortman knew about the young doctor was that he wore stylish clothes, drove a hot Jaguar, and was gay. (This knowledge proved amusing to Wortman when a number of young, single women began peeking into Peter's doorway, finding any excuse to run an errand at that end of the hall. Wortman chuckled quietly to himself when one asked if Peter was available. A straight man, Wortman had been at the clinic for two years and hadn't warranted so much as a glance from these women.)

Early in 1990, Wortman noticed that Peter was taking time off work because of various illnesses. He was told that Peter had been hospitalized for a reaction to medication. On May 1, shortly after his return to work, Peter invited Wortman out for lunch. The two shared small talk at a nearby restaurant, but Peter grew quiet when they returned to the office.

"Jay, the reason I want to talk to you is that I have AIDS," he said. "I have cytomegalovirus retinitis and I've lost the vision in my right eye, and now I think I'm going to be losing the vision in my other eye, and I realize I can't continue to practise. I'm going to need something else to do, so I was wondering if you might have some ideas on the area you're working in. Do you know if there's any work out there in education and prevention, or maybe some counselling I could do?"

Wortman was stunned, saddened, and embarrassed. Stunned because Peter had broken the news of his fatal illness with the matter-of-fact tone he would use describing any of his patients. Saddened because one of his own colleagues was yet another statistic in the AIDS epidemic. Embarrassed because, although he'd worked several years in the AIDS field, Wortman had not noticed the KS lesions on Peter's face, the bad sinus infections, or recurrent fevers. After comforting his friend, Wortman assured him that he would investigate whatever employment possibilities were available in the STD department.

Then Wortman recalled an article he had read in the Vancouver *Sun* earlier that spring, about a San Francisco television journalist with AIDS who was doing a broadcast journal describing his life with the illness. On January 5, 1990, the Bay Area ABC network affiliate KGO-TV had begun the series featuring Paul Wynne, a 47-year-old entertainment reporter who had been out of the media for six years but who had returned to describe his life with AIDS.

Wortman had clipped the article from the paper, wondering if a similar project could ever happen in Canada. It struck him that if such a series could so profoundly affect that many people in San Francisco — where the gay community was far more open and widely acknowledged than in Vancouver — then perhaps the same idea would have an equally positive impact in his own city.

"It was becoming a problem for me that in Vancouver — a city with the highest case rate of AIDS in the country with a very big gay population and a very obvious 'gay renaissance' going on here — that the majority of people in the city still had bigoted views about AIDS and gay people," Wortman recalled later. "We were totally alienated from [gay culture], we had no personal experience or encounter with it. Something needed to be done to put a face on AIDS ... I was thinking if everybody in the city could meet people with HIV or AIDS and relate to them the same way I did, they would go through the same transformation that I went through personally. Their fears and phobias would disappear as they discovered the humanity in people who are different from them."

It occurred to Wortman that Peter Jepson-Young would be an ideal candidate for such a project. "He would be the kind of person who would not scare everyone off — people who already had fixed ideas about gay people," Wortman said. "If someone had affectations or mannerisms, people would react to the superficial aspects of that before finding out that they could relate to that person as a person. That's one of the things I thought was good about Peter for that role." The fact that Peter also happened to be a doctor and had an articulate medical perspective on his own condition would only add to his credibility.

The initial idea was to show both Wortman and Peter, two medical colleagues, having a "discussion" in which Wortman would ask Peter questions about his life and Peter would respond. They would tape segments at various locations throughout the city — at a restaurant on Granville Island, on the beach, in a hospital setting — and the friendly rapport between two men (one straight and healthy, the other gay with AIDS) would presumably destroy homophobia while providing much-needed information about AIDS for the general public.

When Wortman mentioned the idea to Peter, he liked it. He was certainly capable of doing effective AIDS education, and he agreed that a high visibility campaign was exactly what was needed; every day he was confronted by ignorance. Just recently he had been at a small party where a woman who had finished her glass of wine came around to gather other empties. Peter, one of two people with AIDS at the party, gave her a glass and noticed how perplexed she became when she couldn't remember which one was hers. Worried that she might get infected from a glass, she decided to drink beer from a bottle instead.

Peter also had reservations about the television idea. His main priority was to continue professional practice in areas that didn't require use of his vision. The notion of a television journal had entirely different implications. How could he protect his privacy? Was he ready and willing to go public in such a major way? Peter liked the idea in principle but told Wortman he wanted to think about it.

Only when his health began to fail further did he finally warm to the idea. He was suffering bouts of sinusitis and vitreitis (an infection of the fluid inside the eye), and recognized that within a short time he would be completely blind. Fewer work options would be open to him then so why not take advantage of whatever opportunities came up? A TV special on AIDS would be a worthwhile project to keep him occupied for a short time.

With the encouragement of his sister and several of his friends, he told Wortman to pursue the television idea. After dismissing a friend's proposal for a rather sensationalistic TV feature film, Wortman continued to cast around for ideas.

On July 6 he was reading the *New York Times* when he saw Paul Wynne's obituary. Only two weeks previously, Wynne had delivered the opening address for the International AIDS Conference in San Francisco from his hospital bed — the twentieth and final installment of his "AIDS Journal." The series had "won rave reviews from television critics in the area" and its producers had "received scores of telephone calls and letters, a vast majority praising the station for its courage and Mr. Wynne for putting a face on the dread disease." The "AIDS Journal" was described as "stunning television, shocking for some viewers, inspiring for others and a 'reason to get up in the morning' for its dying star."[1]

It occurred to Wortman that the best route for Peter's project was a television station. If Wynne had done it in San Francisco with a local ABC affiliate, why couldn't the same thing be done in Vancouver? The obvious choice for a local station, he decided, was the Canadian Broadcasting Corporation. The CBC was a more commercial version of the American PBS, and its current affairs programs were respected around the world. As well, Canada's chief public broadcaster had so far provided the most balanced, least homophobic coverage of AIDS issues. Wortman had also had some personal involvement with the CBC during the 1987 dispute between doctors and the province over billing numbers. As a media spokesperson for the doctors without billing numbers, Wortman had been impressed by the CBC's sensitive handling of the issue. Now he figured CBC producers would at least be willing to hear his pitch.

The following week Wortman called the CBC and reached reporter Ian Hanomansing, who passed him on to *Evening News* executive producer Graham Ritchie. Ritchie mentioned the idea to field producer David Paperny, who promptly arranged a lunch meeting with Wortman and Peter at a nearby restaurant.

Six months younger than Peter, Paperny was well positioned to take on such a project. In his eighth year with CBC — the last six as a producer working on network current affairs programming in Toronto — Paperny had always preferred the educational approach and longer shelf life of documentary current affairs programming to the "pack" mentality of straight news coverage, and his work tended to focus on society's marginalized (gay teens, runaways, prostitutes) and the extent to which bigotry contributes to such marginalization. He had hoped to continue doing this kind of work as a documentary producer at The Journal — the CBC's national current affairs program — but there were few openings available for advancement in the fall of 1989. When senior current affairs producer Sue Ridout invited him to join the Evening News team in Vancouver as field producer for current affairs programming, he jumped at the chance.

Listening to Wortman and Peter's pitch for a series, Paperny was intrigued by Peter's story. He knew there was much potential for exploitation, however, and he wasn't about to browbeat Peter into anything he didn't want to do. "I was very clear on telling him the ugly side of the medium — that it's exploitative, manipulative, that it would interfere with his privacy, that it can be very sensational," Paperny said. He also made it clear that the CBC would probably not be willing to pay him for the segments, as Peter belonged to a category of news source that executive producer Graham Ritchie referred to as the "newsmaker." It is considered journalistically inappropriate to pay someone who is considered a "subject" and functions as part of the news story.

As a public broadcaster, CBC could not risk making an exception in Peter's case. To do so would presumably reduce the network to the level of *Hard Copy*, *A Current Affair*, and other such U.S. tabloid news programs which pay exorbitant sums to their subjects for the privilege of "exclusive" coverage.² Paperny suggested that Peter "mull it over a few days."

Paperny's enthusiasm for the idea was not shared by everyone in the CBC newsroom. There was general concern that television news was already suffering from AIDS burnout; the disease had generated so much coverage in the last five years that the notion of a special feature on AIDS seemed a bit like overkill. And what made AIDS so much more worthy of coverage than other health problems, like breast cancer or heart disease? Graham Ritchie encouraged Paperny to go ahead and tape a few segments, but gave no guarantee that the *Evening News* would run the footage.

With these comments in mind, Paperny contacted the producer of the Paul Wynne diary, KGO-TV's David Sampson. Sampson encouraged Paperny to let his subject decide where to take the series. "Do it with dignity," he told him. "Try to show your audience, as Paul did, that you can live and thrive with AIDS, it's not just about dying." His advice for Paperny: "Don't have a reporter or an intermediary. It'll live or die according to how well the audience can relate to the subject. And they'll relate immediately and dramatically with your subject talking directly to the camera." Later Sampson commented, "The most important thing for us was to try to break that strong wall that stands between most reporters and their audience, and that's what Paul did so well."

Paperny contacted Peter at home on July 19 and asked if he would be willing to take on a multi-part series by himself. Peter, whose health problems were increasing (that day he began treatments of prednisone — a very powerful anti-inflammatory drug — doubled his dosage of ganciclovir, and was facing a biopsy of his left eye to examine the extent of CMV damage in the retina), received Wortman's blessing to go ahead with the project on his own. The first taping was scheduled for a week later.

❖

J uly 26, 1990
During rush hour in Vancouver's South Granville shopping district, Peter slowly made his way along a crowded sidewalk toward a television news crew. Oblivious to the throng of curious pedestrians around him, he repeated the speech he had memorized for the segment: "Hi, my name's Peter. I'm a physician here in Vancouver, and I'm going to be talking to you about a disease which is affecting more and more Canadians on a daily basis. The disease is AIDS."

His tone was earnest and friendly, but Peter was completely disoriented by his surroundings. He couldn't see where he was going, and it was hard not to trip over the cord attached to the microphone on his shirt as he walked toward the crew. Of all the diary segments, this would prove to be the most difficult to record; the scene required twelve takes before he got it right. "Keep talking, Peter. And just look at the orange card," said Paperny, coaxing his subject with a fluorescent piece of paper beside the camera lens. Later they wrapped up the segment with a scene in Peter's apartment, where Peter described his initial illness and recovery in 1986.

Peter felt good about the taping. He hadn't committed himself to anything regular yet, but he enjoyed working with Paperny and was eager to do some more. Four days after taping the first segment, however, he still hadn't told his parents what he was up to.

When he finally let them in on his plans, over lunch at his apartment on July 30, he delivered the news with a tone of finality. Although he knew that nothing yet was firm at the CBC, he told Bob and Shirley that a series on AIDS would be a perfect way for him to continue medical practice while providing valuable education for the public.

The impact of this announcement was almost as devastating for the Youngs as the revelation that Peter had AIDS. "The way he told us was a little unfair," recalled Shirley. "We went over there to make lunch and visit. Nancy had discussed it with him and he hadn't said a thing to us. And we were about to leave, and kind of as an aside [he said] 'Oh by the way, CBC has asked me to do a show on AIDS, and I've agreed to do it' ... I wrote in my journal: 'My world fell apart today.' I mean, it was dreadful. He had made up his mind, and I guess a lot of it is hurt. We had been loving and supporting, and he hadn't said, 'I've been asked to do this and I know there's risks.' He said, 'I've been asked to do this, and I'm doing it.'"

The Youngs were already preparing to tell friends about his blindness, but they needed much more time for this bombshell. "Probably it was selfish, thinking about how it was going to affect us as well," Shirley recalled. "But it was such a hard thing for Peter to understand — he'd never been a parent, and I don't think he could imagine the powerful protective feeling you have towards your children. It doesn't matter what age they are. You would protect them from everything if you could. The worst scenario in the world had happened to our son. He had a terminal illness, an illness about which there was much stigma. He was losing his sight. He had nothing in his life that was positive, and now we're going to go forth and open our very soul to the world? My God, it was negative — how do you protect him?"

Peter also failed to recognize the impact the revelation of his sexuality had had on his parents since 1986. After their initial discussions in which Shirley insisted it was Peter's "choice" to be gay, he avoided all mention of sexuality with his parents for the next four years. Now he wanted to celebrate his gay pride in public. Was this fair? Once again Bob and Shirley told Peter his homosexuality was a "choice." Peter was enraged.

"I thought I had gotten through that this wasn't a conscious choice," he said. "But it was kind of an issue that was brushed under the carpet if you will. It was like, they were able to take me and my friends and pluck off our sexuality like a piece of Mr. Potatohead and just throw it away."[3] Peter felt that Bob and Shirley had spent the last four years avoiding the reality of his gayness in the hope that both his sexuality and illness would disappear. Initially Peter was willing to put up with his parents' denial because he felt there was nothing he could do to change their way of thinking, but he had become impatient about the issue in recent months. After all the struggles he had been through — the doctor in Mill Bay withdrawing the locum, his supervisor at Government Employee Health Services deciding not to extend his contract, and the various men he had met whose self-esteem suffered because of their lack of self-acceptance — Peter had finally come to believe that hiding his homosexuality was as damaging to his mental health as AIDS was to the immune system. The Gay Games had inspired confidence and pride in him, and he was convinced that a television news series on AIDS — done from a confident, out-of-the-closet perspective — would be a perfectly logical extension of gay pride, something of which even his parents should approve.

Given their previous response, this was a naive assumption. As in 1986, much of the Youngs' fear was based on events in the outside world. After Peter's first stay in the hospital, Shirley had encouraged him to remain quiet about his illness because the Ray family in Georgia had had its house burned down. Now Bob tried to discourage him from going public as a doctor with AIDS because a Florida dentist was recently revealed to have infected several patients with the virus.[4] The timing was bad, he said; as a doctor with AIDS, Peter could easily leave himself open to attack. Bob and Shirley were concerned that Peter would be vulnerable because of his blindness, especially if response to the series was negative. And Shirley was afraid Peter would suffer at the hands of the tabloid media, eager for a scandal. They were also angry that Peter had discussed the idea with Nancy before speaking with them. Nancy and Peter had always been close and their intimacy often seemed conspiratorial to Bob and Shirley.

What bothered them most about Peter's plan to go on television, however, was his willingness to drag *them* out of the closet — as parents of a person with AIDS — without their consent. Peter could easily afford to be blasé about the issue since even his straight friends were of a younger and more liberal generation. Gaining their acceptance was a non-issue. For Bob and Shirley, the fact of Peter's gayness could not be passed off so easily. Telling one or two of their friends that their son was gay and had AIDS was difficult enough in 1986; how were they going to explain his television appearance to everyone they met on the street, as well as co-workers? (Bob was retired from the Royal Bank but Shirley still worked, among a staff of about 50, for the North Vancouver School Board.) And what did it say about their relationship that Peter never told them the truth about his life until there was nothing they could do about it? As in 1986, when the discovery of his fatal illness revealed his gayness, this time Peter had held onto his secret about going public until a painful upheaval had become inevitable. "You didn't think of anybody but yourself when you went ahead and did this!" Bob snapped at his son. "It was goddamned selfish!"

Peter could have spared his parents much anguish by describing the idea in a bit more detail. He had already decided, for example, that he wouldn't use his distinctive surname. And Bob's concern that Peter would use the series as a political soapbox was completely unfounded; if anything, Peter toned down the politics. Simply by explaining some of these issues, Peter would have had much less difficulty gaining Bob and Shirley's support. But he said nothing about the content and there was much bad feeling when they left his apartment that day.

Peter was so despondent the next morning that he cancelled his afternoon appearance with Jay Wortman at an AIDS lecture. He knew he had instigated the fight with his parents, but he was angry that they couldn't see how the value of the series would outweigh whatever personal concerns they had about it. And he was depressed that his relationship with Bob and Shirley had not moved forward since 1986. At this point it seemed that all of Peter and Wortman's careful planning would go to waste.

Two days later Bob called up Peter and invited him to North Vancouver to talk about the series again. Peter declined; he was going blind, so it wasn't exactly easy to get around. Shouldn't they be coming to him? Finally Bob and Shirley returned to his apartment to resolve their differences. "It would have been so simple had he and Nancy said 'Okay, this is what the format is — this is what I'm going to do,' because at this point nobody knew of his situation," Bob said later. The Youngs both knew that Peter's blindness would inevitably push them further out of the AIDS closet, forcing them to tell more people. But they didn't want to be rushed into it.

When Peter assured them that his efforts could mean that other people affected by AIDS wouldn't go through what his family had, they gave him their blessing to do it. Then Bob and Shirley wrote letters to a group of friends and left town for a week's holiday. When they returned they found warm letters of support from all the friends they had written, including one couple who announced that their own son was gay.

Shirley took two full working days to conduct private meetings with each of her fellow employees at the North Vancouver School Board. She was surprised by the response. "I had one of my friends say she thought it would be really difficult for her husband, but that wasn't the case. He was in the office the next day saying, 'Come here, let me give you a hug.' It's quite powerful, you don't expect that response from certain people." Later, one of the Youngs' neighbours from up the street — an older man who had known Peter since he was a child — walked up to Bob as he washed his car and, struggling for words, burst into tears.

When Bob and Shirley agreed to surrender their privacy by accepting his plan to go public with his illness, Peter realized he was about to make a huge transition in his life. After four years of dealing privately with his illness, pursuing his career in the best possible health, he would now be labelled a "person with AIDS" by everyone he met. But such labelling was a small price to pay for the chance to educate the public. Besides, now that he was blind, what did he have to lose?

6

On the Air

With his family on side, Peter could now get on with the
business of taping the diaries. The first two segments of
the series were taped in the last days of July, and three
more within two weeks of the Gay Games closing ceremonies on
August 11.

The mood in the city during this time provided an ideal atmosphere for Peter to come out in a big way on TV. Despite the objections of fundamentalist Christians who regarded the Gay Games as a
"Sodomite invasion" that would corrupt the young and spread disease,[1] most of Vancouver's citizenry rolled out the welcome mat for
thousands of jubilant visitors who flooded the city's core as July
turned into August. BC Transit provided free bus passes for out-of-
town guests; hotels, restaurants, and boutiques dusted off their Super-
host manuals left over from Expo 86 and offered discount rates along
with their smiles; politicians who had scarcely uttered the word "gay"
in their lives embraced the event as a much-needed boost to the local
economy. Even the tabloid Vancouver *Province* jumped on the bandwagon, offering an editorial apology for having previously referred to
the Games as "silly."[2] Nothing, it seemed, could spoil the party for a
movement whose time in the mainstream had clearly arrived.

The Gay Games gave Peter a greater sense of pride and confidence, especially when discussing politics with straight friends. On one occasion a medical school colleague noticed a higher than usual concentration of police officers circulating in the West End. "I guess they have to keep them in control," she remarked, passing by a group of city cops. "Who do you mean by 'them'?" Peter asked. She assumed the police were keeping an eye on the gay participants, to make sure they behaved. Peter bristled. "Listen, that's not why they're there. They're there so that the people participating can feel safe that there's not going to be a lot of gay bashing going on."

"What do you mean by 'gay bashing'?" the friend asked. "What makes you think they're being beaten up because they're gay?"

"Listen," Peter sighed, "when someone's beating you up and calling you 'fag' and stuff, that's pretty straightforward."

While he couldn't participate in the Games as much as he would have liked, Peter knew he was about to take a much greater leap for gay pride. Celebration 90 had created an opening for more positive television coverage of gay issues, at least in Vancouver. Both Peter and Paperny knew their project would be cutting edge television, and they had to go about it carefully.

One scene from Diary 1, shot in Peter's apartment after the Granville Street scene, was eventually cut from the segment because of its heavy-handedness. Peter had escorted David and the cameraman to his apartment, where Peter stood in the kitchen doorway, delivering an impassioned speech about homophobic oppression. "AIDS was first identified amongst homosexual males in large urban centres and subsequently amongst prostitutes and drug addicts," he began.

Because these are people who have not historically been valued by society, this has added a social stigma to the disease which has previously been unknown. It's affected the response of governments, the medical profession, and the general public to this disease. It's bad enough for someone with the HIV virus to face a variety of serious debilitating illnesses and possibly an early death. But to have to do this in light of the amazing weight of social disapproval adds a deadly aspect to the disease which no medicines can remedy.

The message was straightforward enough, but Peter's tone was preachy and self-righteous, his posture arrogant and stuffy. It was a questionable approach given that this was the first glimpse the public would have of the AIDS diarist, Paperny believed. Launching into a lecture on homophobia only seconds after introducing himself could alienate viewers. Besides, each segment would only work if it had one clear focus — in this case, the story of how Peter became ill. Any further discussion would take the segment beyond the length and scope of an average news story and possibly lose the viewer. (The basic content of this speech would be included much later in Diary 44.)

For Diary 3, however, a segment shot at Delbrook High in North Vancouver, Peter put the gay issue into a more personal context, saying he could never come out to his parents because they were "victims of the cultural stereotypes they'd been fed." Of all the diaries in the first five, Paperny recalled, this was the one that could have been pulled for its controversial content. But he was determined to get it through the senior producers because it would set a precedent for future segments. "If I couldn't talk about Peter's life it would no longer be a diary, it would simply be an AIDS primer," said Paperny. "So I fought hard to get that one past."

Evening News executive producer Graham Ritchie worried about the episode's potential to set a precedent for the series as a platform for gay rights. It wasn't homophobia, he told Paperny. He just felt uneasy about a news program doing advocacy for *any* cause. "I wanted it to be the story of one person living with AIDS, but practical things like, 'This is Kaposi's sarcoma,' 'I am going blind' — that kind of thing," Ritchie recalled. "Supper hours tend to be fairly conservative, so it had to be commonplace to the general public. It's only by being commonplace that we accept things and understand them."

If Paperny had not pushed so hard to have the "Growing Up Gay" segment approved, the series would never have lasted as long as it did. As an AIDS primer there was only so much the series could have told its audience about Peter's physical symptoms and various treatments. As well, there is no way to address the topic of AIDS honestly without acknowledging themes like sexuality and homophobic discrimination. So Peter's story had to be treated more as a personal diary than

a primer. In the end, Graham Ritchie agreed that the Delbrook segment was journalistically relevant to the series.

Paperny and Peter spent the next few weeks shooting the remainder of the five segments. When Paperny showed the tapes to Graham
Ritchie and show producer Rik Jesperson, both men, although keen
on the project, predicted a hailstorm of protest on the network's
"Talkback" phone line, a call-in service which allowed viewers to respond to what they saw on the news. Others involved with the show,
like anchor Kevin Evans, believed it would be impossible to avoid a
"death watch" scenario, where the state of Peter's health determined
viewer interest in the series. How would the CBC avoid crossing the
line — as Evans later put it — "between journalism and voyeurism"?

To bolster his cause, Paperny called in local media critic Stan Persky to review the series. Persky liked the concept of an AIDS diary the
moment Paperny described it to him. It was an important issue, he
said, and the television medium offered great potential to educate the
public. The only concern he had as he viewed the series in a tiny
CBC edit booth was whether the man called "Dr. Peter" would be the
right messenger. "The question was, would this guy be a Terry Fox?
Or would he be a Steve Fonyo?"[3] Would he inspire television viewers
with his humility or would he turn out to be a public relations nightmare? When Persky finished watching the tape, there was little doubt
of the answer.

"This is great," he told Paperny, adding that Peter clearly had the
right tone and approach to draw in the viewer. He was also confident
that Peter's status as a doctor would provide added legitimacy, both in
terms of convincing the CBC brass to approve the series and in convincing viewers of the veracity of Peter's message. Paperny was hoping
for a plug in Persky's Vancouver *Sun* media column, but the approval
of a gay socialist heavyweight such as Persky was probably not the leverage he needed to persuade Ritchie and Jesperson to run the series.
Given Persky's bloodhound instinct for sniffing out nasty political
squabbles in large media outlets, however, he would certainly have
fired off an essay if the series was pulled at the last minute.

The final question mark surrounded Peter's insistence that his full
name not be used on the air. Usually the CBC reserved the right of

anonymity for the most extreme cases — battered women, drug addicts, or people whose security is deemed to be at stake. In nearly all these cases, the subject is "blacked out" or not shown on camera at all. Some CBC staff worried that the credibility of the series would be compromised if its subject wasn't willing to identify himself. (How could they guarantee, for example, that their subject was really who he said he was — that he wasn't just some actor portraying a doctor or a person with AIDS?) But Peter's decision was final. Aside from his concern for his parents' privacy, there was his own to think about; now that he was blind, he was concerned that the lack of security in his building and his status as the only Jepson-Young in the phone book would make him vulnerable to unwanted visitors.[4]

Ritchie finally decided to grant Peter's request of anonymity. The segments would have a strong impact no matter what name the subject used, he said, because the issue warranted major human interest coverage. The use of a first-person narrator would be such a novelty in television news that referring to him only as "Peter" was a minor concession in what was expected to be a five-part series.

Sue Ridout, senior producer for current affairs, recommended they run the five segments in one week — one for each news telecast — to launch the fall season. Each night would focus on a different element of Peter's life so that, by the end of the week, viewers would have a good sketch of the subject. As the final tapes were added to the lineup for the week of September 10, a title was chosen: "Peter's Story — An AIDS Diary." From now on he would be referred to on broadcasts as "Peter" or "Dr. Peter."

September 10, 1990
Jay Wortman watched the first segment from his False Creek apartment. He winced as Peter's face came into full view. Oddly detached from the bustling street scene around him, Peter looked old, his eyes were intense but showed no clear focus, and his thinning brown hair was combed stright up from his head. "He looks too frail, he doesn't seem confident enough," he concluded. "He's

going to scare off all the bigots and conservative viewers. He's too vulnerable."

In other living rooms throughout British Columbia, reaction was mixed. Many viewers were touched by the personal story of a man defying his terminal illness; others were outraged by the generous air time allowed an openly gay man talking about AIDS on publicly funded television. Old high school and university acquaintances sat stunned in front of their televisions as they recognized the handsome and popular student they had known as Peter Young.

Finally, puzzled AIDS activists watched the program in fascination. Who was this guy, and where did he come from? Some of them wondered why they hadn't seen him at the PWA Society office or at AIDS Vancouver. Others recognized him as the hunky doctor they had seen frequently at the Vancouver Aquatic Centre. But how did he manage to get on television? And why was he only using his first name?

For Diary 2, Peter was shown sitting on a bench at Jericho Beach wearing shorts and the volunteer T-shirt of Celebration 90. He explained how quickly he recovered from his initial bout with AIDS-related pneumonia and managed to live as close to a normal life as possible for the next three years. Then he described how the disease crept back into his life.

In September of '89 I noticed a subtle change in the vision of my right eye. I saw the ophthalmologist that week and was diagnosed as having a viral retinitis. The virus is a very common one, something most people have been exposed to and it stays in your system. If you have a normal immune system it's not a problem, but when your immune system is screwed up — as is mine — the virus can manifest itself in several ways, one of which is an infection of the retina. Within six weeks I lost the vision in my right eye and then realized there was a problem with my left when I started tripping over the garbage can in my office, and then on one occasion walked into my secretary's desk. She looked up at me and asked me if I had been drinking ...

"When I was first diagnosed, the concept of going blind was too unreal," he concluded, "but it's an eventuality that I have to face now. I'm facing another series of unknowns living in a world of darkness, but it's a challenge that has to be met."

Before the broadcast of Diary 3, Peter sat down with his parents to prepare them for that evening's subject. "I'm going to be talking about something tonight that doesn't really apply to you two completely, but it's something that needs to be said," he explained, adding that growing up gay is difficult for any teenager, no matter who the parents are. Then they turned on the television to see Peter strolling across the playing fields of Delbrook High School, wearing the red "Gay Pride" T-shirt of the English Bay Swim Club.

I grew up in a middle-class family spending my teenage years in this North Shore neighbourhood. [The high school I attended] was a conservative, academically geared school — not a welcoming place for a gay teenager. In a similar fashion, I didn't feel that I could discuss my sexuality with my parents. For me, I'd been gay since I could remember. It was just a normal part of who I was, but I knew they wouldn't take that view. They're a product of their generation and the cultural stereotypes they'd been fed. It was a large part of my life I couldn't share with them and I got to be 29 years old and had never dated women, and they didn't ask. I wouldn't have lied if they had. Unfortunately, they found out in the worst way possible when I became sick with AIDS.

Their initial concern was getting me out of hospital and back on my feet. But once that was achieved, they started to think about the implications of my being a homosexual. I think for them, my being gay was more difficult to deal with than my being potentially terminally ill. They expressed a lot of anger and disappointment. They felt that this was a choice that I had made and because of this choice I was responsible for bringing this thing upon myself and my family. I tried to explain to them that I had no choice in this; my sexuality had chosen me. It caused a lot of problems for a while but things are sorting out. Sexuality isn't such a big deal. It certainly isn't important enough to divide a family.

Peter's thinly veiled anger was apparent to most people who knew him, and it was not an easy diary for Bob and Shirley to watch. "When he said that he had been gay since he could remember, it made me feel as a mother a little sad," Shirley recalled. "When he said 'that was a part of my life I couldn't share with my parents,' it made me sad that our belief system was such that he wouldn't be comfortable if he told us, and we would have found it difficult. But we can't change that."

Meanwhile, Graham Ritchie and Rik Jesperson's concern about an anti-gay backlash proved well-founded. Although there had been much positive feedback from the public, there were also several spewings of hostility on the "Talkback" phone line, and several viewers phoned Ritchie directly to complain. The violent homophobes and Christian fundamentalists were easy to dismiss, Ritchie recalled — they weren't so much interested in the issues as they were in finding someone "official" to scream at. In the early days there were several of these calls, but the number decreased within a couple of months. Presumably the callers were tired of complaining to deaf ears.

However, one type of caller continued to gnaw at Ritchie's conscience. Viewers who adopted the "public broadcasting complaint" would tell him, "You're using my taxpayer dollars to influence my children. How do you justify what you're showing?" Ritchie simply laid out the position he had held since he approved the series: it was not designed as a platform for gay rights but to show what it was like to live with an incurable disease. "And it was a first-hand account, which is rare," Ritchie added, "because it takes a lot of courage to get up like that. Dying is a very private thing."

There were also complaints from the gay community. Less confident gay men were afraid that Peter would say something offensive to straight people, causing a backlash against gays and lesbians, and increasing homophobia. These viewers wanted Dr. Peter to tone it down, but at least two gay callers argued that Peter was being a "Judas" by not using the diaries for a more activist function. "There were some pretty bitter calls from members of the gay community, to the effect that [Peter] was being too clinical and too uninvolved, too emotionally distant, too diffident, and that he was 'playing the doctor' too much rather than the person with AIDS," Ritchie recalled. "And my reaction to that was that it was the very fact that he was a medical person that gave him such in-credible credibility, in addition to the fact that he was obviously a nice person and a good communicator to boot, which meant that he was very easy to relate to."

Ritchie's reaction, and the high number of responses praising the series for its educational value, tipped the scales in Peter's favour. Kevin Evans introduced Diary 4 on Thursday September 13 with the announcement that "viewer reaction has been overwhelmingly posi-tive." Peter, appearing on the rain-swept grounds of UBC, explained his decision to continue practising medicine after he had AIDS.

When I was in high school I had decided that I wanted to become a physician and came to university with that goal in mind. After several applications I was accepted at medical school. When I started medical school AIDS wasn't even an entity, but by the time I'd finished I'd lost several friends to the disease, one of whom had been an ex-boyfriend of mine, and so it was obviously a concern for myself. I went on to do a year's internship in Ottawa and then returned to B.C. to begin my career.

Three months after I finished all of this training, I became sick with AIDS. I was completely devastated to have spent nine years of university and a year of internship to do what I really wanted to do, and to have it cut so short, so quickly. I wasn't sure that I'd be able to work, not only because of my health but also because I was infected with the HIV virus. I addressed this concern to my own physician and to the AIDS care team at St. Paul's Hospital. I was assured that there was no medical reason why I couldn't work as a GP, that I wouldn't be putting my patients at risk, that in fact I might be putting myself at risk by exposing myself to a variety of illnesses.

I got my first opportunity to work three weeks after I got out of hospital when my own physician went on holidays. This was a practice that had a lot of AIDS patients and patients with other HIV-related problems. My family and friends were concerned that I would find this difficult, perhaps depressing, because of my own situation, but I didn't. I was able to help these people and relate to them because of what I'd been through. I discovered that I really loved clinical medicine and I was able to do this until a couple of months ago, but because of what's happening with my vision, I'm not going to be able to do all the things that you do as a GP. I'll be able to do counselling and education and hopefully will be able to continue helping people in this way because that's one of the main reasons why I went into medicine in the first place.

For the final segment of the five-part series, Peter spoke about how much more meaningful his personal relationships had become, and how thankful he was to have led such a normal day-to-day existence despite having AIDS.

I've said that the four years since my diagnosis with AIDS have been the best. It's true. When I was in hospital, the friends who were really true friends rallied around and came to visit. A few of them ended up spending the night while I was in the ICU. That was a gift that couldn't be replaced by flowers or chocolates or a take-out pizza.

When I got out of hospital I made a decision that a lot of people I knew as acquaintances — people that I could have fun with but had no deep attachment to — I decided that I wouldn't take the time to spend with those people. I would spend it with the people who really meant a great deal to me. I became a lot closer to the close friends that I had, and closer to my family as well. The time that we spent together was always very, very precious and much more valued than it had ever been before. You might get to a Christmas and think this is going to be my last Christmas, not in a pessimistic way but in a way that you make the most of it, and you make the most of every day as if it was Christmas.

Having death stare you in the face has a nasty way of putting things in perspective and you sort out pretty quickly what's really important and what's not. Material objects are just things, nothing to get in a fuss about. People become the really valuable commodity. Also, things that you're able to do. I was so weak when I got out of hospital that it was true effort to get from the bed to the bathroom. When I'd regained my strength and I was able to participate in sports and even just go for a long walk, it seemed like such a gift. [It was] very fortunate I think that I maintained my vision long enough to participate in the Gay Games. I volunteered as the physician for all the swimming events and it was such a positive experience.

I want to get involved myself. I want to compete and my plan is that I'm going to start swimming again this fall with a view to being in New York in 1994. That's my goal right now.

The message was poignant, but a lot was left unsaid. In expressing how thankful he was to have "maintained [his] vision long enough to participate in the Gay Games," Peter didn't talk about how difficult the experience had actually been because of how little vision he had left. As for "material objects," the period after 1986 was perhaps his busiest in terms of acquisitions. He had bought a classic Jaguar and a five-year-old BMW during this time, and — as he would demonstrate in the coming weeks — he had saved enough designer sweaters over the years that he could wear a different one for each diary segment over a couple of months!

But these were minor details. Given that he had literally fifteen minutes of fame in which to leave an impression with viewers, it was essential that he stick to the basics of living with AIDS. He didn't have to share every intimate detail of his life with the audience. Was it not enough that AIDS was being discussed on the evening news at all?

Until this point, Peter had assumed the five-part series would be the extent of his TV work, and Paperny had no idea whether the CBC would continue with the diaries on a regular or occasional basis. Kevin Evans reflected this non-committal approach when he concluded the fifth segment: "We'll be checking in on Peter from time to time in the coming months." By early the following week, however, Sue Ridout strongly recommended that the diaries run weekly. Whether viewers applauded or maligned the series, it was clear that people were watching it. Paperny and Ridout recommended that they continue taping diaries for a regular Wednesday slot. That way, viewers would be able to locate it easily and the segments could build a larger audience.

On Wednesday September 19 the first weekly installment of the regular series, now called "AIDS Diary," went on the air.

PART 2

The Diarist

This is one of the hardest letters I've ever written ... It was last fall that I was listening to the TV (from another room) to your program. I had never heard of it. And it only gripped my attention when someone mentioned your age. I thought "Jeez, this guy is the same age as me," and I came in to the room and saw your face. My first feelings were of great sadness. I kept thinking "Wow! Peter got to be a doctor!" and we're so young and all his opportunities are being swept away, when I feel a time in my life of mine just opening up. I thought of calling, but I felt that too much an imposition as we didn't know each other that well. I can't watch the program as it saddens me so much, the finality of this disease. But I felt so much respect for your opening up on a public level to increase all of our awareness.

FROM A LETTER TO PETER BY A HIGH SCHOOL
CLASSMATE, MAY 24, 1992

7

'AIDS is not a focus in my life'

P eter's first weekly installment of AIDS Diary on September 19 began with a startling announcement. "I'd spoken before about the trouble that I was having with my vision and described it as looking through a small window that was getting smaller and cloudier," he said, sitting on a park bench clutching a pair of glasses. "Well, that window's gone now. In other words, I am completely blind."

By the time he made this announcement, Peter had only been legally blind for about two weeks. Yet his tone was remarkably resigned, philosophical and optimistic.

It's not blackness that I see — it's sort of a heavy grey, like being in a very thick fog that you know isn't going to clear. I sometimes wake up in the morning, open my eyes, and expect to see my room, but I don't. I do visualize it, however, and I visualize familiar places and people. The places and people that I haven't known previously, I form mental pictures of. [THE CAMERA PULLS BACK TO SHOW HIS CANE] This is how I'm getting around now. With the help of the CNIB, I've been learning how to use my cane to manoeuvre my way around the neighbourhood while I'm waiting for my guide dog. These glasses I don't need for vision but I wear them for eye protection, to keep branches and things out of my face.

Then Peter told viewers of his plans to set up a counselling practice, join the swim club, learn ocean kayaking and resume downhill skiing in the winter. "Being blind slows you down at a lot of things, but it doesn't have to stop you from doing what you want to do. It's not going to stop me."

Given that no one in the world had ever been cured of full-blown AIDS, Peter's defiance seemed outrageous. But it was clearly a positive force that he used to confront his illness. By accepting that he had AIDS, then carrying on with day-to-day activities, he exemplified his belief that AIDS patients were not victims, as so often reported in the press, but people for whom every new day was a triumph.[1]

Diary 8 (October 3, 1990) provided the first clue that Peter's strength was not entirely based on his medical knowledge and rational will. Recalling a visit to Long Beach on Vancouver Island the spring following his diagnosis, he described the spiritual experience that inspired the meditation he privately referred to as "Affirmation."

When I was in hospital there was a period of time during which it seemed uncertain whether I would be getting out of there at all. My mother, who is a quietly religious woman, had concerns that I didn't have any beliefs in God and that because of this I was going to be very fearful about dying. I explained to her that I did have beliefs and that I wasn't afraid of dying.

I've never bought into organized religion. I've always felt that a sense of spirituality is a much more personal thing. I didn't have a formulation in mind of what it was I believed in but I knew that I had some beliefs. I grappled with this over the next six months and it seemed to all come together for me on one perfect spring day when I was at Long Beach on Vancouver Island with some friends. It was warm. The surf was pounding on the sand and I decided to take off on my own for a while. I stood there looking around and thinking, "How much better can it get than this?" I wanted to be able to recapture this moment for future reference because I knew that I would be facing some difficult times. I also wanted to get a sense of being able to draw in some of the forces that were around me to help me heal myself. So I climbed up on a big rock and laid down in the sun, closed my eyes, and this is what I came up with.

I accept and absorb all the strength of the earth to keep my body hard and strong;
I accept and absorb all the energy of the sun to keep my mind sharp and bright;
I accept and absorb all the life force of the ocean to cleanse my body and bring me
*   life;*
I accept and absorb all the power of the wind to cleanse my spirit and bring me
*   strength of purpose;*
I accept and absorb all the mystery of the heavens, for I am a part of the vast
*   unknown.*
I believe God to be all these elements, and the force that unites them;
And from these elements I have come, and to these elements I shall return;
But the energy that is me will not be lost.

The CBC received dozens of letters and phone calls about Peter's meditation, all expressing empathy for the personal nature of his spirituality and his apparent stoicism in the face of illness. Many people requested printed copies of the words. Whenever the "Affirmation" aired on subsequent documentaries, viewers from across the country would express admiration for its message. "Your poem left me speechless," wrote Melanie Elliot of Halifax after seeing the diary clip on the CBC program *Man Alive*. Elliot, who had once worked at the North Vancouver school board with Peter's mother Shirley, was now suffering from severe epilepsy. She also spoke on behalf of her twin sister, a quadriplegic, when she wrote:

I have taken the liberty of recording your poem on a cassette tape and when I feel the need to be re-energized or refocussed, I listen to it — each and every word. Recently, while an in-patient in the Nova Scotia Rehab Centre, it was a source of balance for me. Progressive neurological and cognitive defects from a "slow virus effect" (post viral encephalitis) have left me with the never-ending process of employing adaptive coping skills and devices.

On occasion I find myself in a negative mindset when I am met with a challenge to find a compensatory strategy to yet another obstacle. Your poem has given me the ability to stand back from my situation and be free of the anger and frustration which cloud my ability to get on with the task at hand.[2]

The only cynical response to the meditation came from Peter's own friends, some of whom chided him for sounding so earnest. "A few of us teased him about [the meditation], because it was so embarrassingly sincere," Flora Hillier recalled. Peter, she said, had rarely discussed his spiritual feelings with friends in the first four years following his diagnosis. Now he was telling the world.

Shirley Young was somewhat amused to be described as "a quietly religious woman." She had always believed in God but didn't really consider herself "religious," she told Peter after the broadcast. But for her and her husband this was a minor detail. The diaries had pulled off the cloak of silence surrounding their son's illness and homosexuality, liberating them in the process. Because of the overwhelming support they had received from friends, relatives, and acquaintances, Bob and Shirley were able to reexamine Peter's gayness with much less of the embarrassment and shame they had felt in 1986. As Peter explained in Diary 7 (September 26, 1990), this would never have occurred had it not been for his decision to go public. Only months earlier, Shirley had wanted to explain Peter's blindness to friends by saying he had cancer.

It was very difficult for my parents to have to deal with this illness, and also to try and come to grips with my being gay. They had this little fantasy, particularly because I was doing so well, that I was going to be cured and that they'd never really have to deal with this or talk to anyone about it. But because of losing my vision, and also because of doing this series for CBC, they were put in a position where they were going to *have* to talk to people and explain what was going on. It was a "coming out" process for them and they began to feel this horrible burden of the social stigma that surrounds AIDS.

This had been a barrier for us previously and it was something that they were going to have to face. They were very afraid of being judged because of my sexuality but ... all they got in response was a flood of warmth and caring and support. There was no judgment.

Anyone, particularly a parent, is going to see this as a child who's been ill, who might be very ill again and might die before his parents and that's not the way things should happen. They're going to look at the tragedy, not at the cause.

Too often the "coming out" process had been depicted in the media as a one-sided event in which it is always incumbent on the parents to "accept" and be proud of the gay son. But in this diary Peter emphasized that parents need encouragement too. In announcing that Bob and Shirley would accompany him at the upcoming AIDS walkathon — a fundraising event organized by the Vancouver PWA Society — Peter explained that "it was actually their idea. I'm very proud of them." The series had also allowed him to open up communication with his niece and nephews, who had limited knowledge of his situation before the series began. As he explained in Diary 14 (November 14, 1990):

The information they wanted was very basic. They're quite intrigued now by the fact that I can't see them and I think they've realized — particularly my niece — that because I can't see them they have to be more physical, more touchy and cuddly. And she'll play games with me, cutting out different things that I have to identify. It's quite interesting. It hasn't affected our relationship, certainly not for the worst, and possibly for the better. I guess they love their Uncle Peter and, in spite of the fact that I'm blind or have AIDS, in their innocence they're very accepting.

In Diary 10 (October 17, 1990), Peter was shown working out at his favourite fitness centre. Wearing a sea-blue tank top and shorts, with U2's "With or Without You" blaring in the background, the AIDS diarist sat on a weightlifting bench and explained how his appearance on the evening news as an openly gay man had helped him overcome his own internalized homophobia — as well as heterophobia.

The straight world has many stereotypes about gays, but also gays have many stereotypes about the straight world and one of the concerns I had was that in this sort of muscle, macho atmosphere of the gym, that I would be very much frowned upon for being open about my sexuality, for being open about having AIDS, that these guys wouldn't want me around, wouldn't want me sweating on their equipment.

The interesting thing is that the response has been completely opposite to what I had feared. The membership and staff here have been incredibly helpful. People have come up and addressed me by name and asked if I could use assistance in getting to equipment or helping me with different weights. It's been quite overwhelming. I've been really glad to see that my stereotypes have been blown out of the water.

For David Paperny, the fact that the diaries had so quickly healed a rift between Peter and his parents, and had reassured Peter about his own acceptance in society at large, was proof that the series was already a success. But that success would not have occurred had it not been for Paperny's own subtle influence and gentle persuasion. He and Peter were, in many ways, ideally suited. Paperny's laidback style put Peter at ease on the first day of shooting, and the two quickly developed a strong rapport. Their shared sense of humour helped Peter relax for each segment so he had no problem sharing some of his more intimate thoughts on camera. Paperny would tease Peter to loosen him up. "Come on Peter, let's shoot this one on your bed," he said when they were taping a diary on safer sex. "We want to get the sexier side of you."

"You can forget *that* idea!" Peter laughed. "My grandmother might be watching." In the end, he was taped sitting on the living room sofa.

Before long they had a routine worked out. Paperny called the day before a shoot to ask what ideas Peter had for that week. Peter would have several topics, Paperny maybe one or two. A couple would be practical so they would decide on one and discuss a general outline. Paperny reported to senior producer Sue Ridout, who provided feedback. If a diary lent itself to a particular location or visuals, Paperny and a cameraman would take Peter there. The entire process usually took about half a day, although some diaries were completed in just a couple of hours. (On occasion they would tape two diaries at a time, even three, but Paperny was reluctant to do so because the quality suffered if Peter grew tired. As well, it was much easier for Peter to maintain his focus if he only had to concentrate on one topic.)

Most of the early segments were made up of a single shot that focussed on Peter, slowly zooming in while maintaining eye contact. Peter couldn't see the camera, of course, but Paperny recalled the advice of David Sampson, producer of Paul Wynne's "AIDS Journal," who told him that it was crucial for the subject to speak directly to the camera in order to grab the audience. Usually a diary required three or four takes, but Peter's near-photographic memory — which had dazzled friends and relatives since medical school — often allowed him to recite a diary in a single take. Every now and then he surprised Paperny by ending a segment with a timely punchline. "It may sound corny and may be a bad pun," was his finish for Diary 15, "but being blind has been a real eye-opener for me." In Diary 31 he concluded that he needed to pay more attention to what his body told him. "And right now," he said, "it's telling me to go climb into a hot tub with my Ninja Turtle bubble bath. If that doesn't make me feel better, what chance is there for modern medicine?"

In the early stages Paperny had to ensure that Peter adapted his language to maintain the colloquial feel of the diaries — it was important to discuss medical issues without using jargon. But Peter was a quick study and was often able to provide social and historical background for what were complex medical lessons, as he demonstrated in Diary 9 (October 10, 1990). Sitting crosslegged on his living room floor, with the cuffs of his blue jeans rolled halfway up his shins, he began his weekly monologue with an historical account of the outbreak of Kaposi's sarcoma. Its spread among New York and San Francisco gay men in 1981, he said, "was one of the first things that indicated that there was something going on in the gay community." Given that KS had previously been common only among middle-aged and elderly straight men in mostly Mediterranean countries, the outbreak of this infection among younger, American homosexuals confounded researchers, said Peter.

It's a different sort of cancer. It's not like what many people think of as a tumour that then can spread to the rest of the body. In this case it's an indicator that there's something wrong with your immune system and so it can sort of crop up anywhere. It doesn't spread like we think of a normal cancer spreading.

Then he explained how he had been diagnosed with KS the previous year. At first there were only a few spots that didn't cause him much trouble, but lately the lesions had begun to spread. With the camera moving in for a closeup of his shins, Peter showed viewers a round, purple splotch on his right leg.

This is what a typical KS lesion looks like. It's generally an oval, purplish spot on the skin and usually just causes cosmetic problems.

But I had a patch on this leg. It was like a little bruise. It was more diffuse than the other one and I guess in the past few weeks, since I've been blind, it's become more aggressive and has spread to cover a larger area. And what it's doing is, it's blocking the fluid flow from the tissues so I can push my fingers into my shin and make a dent there. It also is a little painful. Feels like shin splints. I had radiation treatment on it a couple of weeks ago. It's going to take another eight weeks or so to see the results.

Peter concluded on an optimistic note that would have puzzled scientists and activists alike.

AIDS used to be considered a death sentence. I don't believe that. AIDS is not a focus in my life. It tends to be a bit of a nuisance [but] in spite of being blind and having this problem with my leg, I've got a very full life and generally I'm pretty healthy.

Peter was more forthcoming about his problems with AIDS in a videotaped interview with a former professor. At the end of September he received a phone call from a doctor who had been his psychiatry professor at UBC. Dr. Michael Myers, in addition to teaching and carrying on his own practice, was in demand on the lecture circuit, addressing conventions of psychiatrists and other medical professionals. In his latest lecture he was discussing issues facing doctors with

HIV; his talk included five case histories of doctors with AIDS in the Vancouver area. When Stacey Elliot, a colleague at Vancouver's Shaughnessy Hospital and a medical school classmate of Peter, learned of his lectures, she suggested he get in touch with Peter. In early October they met for the interview.

Psychologically, he told his former teacher, he had felt worse while losing his vision than when he finally lost it completely. On his initial diagnosis Peter said, "You feel like a pariah, you feel soiled. I was afraid people wouldn't want to touch me or hug me." Sometimes the paranoia extended to the comical. "When we left hospital, one of the nurses said 'If there are any spills of bodily fluids, you can clean it up with a bleach solution.' Well, my mom got a bit carried away and our house started to smell like an indoor swimming pool."

The interview marked the beginning of a two-year collaboration in which Myers and Peter addressed UBC medical students and other groups on HIV issues. Myers himself travelled to various cities in Canada and the U.S., presenting the tape to conventions.[3]

By the first week of November, AIDS Diary was receiving national attention. A November 5 story on CBC's prime-time news show, *The National*, covered the development of the series through the first few diaries and commended Peter for his contribution to AIDS awareness. It was a satisfying affirmation of the last two months. Although he hadn't found work in counselling, he was getting plenty of speaking requests around Vancouver and was making new contacts. He was much closer to his parents than he had ever been, and the viewing public showed warm support wherever he went. People approached him on the street, in restaurants, and at the gym to thank him for doing the diaries. And in recent weeks he had begun a new relationship.

Six months earlier the glass had seemed half empty. Now it was running over.

8

'Being blind has been a real eye-opener'

On September 16 — the weekend after the first five diaries were broadcast — Peter was invited by his former lover, Brian, to a dinner party in honour of a mutual friend. Peter and Brian had split up after a brief romance the previous year, and Brian had recently broken up with another man who would also be attending the party, Andy Hiscox. Hiscox was a 42-year-old urban planner who had only recently begun dating men. Peter and Andy had heard about one another through Brian but had never met, so while Peter was looking forward to the dinner — one of his first social outings since going blind — Andy was intrigued by the prospect of meeting the man who had previously gone out with his first boyfriend.

Some of Andy's gay friends were skeptical about Peter's presence at the dinner. Steve Schilling recalled his own complaint when Brian suggested inviting him: "Oh God, not a blind person with AIDS — this is going to be a downer!" He found Peter a charming dinner guest, but was still doubtful when Hiscox began dating the AIDS diar-

84

ist shortly afterward. "What are you *doing?*" Schilling asked Hiscox, who was HIV negative. "Are you a martyr?" It was hard for Schilling and other gay friends — all of whom knew people who had died from AIDS — to fathom why Hiscox would leave one partner with HIV only to go out with another within two months of the breakup.

"Our love and relationship defied logic," Hiscox conceded later. "Here was I, a perfectly healthy person falling in love with a blind man with AIDS. [But] Peter was very healthy when we met and it was hard to imagine that he was sick. Harder yet to imagine that he may die." Hiscox thought his friends were missing the point; he didn't think the fact that someone had AIDS was any reason for not being friends or not associating with him. When Peter told Andy that Brian and Nancy were accompanying him to a film the following week, Andy accepted his invitation to join them. (Although he couldn't see anything, Peter enjoyed sitting in a theatre and listening to a script packed with dialogue, so the group went to see Carrie Fisher's *Postcards from the Edge.*)

Two weeks later, Peter convinced Andy to take him on a kayaking picnic. "I was so busy putting up barriers for why we couldn't go kayaking, and he had none. I kept thinking 'He's blind,' but he didn't have a problem," Hiscox recalled. "His attitude was 'I'll find a way around it.' I knew right then that he was a solution-seeker rather than a problem-seeker." (Later, when Peter felt like going for a bike ride, Andy would rent a tandem bicycle.) In the following weeks Peter and Andy got together as friends and discovered a common appreciation for Cole Porter music, anything sung by Billie Holiday or Dinah Washington, good food, outdoor adventure, and conversation.

Peter was expecting romance when they met at Andy's West Vancouver home for the kayak outing, but Andy maintained a wait-and-see approach to their relationship. All that changed on October 3, however, when Peter and Andy met for lunch right after Peter had taped the "Affirmation" diary. The conversation turned to spirituality and their individual beliefs. Peter told Andy the "Affirmation" and, like many who heard the meditation on television, he was moved by Peter's personal expression of faith. By the time they attended a

Thanksgiving dinner the following weekend, the two men realized they were in love. The following February Andy moved into Peter's South Granville apartment for good.

Hiscox knew there was greater emotional risk in loving and losing Peter to death than there was physical risk of contracting HIV from his new lover. He wondered how he would deal with Peter's illness. Would he be able to care for him? Also, the fear of AIDS transmission was so high among his straight friends that Hiscox felt he couldn't tell them that he and Peter were lovers; he wanted them to get to know Peter for who he was and not in relation to himself. When he had admitted to some of his straight friends that he was gay and was seeing Brian, one told him he didn't want to meet Brian, blaming him for Andy's gayness. Still coming out of the closet and struggling with his own homophobia, Hiscox was worried these friends would reject Peter for the same reason.

For Peter, on the other hand, the arrival of Andy Hiscox in his life marked the end of a lengthy period of loneliness. The first three years after his diagnosis had been happy ones in terms of physical health, but the road toward romantic fulfillment — so often abandoned by single people with AIDS — was a constant struggle.

Initially, Peter had difficulty giving up the sex habits he had enjoyed before his illness. This was hardly surprising, given that many people facing a sudden terminal illness are forced to endure radical lifestyle changes. Seven months after PCP nearly killed him in 1986, Peter was in excellent physical condition. His appetite had returned, he was working out regularly, and he was finally regaining the libido he had lost while in the hospital. While other people with AIDS struggled through long illnesses, Peter felt so good that he may well have credited his AZT treatments for a complete recovery. Thus, when he lost the locum on Vancouver Island because he had AIDS, Peter was determined not to get discouraged by the setback. At the end of May 1987 he packed his bags and joined his best friend, Ross Murray, for his first trip to Europe.

On their third day in Paris, Peter and Murray were at a bar called The Trap when they met a charming young Frenchman named François. Peter was attracted to him, but it was Murray that the beautiful, dark-haired François invited to dinner two nights later. They had planned to spend only two more days in the city, shopping and sightseeing before proceeding on to Spain, but when François agreed to invite Peter along as well, they changed their minds.

Peter's travel journal for June 5 reveals that the dinner in the trendy Montmartre district was more like an elaborate seduction ritual, orchestrated by a couple of highly accomplished Parisian playboys. After François drove the two young Canadians to a friend's richly adorned apartment for drinks ("I'm brought a veritable tumbler full of scotch," wrote Peter. "Uh oh, what does this mean?"), Peter and Murray were treated to an exquisite meal at a nearby restaurant frequented by the rich and famous, before being escorted back to the apartment of 45-year-old Jean, a partner in one of Paris' finer dining establishments.

> Return to apartment for Armanac & drugs — lots of things get strange. Jean disappears. Ross goes to bathroom and François comes to sit beside me and is all over me once Ross returns. I fear for my life. Things are getting stranger. I know we aren't going anywhere because François & Herve [Jean's lover] too stoned to function. Then I go to bathroom and return to find Herve by himself. He says everyone is in the bedroom. I walk in to see Ross' undies being whipped off in record time and Jean is asleep on the bed. Mon dieu, things are stranger still ... The ensuing melee was too nervous and shame-making. It is enough to say that we returned to our hotel at 2:00 the next afternoon — henceforth known as Ross & Pee Wee's big Adventure ...

Murray was disturbed on the way back to the hotel. Once they were alone, he lectured Peter about the previous night's escapade. Why, he asked, did he go as far as he did? Why, in a single moment of drunken abandon, had Peter accepted Jean's invitation to have unprotected intercourse? Why did he just go ahead and do it — no questions asked, no condom, no confession of his HIV status?

Peter, startled by the confrontation, struggled to find a good excuse.

Ross was perfectly right, of course; he should have stopped short of intercourse, or at least told Jean that he had AIDS. But the evening had been euphoric and decadent — not to mention drug and alcohol-drenched, he said. Given this environment (and the aggressive overtures of their friendly hosts) his judgment was not exactly at its best. Besides, what was a sophisticated man like Jean doing having unsafe sex with a young tourist he had met only two days earlier, especially when he had just finished warning his guests about the perils of anal sex in the age of AIDS? Murray recalls that during a conversation at the restaurant only two hours earlier, Jean had told the assembled guests, "You'd have to be crazy to have sex without a condom in these times." And why hadn't *he* said anything about his own HIV status? This was not to excuse his own behaviour, Peter admitted, but to acknowledge that the sex was consensual and both men presumably knew the risks. Peter's perception of Jean was that the man was somewhat creepy and appeared to be daring Peter to "do it," like a 1950s game of "Chicken" between two hotrodding daredevils.

Peter's action in Paris was not unusual for someone facing terminal illness, according to David Richardson of AIDS Vancouver. Richardson, coordinator of the Man-to-Man sex education program for gay men, was the organizer of a 1993 national survey of Canadian gay men's sex habits. The survey revealed that 23 percent of the men in the study acknowledged having had sex without a condom at least once in the last year. Figures specifically for HIV-positive gay men were not available. "Being sick and coming back to health is like a re-birth, and for someone who's facing an uncertain path toward a premature death — who's just gone through a physically and emotionally draining bout with PCP — it's almost predictable that they would want to celebrate that rebirth," Richardson commented on Peter's case. This is not to excuse risky behaviour but to acknowledge that everyone is susceptible to it now and then. As one friend later remarked, "It's a bit like being drunk and getting behind the wheel of a car." Peter, who had rallied back from the edge of death only nine months earlier, was recapturing the hedonistic sense of adventure he had known before he became ill. For a few short moments, only three days before his 30th birthday, he had nearly forgotten he had AIDS.

Still, the criticism of his best friend struck a chord. If he wasn't going to tell his sexual partners of his HIV status, which was his right, he would at least have to refrain from unsafe activities. Back in Vancouver he received another lecture from Murray about the unsafe sex incident. "Enough, already!" he snapped at his friend. "I *know* I'm not supposed to do that, you don't need to tell me a second time." It was frustrating; he knew that what he had done was wrong, and he regretted it, but there was nothing he could do to correct his mistake and he just wanted to put it behind him.

Perhaps partly as a result of this incident, his approach toward long-term relationships was beginning to change. In his pre-AIDS love life he had often found himself with more than one boyfriend at a time (he kept a young pre-med student waiting in Vancouver while he fell in love with Sam in Ottawa), but now he wanted to meet someone to whom he could devote himself entirely and who would be there for him in his darkest moments.

The problem was, he was unrealistic about his prospects and continued to follow the same method of seeking men. It was a path of physical attraction, followed by sex, followed hopefully by things in common, which was supposed to lead to mutual adoration. When that method failed, Peter decided that perhaps a frequent sexual partner would be better than a string of one-night stands. To this end, he placed an ad in the weekly *WestEnder* newspaper, hoping to track down a muscle-bound stud he had met at a log boom on Wreck Beach, a popular nude playground for straights and gays alike, located down a steep, forested hill on the westernmost tip of the UBC campus. "This," he wrote in his diary, "after returning repeatedly to the same log boom" in search of the man.[1]

When he met the gorgeous, moody Marc in New York City in late 1987, Peter thought he had found what he was looking for. He had gone to New York to visit friends for a few weeks while considering his work options, and first spotted Marc at an upscale bar for gay professionals. The two didn't meet until a party the following week, where Peter recognized the handsome strawberry blonde man who had returned his gaze at the Eagle and Spike. This time they chatted at length and Marc asked for Peter's phone number. The following week, on September 28 — a year to the day after he was hospitalized with PCP — Peter spent the night at Marc's apartment.

The two men began dating regularly and working out at the gym; by October 4 Marc asked Peter to move in with him. "He [was] obviously starting to fall in love," Peter later wrote in his diary. "I didn't know what to feel or say."

Evidently he didn't say very much. Peter didn't feel as strongly about Marc once the relationship began; as far as he was concerned, the idea of being in love was as good as the real thing. Only later, when Marc followed him back to Vancouver at the end of October to meet his friends, go to a Hallowe'en party, and share a two-day trip to Whistler ski resort, did Peter begin to fall for him. But he made one crucial mistake that ultimately led to their breakup. Although the two had already discussed their fear of HIV infection, Peter only decided to tell Marc that he had full-blown AIDS on the day before the Whistler trip.

Later he admitted to Phil Sestak that he didn't tell Marc about his HIV status earlier partly because they "wouldn't have been able to share the good times" if he had. Peter had spent the first year after his diagnosis wondering if he would ever be able to have a long-term relationship. Once he did meet someone special he was desperate to hold onto him. He was afraid of rejection and wanted Marc to love him for who he was before he told him he had AIDS.

Even after he broke the news and Marc began to withdraw, Peter refused to believe the relationship was doomed. Within two weeks of Marc's return to New York on November 7, Peter followed him back, determined to keep their promise to move in together. At first Marc gave no signals that he wanted the relationship to end. Peter moved in to his Chelsea district apartment, located within six blocks of Macy's, the Empire State Building, and Madison Square Gardens, and worked on odd jobs and construction while redesigning the apartment. But by late January, as the two men vacationed together at the Caribbean resort of Antigua, Marc was already distancing himself from Peter.

Before long his indifference became unbearable. One night Peter wept on the phone as he called his UBC chum, Flora Hillier. "He was crying his eyes out," she recalled. "They had been at a club and Peter said 'Let's go home.' And Marc said, 'You go on, and maybe I'll bring you a surprise' — meaning a guy they could share — and Peter didn't want that. And he had to get off the phone because Marc did in fact come home with someone else." Peter was confused by Marc's change in attitude, and Marc never did communicate what was wrong. By April Peter was back in Vancouver, wondering how he could have done things differently.

He wouldn't have that problem with Brian, who told Peter he also had AIDS when the two met in the fall of 1989. Instead, this new relationship was plagued by fundamental differences in response to their illness. Like Peter, the healthy Brian was a muscular Adonis who knew how to attract people with his good looks. But Brian had difficulty accepting Peter's losses as well as his own. He was never able to adapt to his illness and couldn't stop dwelling on his anger, constantly speculating about who had infected him with AIDS. While Peter learned to accept the loss of his gym physique and youthful good looks, Brian resented the fact that doors no longer opened for him as they once did. While Peter embraced every moment of travel as if it were his last, Brian spent an entire holiday in Palm Springs complaining about a rash.

By the time he broke up with Brian in early 1990, Peter realized the common factor in all the men he had pursued: all physically attractive, they appeared to be strong and in control but had difficulty expressing their true feelings. They were a bit like Peter himself.

Now that he was blind and his AIDS was no longer invisible, Peter had little choice but to open his heart to those people who were attracted to him for who he really was. He was no longer capable of reacting to superficial impressions and had to rely on the subtle nuances of language, voice, and touch. Andy Hiscox may have been a Robert Redford lookalike according to Nancy, but what most mattered to Peter was that he was a good-natured, caring man — one of the first romantic partners with whom he felt completely compatible. In Diary 15 on November 21, Peter shared a rather muted version of his joy with CBC viewers.

After I lost my vision a friend of mine asked me one day if I was more lonely now that I was blind. It was a very interesting question. I hadn't thought of it in those terms before, but I knew exactly what he meant. I was always someone who was a real people watcher. I enjoyed watching people picking up social cues, visual things. But now when I'm in a room with people I can hear their voices but I can't see them, and if they're quiet I don't necessarily even know they're there. One time I went into my doctor's waiting room and just about sat on someone who was reading a magazine and wasn't aware that a blind person had come into the room.

Another thing I hadn't thought about before was what it was going to be like to meet someone who I'd never met. Now the people who I knew before I, of course, could picture them as I had last seen them. But someone I'd never seen, I was assessing on a completely different level. Naturally I pay more attention to voices now but also I get an idea of what the person is like just, well, basically, I guess what comes through is who they are.

In the time that I've been blind I've met a few new people including one in particular who's become very special in my life and it's interesting because I've never seen him so I wasn't able to form an opinion based on the superficial things, on his appearance, the clothes he wears, the car he drives, etc. Instead what comes through is just a very clear picture of what a great person he is. It may sound corny and may be a bad pun, but being blind has been a real eye-opener for me.

A ndy wasn't the only new "significant other" in Peter's life. For several months he had been getting around with his cane while he waited patiently for approval from Ottawa for a guide dog. The December 12 diary began with a beaming and triumphant Peter shown standing on a sidewalk in the wealthy Shaughnessy district.

When I first lost my vision, I had a mobility instructor come out from the CNIB. We sat down and discussed some of the options that were available for visually impaired people to get around. Of course, there was the proverbial white cane but he told me about a bunch of high-tech options which I had never heard of. One of them was a set of, well, what would look like glasses and they emitted an ultrasonic signal that fed into a little speaker that was in your ears and that you could get an idea of what was ahead. Another one was a laser cane. All I could think of was, I'd be drifting down the street sort of dressed like Darth Vader with this glowing stick, able to annihilate anything in my path. That image certainly has its attractions on some days. I decided, however, to go for a more low tech option. [HE LEANS DOWN TO REVEAL A BLACK LABRADOR RETRIEVER, WAGGING ITS TAIL AND LICKING HIM. HE CARESSES THE DOG.]

This is Harvey. Harvey is a Canadian Guide Dog for the Blind. I just got Harvey a few days ago and right now we're ... well, actually it's me that's being trained. Harvey's already trained. Harvey's from Ottawa. He used to be a cabinet minister but he decided to quit politics and get a real job. Right, Harvey? Let's go. [THEY WALK AWAY FROM THE CAMERA WITH PETER ENCOURAGING HARVEY]

Maggie Johnston, recently transplanted from Britain, met Peter in October to prepare him for guide dog training, and on December 4 she returned with Harvey. Peter gave Harvey an old Cashmere sweater to keep in his bed. It was a piece of himself, with his scent, that would quicken the bond between them.

Dog and master learned quickly — it was as if Peter had been blind for years. "Basically, the arrangement is that he's the pilot and I'm the navigator," he said in a later diary, adding that Harvey's ability to determine safety on the street and alert Peter to obstacles had given him much more confidence.

There were some funny moments in their training. One snowy day as Johnston and CNIB mobility trainer Jay Wadsworth were taking Peter through traffic training — in which Johnston repeatedly drove a van toward Peter and Harvey as they left the sidewalk, to test Harvey's reaction time — a man who had been watching the scene ran out of his house and threatened to call the police. "How dare you run at a blind man like that?! And it's not just any blind man, it's Dr. Peter!" he shouted at Johnston. Peter and Wadsworth stifled their laughter and ran around the corner, leaving Johnston to defend herself. "It's okay, she's with us!" they said finally.

If the man's concern for Peter's welfare was an amusing misreading of the situation, it was also a reflection of Peter's growing profile. Since the series began he had become something of a minor celebrity in his own neighbourhood, with people stopping him on the street to say hello or comment on the series. While not all of the comments were positive, he was humbled by the concern shown by many. "People don't really know what they have inside until they're challenged," he told the *Sun* in the first local print coverage of the diaries. "If five years ago, you'd said to me I'd have AIDS within a year, I might have said, 'I can't cope with that.' Then, once diagnosed, if you'd said, 'In four years time you're going to be blind,' I might have said, 'I don't think I can cope with that.' But things crop up and you just deal with them. I'm not convinced I'm an exception."[2]

By Christmas Peter felt confident he would be able to cope with just about anything that happened to him. Despite having gone blind, and although he required a new drug — alpha interferon — and radiation therapy to treat the KS which was spreading on his legs and pelvic region, his spirits were high heading into the new year. His knowledge and experience were in demand on the speaking circuit, his diaries were developing a larger audience, he had fallen in love, and now he was sharing his apartment with a loyal guide dog. For the first time in his life he felt as though he would never be alone. His Boxing Day address on AIDS Diary, taped before sparkling candlelight, was like a thank-you card to his viewers.

When I started doing this series with the CBC a few of my friends wanted to know what it was I was going to get out of doing this. I wasn't getting paid and a lot of people felt that I was making myself needlessly vulnerable by going on the air and talking about my situation, my sexuality, my having AIDS. But it's provided me with satisfaction in a variety of ways.

First of all, it allows me to practise medicine in a different way than I did before. I'm able to hopefully educate people, and more people than I would be able to do just working in an office, which is something I can't do now that I'm blind. I've also had a lot of personal feedback. People coming up to me on the street, in restaurants, at the gym, just to say thank you for what I'm doing, to say that it's having an effect. Some people share very personal stories. They may be affected themselves, or they may have a friend or a family member who's affected, and that's been a really positive experience. I guess the other thing is that I've been able to lay myself out, my most vulnerable side, to public scrutiny and not be rejected, and not only not be rejected but also to get positive feedback. People coming and saying, "Wow, that's really great what you're doing." And that's very empowering. It's, I guess, become part of my own healing process and I suppose that's what the payback is for me.

9

'I've never bought into organized religion'

E arly in the new year, Peter received a call from Neil Gray, rector of St. Paul's Anglican Church in Vancouver. Was he interested, Gray asked, in being the keynote speaker at a church conference on AIDS? The conference, sponsored by the Anglican archdiocese of New Westminster, would attract 125 church members from around the Lower Mainland to address the church's response to AIDS, while offering many of the clergy and lay people present their first direct exposure to someone with the disease. Peter, who was raised an Anglican but quietly abandoned the church in his teens, jumped at the opportunity.

Peter had first met Neil Gray in fall 1989 when Gray — then assistant priest of St. Paul's Anglican Church and chaplain for Anglican patients at nearby St. Paul's Hospital, a Roman Catholic-run institution — was sharing a quiet moment with an AIDS patient of Phil Sestak. Peter, relieving Sestak, stepped into the room rather abruptly to examine the patient. "Who are you?" he asked Gray, interrupting their discussion. "I'm the chaplain, and I'm not finished yet," Gray replied icily.

A few weeks later Gray was at a Calgary AIDS conference for social workers, medical professionals, and clergy when he spotted Peter at a lecture on The HIV-Positive Caregiver. Gray had delivered his own lecture at the conference, on the church's neglect of people with AIDS, and he shared parts of it with Peter.

"I am impatient with a church that does not relate to life as it is lived," Gray wrote. "People with AIDS are dealing with deeply philosophical issues — pain and suffering, disfigurement, lack of control and independence, weakness, guilt, death, judgement, heaven and hell. The Church claims to have insight into these, but they are often either in jargon (salvation, atonement, redemption, or incarnation) or in poetry and metaphor (especially in talking about Heaven) ... I am angry at the way in which religion frequently masks the face of God, particularly in the AIDS crisis."

Peter was impressed. Sharing the flight back to Vancouver, he described the last three years of his life to Gray and expressed his desire to continue practising medicine despite having AIDS and problems with his vision. Impressed by his wit and candour, Gray suggested they get together for lunch, but the two didn't see each other again until the following April when Gray found Peter's name on his hospital visitation list. He shook his head in wonder; in a few brief meetings Peter Jepson-Young had transformed from a prickly doctor to a thoughtful conference delegate to a needful patient.

"You never told me you were Anglican," Gray said when he went to visit him at St. Paul's. "Well," Peter smiled, "I had to put *something* down. I was baptized in the church, but I have a problem with organized religion."

A year later Gray sat on the committee responsible for selecting speakers for the Anglican conference. Both Gray and Peter knew that HIV education in the church would be more effective if presented by someone with AIDS, and Gray, who had seen Peter's diaries, was convinced the young doctor made an ideal speaker. Peter's "Affirmation" had neatly expressed the kind of body/spirit linkage that Gray had always been eager to address in the church. God doesn't make rubbish, the "Affirmation" asserted; God makes beautiful things.

Surely the church in the 1990s could learn a great deal from this message, even if it came from a gay man with AIDS?

While Peter looked forward to the conference, he couldn't help feeling a bit apprehensive. Like many gay men raised in Christian families, he had rejected the church before it could reject him. Confirmed an Anglican at age twelve in Nanaimo, he stopped attending services once his family moved to North Vancouver in his mid-teens. It wasn't so much that religion had actively oppressed him as a gay youth; it was more that his own sexual feelings were irreconcilable with organized Christianity's assumption that all God's children are heterosexual. The more he partook in church rituals, the more he felt he was living a lie. "By the time I was confirmed I pretty well knew where I was at in terms of my sexuality and basically didn't want to be faced with being told [that] who I was was wrong or sinful," Peter later told a reporter. "It's kind of: 'I'm getting the impression I'm being rejected, so I'm rejecting you.' I think that's very common."[1]

Now that the church appeared willing to extend an olive branch to people with AIDS, Peter was willing to endorse the conference in the diary preceding it.

I think there's a lot of ways the church could be involved in helping with the crisis that we're suffering with AIDS. On one hand, I think clerics are much better trained to deal with death and dying and could be very helpful to both patients and physicians in dealing with this aspect of AIDS. On the other hand, I guess historically the church has been involved in perpetuating the homophobia that exists in our society. But the fact that they're going ahead with a conference like this proves to me that they're interested in what's going on, and they're interested in increasing their understanding of this particular situation.

It's very important for many people — particularly those who've been very involved in the church during their lives — not to feel judged when they're in a situation such as having AIDS and they want to be able to approach the church and feel that they're going to get a warm reception, and that they're going to get help and love and care, and not judgment.[2]

Peter's one-hour talk at St. Martin's Church in North Vancouver was punctuated by colloquial expressions and humour that relaxed the delegates and prompted occasional laughter and applause. "I think you might be wasting your breath trying to convince a horny sixteen-year-old not to do it," Peter told the crowd. "Yes, you can talk to kids about abstinence, but at the same time, you have to arm them with the facts." And the facts, as Peter revealed, were sobering; the last six months had seen a 50 percent increase in HIV infection on the North Shore. This area north of Vancouver with a population just below 150,000 now had at least 200 HIV-positive and 35 AIDS-symptomatic residents. AIDS was much closer to home than many would like to admit.

Peter's rediscovery of the Anglican church was ironic, given how recently he had told his TV audience that he "never bought into organized religion." Two years after he spoke those words in the "Affirmation" diary, Peter would arrange his own Christian burial with an Anglican funeral and a public memorial service including official blessing by the archbishop, choral arrangements of Beethoven's "Ode to Joy," and a reading from the Bible.

This final return to the church was not so much a death bed conversion as a "coming home" or reconciliation with a religion he could never fully embrace in life. Even during the two years of AIDS Diary, his involvement with the church was limited to a few appearances before Anglican congregations. If not for his chance meeting with Neil Gray, he might not have reopened his dialogue with Christianity.

Peter shared Gray's distaste for the church's preoccupation with power and control. "A lot of Christian imagery and metaphors are all about power and domination, and they're all male, i.e. Lord, King, Master, Almighty," Gray recalled later. "Peter and I spoke often about finding metaphors for God that include rather than exclude, that create rather than destroy, and that liberate, rather than control." The power of Peter's "Affirmation," Gray explained, was that it defined God as a "mystery whose self-definition is Love." Gray believed Peter made a valuable contribution by humanizing this mystery. By placing more emphasis on natural elements (earth, sun, ocean, wind), the "Affirmation" defined "God" in more worldly terms. This had the effect of making spirituality more appealing to a larger television audience. It also left room for the Christian church to "reclaim the vocation it had misplaced or abandoned" by making people more comfortable about turning to the church for help.

The "Affirmation" was not the only diary segment that touched on spiritual issues. While Peter's meditation captured the tactile, physical aspects of his spirituality and his personal belief in a higher power, other segments used anecdotes to discuss ethical and moral issues. In one, Peter explained how an experience at UBC ten years earlier helped him put his own pain into perspective. Like the "Affirmation," it was a story that gave him strength.

> I was walking into the gym at UBC, and coming down the other side of the staircase was a man who was more disfigured than anyone I had ever seen before or since. He'd been in a very bad fire or an explosion. His face appeared like moulded plastic. One of his eyes, I believe, was false. He had virtually no ears and the hair was perhaps a wig or something other artificial. One of his arms was missing from the forearm down and the other hand was like a ball of flesh. He was bouncing down the stairs, whistling away and he saw me staring at him. I couldn't help it. He acknowledged me. He looked at me and nodded his head and said "Hi," and kept on going. I stood there. I was completely overwhelmed. It was a very humbling sort of experience. The whole thing perhaps only took about five seconds but I've never forgotten it and never will. I've thought of him often over the years.
>
> When I was in hospital I thought about what I was going through and how it could hardly compare to the physical and emotional pain he must have suffered recovering from his injuries. It gave me a gift, a gift to look within myself. Call it strength if you like, but whatever it is it helps me keep going.[3]

In the weeks that followed the St. Martin's conference, Peter came up with more provocative lessons. These segments offered viewers a chance to challenge their way of looking at the world. Over two weeks in February 1991 he pondered how people deal with, or deny, ill health and death — their own or that of friends and family.

Last week I was in to see my doctor. It had been a particularly tough week for him: he lost four patients to AIDS in that week alone. The same day I was in to see someone in hospital, someone who is losing his vision. This comes heavy upon a bunch of other problems for him and he is very afraid. He's afraid of losing his independence, amongst other things.

AIDS is a disease of losses. It's not unique in this; there's certainly a lot of other diseases this is true for — cancer, rheumatoid arthritis, diabetes — but with AIDS it seems to be particularly concentrated. You may not lose one friend to this, you may lose many loved ones, even family as well. And there are personal losses when you are affected. Certainly there's the loss of your health ... a loss of independence and a loss of control. And all of the fear and helplessness and frustration that go along with that. I've experienced a lot of this myself, but I think in a way I've been lucky in that some of the losses I've had to face have come one at a time. For example, the year over which I was losing my vision — that was really the only loss that I had to face. It was a lot to deal with at the time, although once it had actually happened, the reality of it wasn't as bad as I had imagined. The enemy was there to deal with and once the vision was gone I was able to cope with the blindness and get on with things.

But for people sometimes, these losses come one on top of another, so many that it gets to be overwhelming. I've certainly seen this with some patients; it just becomes all too much to cope with, so that when they come to face the ultimate loss — their own death — this comes sometimes with a sense of regaining control and, in many cases, a great sense of peace.[4]

The second of these two diaries encouraged viewers to cherish the time remaining with friends and lovers who are dying.

The first Christmas after I was diagnosed with AIDS, I got this game called Scruples. It's one of those games where you're given difficult questions and you have to come up with some sort of answer and it's supposed to incite lots of argument and that sort of thing. One of the questions that came up when we were playing was: "What would you do if you fell in love with someone and then found out that they only had six months to live?" Well, it broke up fairly shortly after that and the game went missing and I've never seen it again. And I was probably the only one who was interested in finding an answer to that question.

It seems that there are a lot of people who have, I guess, difficulty dealing with illness and death and so when they have someone who becomes ill — whether it's AIDS or cancer or whatever — they take to the hills, because they really can't cope with the situation. It doesn't necessarily have anything to do with what the cause of the illness is; it's the outcome that they're concerned about. They may be very afraid of getting close to someone or staying close to someone who they might lose in a week, a month, in a year.

I guess it's an attitude that I've never really understood. Particularly it came home to me the other day. I spent a wonderful day with a friend of mine and then he got home to find a message on his answering machine that someone he had cared for very much had just been killed in a very freak accident. Someone who was perfectly healthy, perfectly alive, active, full of promise — gone, without a chance of really having been able to say how much he cared. Or to say goodbye.

There's no way you can protect yourself ... against that kind of loss. So why be selective for someone who you know might have something wrong with them, who you know you might lose, so you decide — yourself — to get rid of them before their death? It may be hurtful to the person you're walking away from, but I think it's very hurtful to yourself, and you're the one who's going to be the ultimate loser.[5]

A year later, Peter related a story he'd been told about how one woman discovered that one of her sons was gay. The parable would have worked well as a homily on unconditional love.

She's got two sons — the older one heterosexual and the younger one gay. When the two boys were in high school, the older brother had been thumbing through his younger brother's room one day and found some male pornography. He took this to a friend of his and said "You know, I think my brother's queer." So the two of them went to school and they started telling other people at school about this.

So one day the young son comes home and tells his mother that he's really upset and would like to run away and maybe even kill himself. And when she asked why, he told her that he was gay and that his brother and his friend had found this stuff in his room and were telling people at school. So the mother went to the older brother and his friend and said "Is this true? Did you find this stuff and are you telling people these things?" And they said "Yes." And she said "Well, the magazines that you found — those belong to me and I hid them in your brother's room so that your father wouldn't find them. And I'll thank you two to keep your nose out of other people's business."

Well, needless to say, the two boys were rather dumbfounded. I don't think that most parents would be either that quick-thinking nor that selfless that they would be willing to put themselves on the line like that. She may not have understood the whys and wherefores and hows of her young son being gay. But she understood that he was suffering a lot of anguish because of it, and she dealt with it in the best way she knew how. If that isn't an example of unconditional love, I don't know what is.[6]

Peter's forthright manner didn't always win over his religious audience. On February 24, 1991, when he got up to address the congregation of St. Margaret's of Scotland Anglican church in Burnaby, his opening line went over like a lead balloon. "You know, I never thought I'd be addressing a church congregation on a Sunday, but the Lord really moves in mysterious ways," he said to a hushed audience. ("I didn't have the benefit of seeing their faces," he recalled later, "so I was sitting there thinking, 'This is really a tough room to play'.") On a later diary, he explained his use of humour in a church setting:

Someone pointed out to me afterwards that perhaps these people — although they might see the humour in what I was talking about — might be afraid of laughing because it might be seen as being inappropriate in the circumstances. But what I was trying to do was invite them to laugh, to invite them to find humour in association with the tragedy of the situation. It's a very important coping mechanism for me, and also I think for the people around me, to have a balance there. I'd rather be remembered for the fun and the humour that I've been able to share with people than the tragedy of what's been happening.[7]

For some Christians, however, the problem wasn't so much the message as the messenger himself. Peter's spiritual credibility, as far as they were concerned, would forever be tarnished as long as he did not renounce the decadence of his past.

One correspondent, responding to Peter's diary about the woman who discovered one of her sons was gay, had an entirely different interpretation of the mother's act of selflessness. "When you spoke of those brothers — the youngest of which had some male pornography books in his bedroom," said the elderly man in a 90-minute cassette mailed to Peter care of the CBC, "you made no suggestion that it might be a good thing if young boys don't get interested in male pornography ... To be a practising homosexual, one must deny the existence of God."[8]

Some Christians pitied Peter for being gay, others thought he would burn in hell. Many wrote lengthy letters to the CBC in an attempt to convince him to repent, and almost all cited passages from the Bible to make their case.

> Peter, sir, go to Jesus, admit and confess your erring ways to Him and ask Him for forgiveness, to be washed in the precious Blood of the Lamb. For, "if a wicked man turns from all his sins which he has committed, keeps all My statutes, and does what is lawful and right, he shall surely live; he shall not die. None of the transgressions which he has committed shall be remembered against him; because of the righteousness which he has done, he shall live ... " (Ezekiel 18: 21-22, 24, 31-32)[9]

Peter never responded to any of these letters. He found them at turns sad, touching, and amusing. He realized, when they were read to him, that his self-esteem as a gay man had risen to the point where he was immune to the judgment of other people. Besides, the letters were written from a Christian perspective miles apart from his own. Although he had reestablished ties with the Anglican church in which he was raised, he always had enough confidence to realize that a healthy spirituality didn't necessarily depend on church involvement.

"Some people think I'm going to hell in a handbasket," he told viewers in Diary 68 (December 18, 1991). "Sometimes it seems that I'm quite misunderstood, but those [letters] I think are in the vast minority."

10

The Mister Rogers Approach

I f his church audiences appreciated the sense of humour Peter employed to get his message across, most people with AIDS probably identified with his diary topic of February 13, 1991: anger. In opposition to the message, his tone was, as usual, that of the calm, cool rational doctor pronouncing his diagnosis. It was a style that had become Peter's trademark, something the *New York Times* described, several months after his death, as "a kind of 'Mister Rogers Explains AIDS' approach."[1]

I'm going to talk about anger today. There's certainly a lot of sources [of] anger for people who are infected with HIV or who have AIDS. There's that global anger — the "Why me?" kind of feeling; there's anger that comes out of fear and anxiety ... there's anger that comes from physical pain, and sometimes from being told by your caregivers that you're getting enough medication when you know you're not — *you're* the one who's in pain! There's anger with the medical profession, anger with drug companies, governments, moralistic and indifferent politicians; sometimes there's anger that's turned in at yourself. Many people who are gay haven't really dealt with that and they're often angry with society because they're rejected for being gay and then having AIDS on top of it is just a double rejection.

I can certainly relate to a lot of these feelings; I've experienced a lot of them myself. Facing a bureaucracy that always says no, or getting an answer like, "There's a Royal Commission looking into that and we'll have an answer for you in eighteen months" — well, hell! I might not be around in eighteen months, and the answer that you're going to get as likely as not is what common sense would have dictated in the first place. And then you get angry because you realize there's nothing "common" about common sense.

I often get asked what I think about groups like ACT-UP, which is a fairly radical, gay AIDS activist group. Well I certainly understand where their anger comes from, and I also understand that there's a lot of people who are very desperate and have absolutely nothing to lose by being violent.

Myself, I try and deal with anger in a variety of ways. Being brought up a good WASPy boy, I was sort of taught to grit my teeth and develop an ulcer. Now I blast someone if they deserve it and it feels good. Other times I'll exercise, work out — get rid of my anger that way — or sometimes meditate.

Anger's a very powerful emotion. It can tear you apart; it can be very destructive. But if you can get some control over it, you can get rid of a lot of it and turn what's left into something good.[2]

While Peter had no intention of using the diaries as a platform for his own personal anger, there was no shortage of opportunities to do so. He grew particularly indignant when confronted by the AIDS ignorance, insensitivity, and homophobia of his own chosen profession. In mid-January, at a seminar of first-year medical students, Peter was told by a couple of student organizers that their instructor of cardiopulmonary resuscitation had advised them not to treat anyone with track marks or any other indication that they might be at risk for AIDS. Peter could barely contain his venom as he responded to this attitude in Diary 24 (January 23, 1991).

I thought, "What a great way for some future doctors to find out about AIDS — from someone who obviously knows nothing about the disease." I've run across this kind of attitude before with some health care workers. Just over a year ago I attended a conference on doing some special work with emergency personnel. The fellow who taught the course had done a poll in the United States and had found out that the worst scenario for ambulance drivers was to have an AIDS patient with a severe bleed. I thought, "Get a grip, you guys! You obviously aren't treating this situation seriously. You'll go out and scrape someone off the road that you know nothing about and not be concerned, but you're handed a situation where you have an AIDS patient, you know exactly what precautions to take, but you're still getting really strung out about it." I guess the worrisome thing is that those precautions aren't being taken with *everyone* as they should be so that you can't make a mistake.

I've even run across this kind of attitude from other doctors. Fairly recently I got a referral letter from a surgeon who didn't want to do surgery on this particular patient. There were lots of good reasons for not doing the surgery, but the doctor listed the HIV status of the patient as one of those reasons — NOT a good enough reason! ...

I guess I get concerned sometimes that intravenous drug users, or gay people are discriminated against because of the possibility that they might carry AIDS. But I wonder, is the discrimination on the basis of the disease or on the basis of these people's lifestyles?

Despite Peter's frequent critiques of this nature, some gay activists in Vancouver complained that AIDS Diary was too upbeat and optimistic, that Peter was too comfortable in his own life to adequately express the anger and frustration that most people with AIDS experience daily. But Peter was not about to adopt an angry persona simply to satisfy an activist agenda; the easy-going, calm tone was closer to who he really was. While there was always a risk of glossing over the harsher realities, he felt he was a far more effective educator when he used humour rather than rage when bashing the government or lecturing about the evils of homophobia. A strident approach would not only obscure the message he was trying to communicate, it would drive away viewers by the thousands. Peter was always aware that his audience was much larger than the gay activist population. He also realized from the beginning that people with little understanding of AIDS or the people suffering from it did not want to be bombarded with strident politics, gruesome displays of physical decay, or maudlin expressions of personal grief.

At one point Peter was asked if having AIDS ever made him feel angry and, if so, why that emotion wasn't coming through in the diaries. "I explained that it was very important to keep those emotions in control, particularly the anger," he said in a later diary. "Anger can really distort the story you're trying to tell. Anger doesn't pervade my life, and therefore I don't think it should pervade the diaries."³

As well, it was easier for Peter to express emotions other than rage. He had always preferred laughter to confrontation, and making people laugh was a skill he had cultivated early in life — first as a child prankster, then as a "ham" actor at UBC medical school skit nights, and later as he struggled for his life at St. Paul's Hospital in the fall of 1986. Peter would crack up his friends at the slightest prodding and he saw no reason why he shouldn't do it with his AIDS Diary audience. He believed laughter was good medicine.

The results of this choice of treatment were on display in early March when he fulfilled his earlier diary promise to go downhill skiing. His afternoon on the slopes at Blackcomb Mountain ski resort, captured on Diary 30 (March 6, 1991), was a triumphant moment of courage, but it was also hilarious. Peter's voiceover described how strange it felt to "have to come up 6000 feet, strap on a couple of narrow boards to my feet, [and] stand at the top of an icy incline before I can take off and do something on my own. But that's what's happening." Then, with the camera following him, he showed his viewers the world from a blind man's perspective.

I'm able to head down the hill — completely unattached to anyone else or anything else — and be able to move and feel the hill, feel the turns, with complete freedom. It's almost like seeing again.

It's quite an amazing and exhilarating sense. It's hard to compare it to anything else. Okay, I'd be kidding myself if I said it wasn't stressful. It's not only stressful for me but also for the people I'm skiing with. It does take a bit of a team effort. But it's sure worth it.

Okay, I've hit one tree so far, but it wasn't that bad. And I was feeling a bit out of breath, and I don't know whether that's physical exertion or sheer terror. But I'm getting used to it. And the whole concept of having that freedom again really opens up doors. I feel now that the only limitations I'm going to have are the ones I put on myself.

Now all I have to do is convince them to let me drive home.

T he physical exertion may have been a bit much given that it was his first time on the slopes since going blind the previous year. A few days after the ski trip he woke up "feeling much like a bag of wet oatmeal — actually, an achy, grumpy bag of wet oatmeal." The KS on his arm had required radiation treatment at the cancer clinic, and he was still feeling fluish from the radiation although otherwise he was in fairly good shape. He'd started taking alpha interferon in late January — combined with AZT, it was said to be effective in battling KS. Since beginning the treatment many of his lesions had shrunk and some had disappeared altogether, so he decided he could afford to relax about his health for a while, as he told viewers on March 13.

> My tendency in the past used to be that I would agonize over whether feeling crummy was a result of physical doldrums or psychological ones ... More recently though, I've been feeling that I should be kinder to myself. I've never been a very good patient — never someone who's been able to just relax and take it easy very well. But more recently I think I should be listening to what my body is telling me. And right now, it's telling me to go climb into a hot tub with my Ninja Turtle bubble bath. If that doesn't make me feel better, what chance is there for modern medicine?

But dealing with the ups and downs of Peter's health was not always easy for his caregivers. It was sometimes hard to know, for example, when he truly needed help and when the slightest bit of assistance could be a nuisance. "I remember when my sister was first visiting me when I'd first lost my sight," he recalled in Diary 23 (January 16, 1991). "I couldn't get up to go out of the room without her rushing over and taking my arm. Quickly she came to realize that I was going to have to manage on my own and I was going to be able to do so." It was the same thing with having AIDS, he said.

> Sometimes you'll go out and someone will hand you an apple juice when you

really want a beer because they don't think you should be having it, or a group of friends may be going out late at night and they won't ask you along because they figure you should be in bed, or you get an extra scarf wrapped around your neck when it's a little chilly outside. You appreciate it but at the same time you want them to lighten up a little bit and realize that you're just a person who's trying to get on with their life and really don't need all those extra special considerations.

Then there was his own capacity to be demanding. There were times when his craving for a certain kind of food was so strong, Bob Young recalled, that he wouldn't be satisfied until every possible venue was explored in searching for it. In the winter of 1991 he had two rooms in his apartment repainted, insisting that they be the "right" colour even though he was blind.

Peter understood how frustrating his demands could be for family, friends, and caregivers. As a doctor he had met more than his share of difficult patients.

There was one in particular who, when his name showed up on the patient roster in the morning, would just ruin my whole day. I found him a particularly difficult person to work with. When he got very sick, I had compassion for his condition, but it didn't make me like him any the better. And I had all these awful feelings to struggle with — all this guilt and this sense of inadequacy, because I had these feelings about him.

Now I know that when I feel uncomfortable, there [are] days when I can be a real jerk as well. And I don't like myself when I'm like that. And when I get to the point where I feel like I'm being difficult, I usually say to people, "Am I being a pain to be around?" And they'll tell me, and that helps me snap out of it. When you're trying to look after someone who's very ill, telling them they're a jerk isn't going to make them any sicker. And possibly, it's going to help both of you get through your day a little better.[4]

Also adding to his frustration were financial worries. The provincial government was not willing to pay Peter to work as an AIDS counsellor in a private practice, so several friends acted on his behalf. Michael Myers wrote to the Medical Services Commission (which approves billing numbers for counselling in B.C.), outlining both the need for "state-of-the-art HIV counseling" and Peter's qualifications for such work. The denial of a special categorization of billing for Peter, he said, "represents, in my mind, a form of employer discrimination against physicians with AIDS."[5] The MSC, in its response a month later, repeated its policy that "special exceptions ... would not be appropriate,"[6] so Peter's ability to work as a counsellor was strictly curtailed.

In January 1990, knowing that his vision was deteriorating, he had applied for benefits through a disability plan available through the B.C. Medical Association, the doctors' professional association in B.C. His application was denied on the advice of the BCMA's insurance company because he had already been diagnosed with a terminal illness. After Peter wrote a letter to BCMA president Hedy Fry, explaining his predicament, Fry brought the issue to the executive. But while the executive was sympathetic to his cause, she said later, it could not convince its insurance company that Peter was a worthy recipient. "One of the problems that we unearthed [was that] apparently, when Peter had applied for disability insurance, he was already HIV positive [and] he was a new physician, he had not practised for long," recalled Fry.

Eventually, the BCMA executive met again and decided unanimously that Peter would be recommended to the B.C. College of Family Physicians and Surgeons as a worthy recipient of the Physician's Benevolent Fund. On May 1, 1991, the College approved a monthly bursary of $2000 be paid until Peter's death.

Peter's campaign for benefits was not as urgent as it would have been had he worked in a field other than medicine. Despite having been unemployed since the previous June, he still had enough savings from three-and-a-half years of contractual work that he could afford (with the help of Andy Hiscox) to fly to New York and take other trips to the U.S. (His European trips were covered by the conference organizers who were flying him in as a speaker.) Before long he was also being paid $550 a month by the Ministry of Health on a short-term contract basis for his educational work in the schools. But this was considerably less than the $1800 per week he was earning until his contract extension with Government Employee Health Services was withdrawn in the spring of 1990. Since July 1990 — the same month he began taping AIDS Diary, for which he was not paid — he had faced unemployment, with living and medication costs of up to $2000 per month.

So while the benefit package offered by the College was a welcome one, the struggle to get a counselling licence had been a sobering lesson for Peter. In a letter to Hedy Fry, he thanked the BCMA president for referring him to the College but expressed disappointment that, "I have received little support of any kind from my medical colleagues. I am quite dismayed that one of the wealthiest professions in this country can be so lacking in initiative to assist a colleague in a time of need."[7] Given the overwhelming response to his diaries and public speaking engagements, he wondered why the BCMA took no public stance in support of his efforts to be certified as an AIDS counsellor.

Peter alluded to this struggle in a diary the following September, but he never took shots at the BCMA in public. Instead, he couched his predicament in more reasonable terms. "I've got nine years of university and five years of clinical practice — a lot of knowledge and a lot of skill, and I'm very frustrated that I'm not allowed to use that knowledge and that skill in order to make a living ... I sort of feel like I'm an untapped resource."[8] Clearly, Peter had learned how to channel his anger for television consumption.

11

Taking It to the Schools

For Peter, the most rewarding result of the diaries was public discussion of AIDS issues. He wanted to increase awareness in as broad a spectrum of society as possible. What he never expected was that his experience with AIDS would become such an example for people with other illnesses, that people with heart problems, cancer, or Lou Gehrig's disease would see him as an inspirational leader.

This was especially the case at the B.C. Cancer Agency, where Peter was treated for Kaposi's sarcoma. The cancer clinic provided a more casual atmosphere than the average hospital, with patients playing an active role in their own treatment and many developing strong bonds with their caregivers. Peter had a legion of devoted fans at the clinic, and he and Harvey were greeted warmly whenever they arrived for an appointment. BCCA staff and patients appreciated Peter's on-air discussion of anger and loss, his courageous response to his own blindness, and his practical advice regarding diet and drug therapies. Many of them could relate to his frustration about AIDS myths, and many more found inspiration in his "Affirmation."

They were also grateful for his efforts to provide better access to information for cancer patients. For example, his casual suggestion to start a bulletin eventually resulted in *Living Well,* a quarterly newsletter for people living with cancer. Its inaugural issue featured a front-page article in which the writer summarized Peter's role in expressing the common experiences of people living with AIDS and/or cancer.

> Where cancer was once the C-word, AIDS is now spoken about with a whisper or wince. This sharp pin of an acronym pricks our preferred silence on sex and sexuality. Some people find the reality of AIDS too sharp. Bodies still young enough to know the easiness of vanity are ravaged of all pretense. Weight loss, hair loss, blindness, cancerous lesions, dementia are too obvious to deny. And AIDS mocks the healthy with its mysteries and pervasiveness. This modern age of medicine was supposed to be safe from epidemics. AIDS startles our complacency. We want to turn away. We want to panic. Peter prefers calm to rage ... His many years as a doctor counsel him to moderation. He knows that AIDS is a disease having no bias or intent.[1]

This uncanny talent for communication, particularly Peter's ability to reflect common experiences among different people, was featured on *Man Alive,* the CBC network's current affairs show. Peter's April 3, 1991, appearance on the show gave him a national profile. With clips from the diaries and new interview footage, this prime-time documentary feature provided the same gentle self-portrait of life with AIDS that Peter's B.C. viewers had grown to appreciate.

The broadcast resulted in an avalanche of mail. A 55-year-old actor from Ontario's Shaw Theatre Festival wrote Peter from Niagara-on-the-Lake: "You did every gay man a special service in our struggle for acceptance because we all saw this beautiful human being talking openly and calmly about his lifestyle & illness & we were all touched and wanted to know this attractive, bright special person." The man, a volunteer buddy for the AIDS Committee of Toronto and a board member of a housing organization for homeless people with AIDS, taped the "Man Alive" program and promised to show it to the entire Festival cast.

Other letters brought home the fear, isolation, and despair of the disease.

Dear Peter:

Last week I watched your program. At first I did not want to watch it. My son has AIDS. He has the same symptoms you have. All he gets is radiation for the worst one. There must be something else to treat them. I do admire you so. You are so hopeful. You gave me some hope too.

I feel so helpless — not to be able to help him. You mentioned the study the Canadian government is doing on alpha interferon. Is there any possibility we could get some help from there? I know it would cost money — but we would get it from somewhere. Please, please, do give us some hope. We are all positive most of the time. It is not always easy. I love my son — and it is just too much to bear sometimes.

Dear Doctor Peter,

First, I admire you for having the courage to admit yourself in front of everyone, you have done a great service to everyone in showing what can happen if we give in to ourselves. This has probably saved many lives, as people who watch will think twice.

I myself will remain pure till there is a cure, life is just not worth risking. Just a glimmer of hope: maybe there will be a cure before you pass over, and you will recover soon ... I myself think life is best left to the imagination unless you wish to have children. Maybe this virus has some positive things to it as this so-called revolution should be headed back in reverse. Madonna saddens me, she is so up front on the topic.

Best, I do not wish to give my name as I am still pure and in my 30s.

P.S. My wish would be granted if you read my letter on your Diary.

Peter received many letters like these. He often responded by telephone to those who were genuinely seeking help, but others like the "pure" correspondent of unknown gender above, or the many concerned Christians who damned him for being gay, appeared more interested in converting him to their religion than in listening to his message. Peter never let this bother him; he knew the diaries were having a positive impact where it mattered.

Following the broadcast of "Man Alive," he received many more public speaking requests. He accepted almost every invitation, knowing that by extending his AIDS education message beyond the television set he could offer thousands of people the chance to encounter someone with AIDS in the unthreatening environment of a public forum. High school students were among his favourite audiences. As he explained in Diary 17 (December 5, 1990), adolescents were usually far more frank with their questions than adults.

You have to kind of gear your talk depending on the group. High school students tend to be very forthright and blunt, but sometimes that's easier to deal with. The adults tend to be a little more guarded in the questions they ask and maybe a little more reluctant to ask the questions. I've been a bit surprised too at the misconceptions that still exist with the adults about the transmission of AIDS, particularly when you're talking about AIDS in the heterosexual population. I had a woman say the other day that her doctor told her that women can't give AIDS to men. Well I corrected her on that misconception.

I've been pretty impressed on the whole on how much the kids know about AIDS and safe sex. A lot of them seem to really feel that it is a risk for them. They seem to have a pretty good grasp of what is high-risk and low-risk activity, and they seem to be aware of the fact that you can't get AIDS through casual contact. You talk to them about sexual practices and sometimes it makes them nervous and embarrassed. I can't see their faces but I can hear little comments in the background like "Eww, gross!" and nervous laughter ...

A lot of people feel that someone such as myself shouldn't be talking to teenagers about sex and condom use, that if you ignore their having sex, that it isn't happening, or that if you talk to them about it you're somehow condoning. But the way I look at it is that the more information they have, the wiser choices they're going to make when they get out there and start experimenting with their bodies and hopefully that can prevent even one kid from ending up in my situation.

Like most high school guest speakers, Peter covered all the standard expertise of his field — in this case, basic methods of HIV transmission — while sharing personal experiences with the students.

When I was a kid, formal sex education was pretty slim. We depended on learning about things in the playground or the back lot — just about anywhere else but school. We were given a rough idea of what this "plumbing" was all about, but not necessarily the mechanics of how it all went together.

I can remember line drawings of the female reproductive system. They always looked like some kid's rendering of Bullwinkle the Moose — totally disembodied from a person, like they were some separate entity. Today there are some good family life and sex education programs for the schools, but it doesn't seem that there's anyone paying attention to whether these things get carried out or not.

When you're fifteen or sixteen, you're going to spend most of the rest of your life being sexually active ... If you were a kid this age wanting to drive a car, you'd have to get a learner's permit, take some lessons, write an examination before you could go out and do it. But with the kind of education we're giving these kids, it's kind of like showing them how to use the starter button but not how to use the clutch or the brake.[2]

By spring 1991 the AIDS Vancouver speakers' bureau already had several representatives circulating in the school system. Few of them spoke directly about their own sexual orientation, but Peter never hesitated to discuss it; having already come out on television, he had no difficulty sharing his thoughts on sexuality with students.

In the last week of April he took his AIDS awareness campaign to Vancouver Island, where he had spent most of his childhood. The students at Nanaimo & District Senior Secondary (NDSS), like many of the groups he addressed, were often bold in their questions. It wasn't long, for example, before someone asked him how many boyfriends he'd had. "I've had a few long-term relationships," he replied, blushing, "and some not so long term." How did he get AIDS? "I was seeing someone in the late seventies who died of AIDS in 1985," he began. "It's quite possible that I became infected through having sex with him. But it's possible that there could have been maybe more than one person that I was involved with that had this infection. I can't say for sure." Did he infect anyone else with it? "I don't know. I can say that I had — I guess for about a year and a half before I got sick — been seeing someone, and this was before we really were talking about safer sex, so we had unsafe sex for that year and a half. Now I know I was infected for that time. We had unprotected sex on many occasions, and for whatever reason this person didn't become infected, and I'm very glad of that."

When he told the group he had found a new lover, one girl scolded him for continuing to have sex, adding that he "should know better" as a doctor. Peter responded by gently reminding her of safer sex methods, adding that, in any case, there is more to hot sex than anal intercourse: "Let's broaden our definition a bit, shall we?"

When he looked at *Playboy* magazine as a teenager, Peter told them, it wasn't the centrefolds that turned him on — it was the Marlboro Man in the accompanying ads. After asking how many people in the room were left-handed, he pointed out that the same number of people would one day identify themselves as gay. "So, if you're throwing around words like 'faggot' or 'dyke,' you could be hurting someone — your best friend, someone in your family."

Because he had AIDS and was up-front about his sexuality, Peter left himself open to judgment about his sex habits, but he made no excuses or apologies for his life before 1986. He had been carefree, he said. Even when he was a resident medical student at St. Paul's Hospital, the facts about HIV transmission were only beginning to be discussed. Now that the methods of transmission were known, he felt it was his duty to share this knowledge with other young people.

Despite the nervous giggles or hushed silence that his anecdotes sometimes provoked, Peter's opposition from students was limited to a few dissenting voices at the back of school auditoriums. At NDSS the group was so large that a few negative comments by a couple of macho boys were enough to distract other students. "One of the things that I learned from my experience was that I didn't want to end up talking to 400 Grade 10 students in the gym," he said in a diary the following year. "It's not a very conducive environment to learning."

Another problem with this format, Peter told his Nanaimo hosts, was that fifty minutes was not enough time to discuss homosexuality apart from its relation to AIDS. With so many other issues to address — HIV transmission and prevention methods among the most important — it was difficult to argue on one hand that anyone can be at risk, and then have time to explain why homophobia was wrong. Peter realized that many students believed "Gay = AIDS" and this was all the more reason to discuss sexual orientation as an issue separate from HIV.

Peter McCue, Nanaimo district coordinator for the provincial Family Life program, agreed. "One kind of backlash [from students] would have been around saying that 'AIDS is not a gay disease,' and then not addressing that being gay doesn't mean you're going to become HIV positive. Because there wasn't an opportunity to do the follow up [on sexuality] that was necessary," added McCue, "I think that raised the level of apprehension for some of our kids — like, 'Who else in this room is gay?' People may be at their most homophobic at that age level, and if you discuss gayness as normal even at levels lower than 10 percent, people will start looking around and making stereotypical perceptions, whether they are or aren't. Even if they don't fit the stereotypical view, they feel themselves as being very vulnerable."[3]

At the very least, Peter's amiable presence in the classroom provided gay students with a much-needed role model, just as the football player Dave Kopay had been such an example to Peter when he was a teenager. Various studies had linked high teen suicide rates with anguish over homosexuality, and this was no doubt due to feelings of isolation and the lack of information available.

Discussion of sexuality raised the level of apprehension for the students' parents, as well. Many parents believed it was still possible to conduct sex education with the approach used in the 1950s and 60s, with no reference to bodily experience at all, heterosexual or otherwise. Not surprisingly, Peter's visit to Nanaimo area schools became the target of parental paranoia about sexual orientation. The complaint occurred shortly after Diary 38 (April 17, 1991) went to air. In the diary, Peter is shown standing at the edge of a school playground, describing the innovative sex education program in Nanaimo.

Available to the kids was a bunch of information — posters and pamphlets and things — on a variety of subjects, one of which was human sexuality.

There was information on heterosexuality, bisexuality and homosexuality. I thought "Boy, times sure have changed from when I was getting my sex education." I can remember when I was about eleven — we were shown a film called, I think, "From Boy to Man." And it basically explained that we were going to get bigger and hairier and smellier. But that was about it. There was no discussion about human sexuality of any kind.

You can imagine, at that age, knowing I was attracted to members of my own sex, what I must have thought. I really felt that I was the only one. There seemed to be nowhere that I could get the information and certainly it wasn't a subject that people talked freely about ... I'm glad to see that times are changing and this information is more readily available to the kids who really need it. Just by talking about these things, we aren't necessarily condoning them. But at least we're informing the people for whom this information is important. I'd like to think that kids today can grow up much better adjusted, feeling less alone and less isolated than I had, twenty years ago.

The sight of an openly gay man encouraging liberalized sex education was more than one Nanaimo woman could handle. Mary de Vries, who had children attending NDSS, had no idea that Dr. Peter had come to Nanaimo until she watched the 11 p.m. news final on CBC. Distressed that she had not been informed of this event, she contacted both the NDSS principal and Peter McCue, to whom she had previously complained about the school district's sex education program. She reminded McCue of her right to opt out of the Family Life program; if she had known that sexual orientation was going to be discussed, she told him, her family could easily discuss it in the safety of their own home. Why did she have to find out these things on the evening news instead of from the school district? McCue acknowledged the school's responsibility to inform parents, thanked de Vries for raising the concern, and promised to send a memo to district schools on the issue.

Not surprisingly, one of the issues that most upset de Vries was Peter's support for the installation of condom dispensers in the schools. The issue came up again the year after Peter's first appearance in Nanaimo schools when a talk by Shirley and Nancy at a local church meeting prompted a strong protest from a woman named Mary Lindsay. Lindsay, who had no idea who Dr. Peter was until someone explained his connection to Shirley and Nancy, was stunned by Nancy's call for condom dispensers in schools and by her suggestion that education, not abstinence, was the best way to combat AIDS. "I am truly sorry for you and so many others as you face a horrible death, and I have the greatest compassion for your parents as I have four children of my own," Lindsay wrote Peter, following her introduction to Shirley and Nancy. "I was asked what I would do if it were MY son who has AIDS, and of course my pain would be unbearable, but the point that was missed was what I would have done when I learned my son was living that perverted lifestyle?"

Instead of taking such comments personally, Peter preferred to make an example of homophobic ignorance. A conference of rural nurses he attended at a resort in central B.C. during May, for example, illustrated the continuing need to educate the educators and caregivers.

One of the women who organized [the conference] brought along her thirteen-year-old son and a school chum. They had a great weekend — all sorts of things for them to do — and when they got back to school they had to write a report on what they had done over the weekend. The one fellow mentioned in his report that he had met Dr. Peter ... and that he had helped me find my way around. Well apparently he arrived at school the next day and one of his teachers wouldn't come near him, wouldn't even hand out a paper to him. And he was very confused and went home and asked his mom what was going on.

Unfortunately, people like doctors, nurses, teachers, because they're educated, a lot of people feel that they know something about these things. Well in many cases they don't. They all have their own opinions, but often those opinions are very wrong. For example, I graduated from medical school in 1985, and we had no formal teaching on AIDS, so you can imagine that anyone who's graduated then or before — and that represents most of the doctors practising — these people have no more information about HIV infection than Joe Public, unless they've made a special effort to learn. And most don't.

Now, I understand that in Washington state last year, they passed a law that anyone who needed licencing to practise their job — whether you were a surgeon or a vet or a hairdresser — you had to have seven-and-a-half hours of instruction on HIV infection. That's pretty wide-sweeping legislation, but maybe not such a bad idea. When I hear the stories of the ignorance that's still out there, I realize how important it is, to get the education done. The problem is, how?[4]

Peter also recalled an incident at his sister's home in Nanaimo in which his eight-year-old nephew had returned from a soccer game and described how one of his teammates had kicked a boy from the opposing team.

"Why did he do that?" Nancy asked her son.

"Because the kid's a gaylord."

"What does that mean?"

"Well, you know," her son shrugged. "A gaylord, a homosexual." Peter was not surprised by the incident. Given that his young nephew had shown so much compassion toward him since learning he was blind and had AIDS, it was clear he didn't understand what he was talking about. He was simply mimicking the catcalls of other children.

At the [B.C. AIDS Conference in November 1990] there was a speaker who was talking about the development of homophobia in the North American male. Homophobia refers to the irrational fear and hatred of people who are attracted to members of their own sex. In this particular circumstance, he said that as little boys we go to school and we quickly learn that the worst thing that you can call someone is a "sissy" or a "fem" or a "fairy" — something that denotes culturally defined female behaviour in a male. That in itself speaks volumes about our society, I think.

In any case, you go through school with this as being the worst in your arsenal of insults. And then you get to puberty and sexuality starts rearing its head in a variety of forms. And a connection is made between homosexuality and being a "sissy" or a "fairy." You've already set up a pattern of hating anyone who's a "sissy" or a "fairy" and therefore you hate someone who might be perceived to be homosexual.

This is particularly a problem for someone who finds themself attracted to members of the same sex. It sets up a pattern of self-hatred, and also a pattern of hatred of any potential partners, and therefore all kinds of problems with relationships.

Prejudices like this get going, they gain momentum, and they persist in our society. Often no one questions why, and certainly no one can pinpoint any contributions that they've made to our society. But I think at least acknowledging them is a first step, and a first step can be made to alter the perpetuation of these very destructive and damaging attitudes.[5]

U p to this point, Peter's health had not interrupted his public appearances, but on May 15 he addressed viewers from the same hospital room where he was first diagnosed with AIDS in 1986. His health was fairly stable when he began alpha interferon treatments in January, but he soon began feeling a general lack of energy and lost a few pounds. By the end of April he decided to switch to chemotherapy. Because chemotherapy can slow down the production of infection-fighting cells in the bone marrow, he developed a fever and was admitted to emergency at St. Paul's on May 9.

Moments before the CBC crew arrived, Peter felt a wave of nausea and had to run to the bathroom as David Paperny walked in. Ever the consummate professional, he managed to compose himself within a couple of minutes and was able to deliver a lucid monologue about what was happening in his body.

They did some blood tests, and they found that there was bacteria growing in my blood. When you have very low white blood cell counts, you can get an infection such as this from something as simple as a shaving cut or a pimple. If there's nothing there to fight off the bacteria, they get into your blood, get frisky and start multiplying like rabbits. And then you end up here.

There's a lot of other scary possibilities when you have a fever and AIDS. I didn't have any other symptoms — no pain anywhere — so they really didn't know where to look immediately. They cultured everything, and they wanted to rule out the possibility of all kinds of nasty things.

The infection that I have is a common one: it's a skin bacteria called staph, or staphylococcus, and it's easily treated with intravenous antibiotics.

It's certainly not going to do me in, but tomorrow's lunch — the salmon surprise — just might.[6]

When he was discharged from St. Paul's on May 17, Peter still had trouble with his medications. The average T (helper) cell count is between 450 and 1300 cells, but Peter had only ten when he addressed viewers in Diary 41 on May 29. The AZT wasn't working anymore, he explained, so after a brief "drug holiday," dideoxyinosine — an infection-fighting treatment otherwise known as ddI — would be next on the list. "It seems like we're doing a juggling act, and essentially we are. Maybe I'm a bit of a guinea pig, but I think there's more comfort in knowing that you're doing something than nothing."

It had been a nasty scare but Peter was on his feet again within days of his release from St. Paul's. He could look back on the first half of 1991 as a productive six months: he had gained national attention for the diaries, built bridges with people suffering from other illnesses, and had brought valuable AIDS awareness into the education system while stimulating a debate on sexual orientation in the schools. As he approached his 34th birthday, Peter could have sat back to savour some of these achievements. As always, however, he didn't have time to relax.

Portrait of a future diarist. Peter Young at age three, in Penticton, 1960. "An expressive boy with a vivid imagination," he began keeping a personal journal at age eight.

This 1968 family photo in Nanaimo shows Peter, eleven, beside sister Nancy, thirteen. A practical joker with a " mischievous sense of humour," Peter displayed a natural curiosity that would later serve him well as a doctor.

Grade 10 school photo from Woodlands
Junior Secondary in Nanaimo, 1972. At
age fifteen, Peter had already suffered the
homophobic verdict of Ann Landers:
"Twisted and sick," she wrote, homosexuals
"want desperately to be like everyone else."
Until he was nineteen, Peter followed her
advice to stay in the closet.

The charmer, circa 1985.

126

Doctor Peter at last! In spring 1985, after nine years of study, Peter (second from left) is ready to begin practice as a physician. Fellow UBC medical school graduates Stacey Elliot, Debbie Bebb, and Richard Bebb remained close to Peter during his lengthy illness.

On the Howe Sound Crest Trail, September 16, 1986. AIDS was already ripping its way through his body but Peter had no problem making it up the mountain during a hiking trip. Soon after this hike he could not "climb a flight of stairs without stopping for breath," and on September 28 — twelve days after this photo was taken — a violent bout with Pneumocystis carinii pneumonia nearly killed him.

127

Holidaying in the resort village of Ibiza, Spain, a popular spot for gay men, in June 1987. At 30, Peter had recovered from a near-fatal bout with AIDS-related pneumonia less than a year earlier and — despite his medical knowledge — still believed he could "beat this thing."

Best friends. Ross Murray with Peter on the Oregon coast, Thanksgiving weekend, 1989. Peter was already losing the vision in his right eye.

Andy Hiscox with Peter at Bob and Shirley Young's home on January 12, 1991. Hiscox, 42, had only recently begun dating men when he first met the AIDS diarist in the fall of 1990.

On the slopes at Blackcomb Mountain resort, March 1991. Fulfilling an earlier promise to his viewers, Peter prepares to go skiing for the first time since losing his vision. He's flanked by CBC cameraman Pat Bell and AIDS Diary producer David Paperny.

The walking laboratory. Peter with his seeing-eye dog Harvey in the spring of 1991. As a medical doctor, Peter strongly supported the pharmaceutical industry. But he occasionally had his doubts. "I'm starting to feel a bit like a human toxic waste dump," he said on Diary 67, "and I wonder how much my body can tolerate pollution with all these different types of quite harmful medications." A complete catalogue of prescriptions would have been difficult to compile for this book, says his doctor, Phil Sestak, because between 1986 and 1992 Peter went through literally dozens of different drug therapies.

The AIDS diarist turns 34. At a surprise birthday party in Nanaimo, Peter is joined by his parents, Bob and Shirley Young, with family friend Olga Barnes (second from left). With them are Peter's niece Rebecca, nephew Ryan, and David Paperny's daughter Anna.

Peter's fondness for animals was clearly displayed in his affection for Harvey, a constant companion during his last two years.

On Vancouver Island's Long Beach with David Paperny in February 1992. Peter revisits the site that inspired his "Affirmation." Paperny's sensitive approach was a critical factor in Peter's decision to go on television. "I felt right from the first time we met that I could trust him," Peter recalled in the Witness documentary. "And the sense of trust has remained with us."

September 14, 1992. Peter, with Logan McMenamie, Harvey, Shirley and Bob Young, visits the Vancouver Island churchyard where he would be buried two months later. For Peter, the choice of this gravesite — with the blessing of the Anglican church — was like a "final homecoming."

132

12

The Fruits of Fame

T he day he left St. Paul's, May 17, 1991, a feature article on
Peter appeared in the *Georgia Straight*, Vancouver's weekly
entertainment tabloid. Peter had done the interview long
before he was hospitalized and was confident that he hadn't been too
revealing, but he found out otherwise when Andy arrived to take him
home. Andy was visibly upset. Peter had told the writer that being
HIV positive does not mean the end of one's sex life, adding that he
had begun seeing a man seven months earlier who was HIV negative.
He had not mentioned Andy by name but he might as well have; all
of Hiscox's friends knew he was living with Peter, so the article's
disclosure that the AIDS diarist was not single would have confirmed
their relationship.

Andy was worried about the article's impact on his continued involvement with straight friends and business associates. "A lot of people don't realize that, less than twelve months earlier, I had been on
the other side," Hiscox said later, referring to his previous romantic
involvement with women. "I hadn't been used to being looked on as
a gay person by non-gay people." Even if his friends didn't reject him
or accuse him of having lived a lie, they, and Andy, still faced a
lengthy period of adjustment to his new identity. "I tried hard to be-

lieve that being married to a woman would be possible but every time it came in the vicinity I couldn't see myself there, knowing that it was really a man that I wanted to be with," he recalled. "[But] it was hard for me to look into my gay side because my image of a gay person was not me."

Though Peter had never been sexually attracted to women, he was sympathetic to Andy's dilemma. He apologized and promised to be more careful in the future, but couldn't help feeling disappointed; he had always hoped that one day he would be able to publicly acknowledge his relationship with Andy, perhaps even on the diaries. By introducing his lover to viewers, Peter could send an important message to other people living with a fatal illness: that it's never too late to fall in love, and that one should never assume that an AIDS diagnosis precludes meeting a partner.[1]

Peter's surprise birthday party on June 8 was a reminder of just how far he had come since his own public disclosure of being gay and having AIDS. When he arrived at his parents' home that day, he was met by 60 people including family friends, medical school companions, and current acquaintances, gay and straight. The presence of so many different friends in the same place was a humbling experience. "My mom really pulled a fast one on me," Peter marvelled in the following week's diary.

> I don't think it could have happened a year ago — before I started doing this series with the CBC, before my parents really came to grips with my situation and started sharing what was going on with me with their friends and so on ... I'd like to think that there aren't too many people out there who are HIV infected, or their families, who are living in real isolation with this problem. When there is so much warmth and compassion. I really hope that all of that's available to everyone if they decide to look for it.

It was a noble, if somewhat naive sentiment. Many people with AIDS were condemned to isolation by families that rejected them. Others, with no families at all, were isolated by poverty. And as Peter had already told his viewers, turning to one's family for support can sometimes be scary, even if family is the most likely place to find it.

On June 19 he explained how social shame often prevents people with AIDS from reaching out, even to those who would support them.

> It wasn't that long ago that I was peeling the labels off my empty AZT bottles before I'd throw them out. I don't know what I was thinking, as far as who was going to find them or what they were going to do with the information once they found it. But that kind of paranoia really does exist for people with HIV infection.
>
> Many people are very self-conscious about being seen going into St. Paul's Hospital to have blood tests or pick up medications. They're afraid of who they might run into or who might see them go into the building. And all of this comes from an aspect of AIDS that is much more than an infection that can cause severe illness and death. It has to do with who was affected by this illness initially: gay people, drug addicts, prostitutes. People not at all valued by our society. And because of who it affected to start with, that very much affected how everyone reacted.[2]

It was similar to the speech he had delivered while shooting the first diary in July 1990. At that time, his lecture about homophobic prejudice in society was considered a diversion from the real goal of "Peter's Story," which was to describe one man's life with AIDS. Forty-three segments later, however, that same speech was a reflection of the growing influence that Dr. Peter was enjoying as a media critic and AIDS ambassador.

As an ambassador, Peter now had an international profile. Early that spring David Paperny received notice that AIDS Diary had been selected for a screening at Input 91, an international conference of public broadcasters taking place in Dublin, Ireland, in mid-June. The annual event was a week-long gathering of 600 of the world's highest calibre public television producers to view selected pieces and exchange ideas about innovative television. Paperny had attended a similar conference as an observer in Montreal in 1986, but now a project of his had been selected by an international jury. Normally producers were not accompanied by the "talent" — the feature subject — of their work, but when he learned that AIDS Diary had been chosen, Paperny convinced the CBC to send both Peter and himself to Dublin on June 14. Although the diaries were not screened until the second-last day of the conference, Peter was in demand the entire time he was there. Producers from France and Germany, many of them gay, were impressed by his out-of-the-closet stance in the diaries; one of them even selected the series for another presentation in Paris. Peter, for his part, was struck by the universal appeal of the diaries.

Following the conference, Peter and David — along with Andy Hiscox and Audrey Mehler, Paperny's wife, who had arrived just in time to see the screening of the diaries — travelled around Ireland. Before leaving Dublin, Paperny arranged for a CBC crew from London to fly in and videotape Peter describing his impressions of a foreign country.

My impressions of the place are completely dependent on my other senses — on what I can hear, smell, taste and feel. What I can hear is a fairly bustling city. Not too noisy, but still busy. The traffic is coming at you from the opposite directions, and that's a bit disconcerting. What I can feel — well, the cobblestone streets are much more interesting to walk on than the regular pavement at home. What I can smell — well, aside from the stinky double decker buses, not much except fairly clean fresh air and every now and then a whiff of the sea. And what I taste? Well what more can I say than Guinness and Bushmill's? ...

I guess I'd be lying if I said that I wasn't sorry that I can't see the place. I'm sure there's so many wonderful things to see. I'm still managing to put together an image. A lot of it's dependent on pictures and films that I'd seen before. I'd often thought that it may be too much hassle to travel blind, because you wouldn't be able to really see things. But I've got a different sense of appreciation of what's out there. And I find this to be a very warm and comfortable place — somewhere I'd like to come back to.[3]

Despite his busy schedule and travel itinerary, Peter could never ignore his health for very long. Back in Vancouver in July he continued his prednisone and chemotherapy treatments, and took antibiotics for recurring sinus infections. He began taking ddI, another anti-viral drug, but had to drop that medication within five days because of muscle aches and pains. When he was feeling healthy and energetic, Peter could not detect many of the exterior changes happening to him, such as the spread of KS lesions and the cataract in his right eye. By August, though, he felt the swelling in his right hand from the KS, and his left leg had become much thicker than his right one.

"[The KS has] plugged up the lymphatic system so that the fluid doesn't drain out as it used to," he explained on Diary 51 (August 7, 1991). "When I talked about it before, it was just the lower part of my leg that was the problem. Now it's moved right up to the top." His knee was difficult to bend and the foot was puffy — there were only a couple of shoes he could fit it into — and KS on the sole of his foot could be painful.

> We've tried a numbers of ways to battle this. The interferon didn't work. The radiation did, and I just had some more of that, right in here [HE POINTS TO HIS GROIN AND ABDOMINAL AREA], hopefully to shrink those lymph nodes ... You just have to keep plugging away at some of these things, trying different therapies, and piecing things together so that you get a battle plan that works for you.

Despite the discomfort, Peter managed to take a brief trip to New York with Maggie Johnston, his guide dog instructor from Ottawa who had become a close friend since she had taken Peter through his training with Harvey the previous fall.

Johnston was amazed by Peter's level of recall while on vacation. In his first trip back to New York since 1988, Peter had no trouble remembering street corners, addresses, and other landmarks as he escorted Maggie around New York City for her first visit. It was supposed to be Maggie leading the blind Peter around the city, not the other way round![4]

Also amazing was the way travel seemed to rehabilitate Peter. As on many of the trips he had taken since falling ill in 1986, his health improved shortly before he left Vancouver and remained stable throughout his stay in New York. When he returned home, however, the fevers came back and his energy level flagged again.

For his last diary of the summer of 1991, a weary-looking Peter was shown sitting at the steering wheel of a vintage fire engine in Stanley Park, site of the fifth annual walkathon for the Vancouver Persons With AIDS Society. (The walk date, September 29, was also the fifth anniversary of his own diagnosis.) Peter had said very little on behalf of organized AIDS groups to this point, but this time he took full advantage of his television platform to slam homophobic resistance to the PWA Society's fundraising efforts.

"AIDS organizations have always had a tough time getting money — whether from government, the homophobic world of finance or big business, or from so-called society," he said, recalling a fundraiser he had been involved with the previous spring. The dinner and dance at the Granville Island Hotel was a benefit for the short-lived Foundation for Immune Diseases.

> We had a society liaison person who reported back to us that several society matrons were heard to say that they wouldn't support this event. The tickets said that there was going to be dancing, and they wouldn't support an event where men might be seen dancing together. Give me a break.
>
> Organizations such as the Persons with AIDS Society and AIDS Vancouver help people like me keep healthy, keep well-informed, and they help our family and friends deal with the tough times. They also educate our children ... If it weren't for organizations like the PWA Society and AIDS Vancouver, I probably wouldn't be sitting here five years after the fact, and I certainly wouldn't be walking in this year's walkathon.[5]

The walkathon, Vancouver's prime fundraiser for AIDS awareness and support services, had recently expanded from a small community benefit to a massive media blitz, raising more than $100,000 in pledges the previous year. This would not have been possible without an extensive public relations strategy that included television and radio ads and public service announcements, a celebrity barbeque with TV personalities, and a concert in the park. By asking Dr. Peter to deliver the keynote address, the PWA Society recognized the value of his increasing public profile.

In the diary following the event, Peter praised the organizers for the large increase in walk participants and proceeds. "The politicians seemed to turn out in full force this time, as did the media," he said in a monologue shot in a CBC edit booth. "And it seemed to me that over the past year, the media — at least locally — are covering AIDS issues much more responsibly, with much less hysteria and sensationalism." It was a naive generalization, and his optimism would soon prove unfounded.

PART 3

Politics And Power

There has to be a time, I think, when Martina Navratilova will be able to show up at court side with her fling of the day, give her a kiss and go on to win Wimbledon, and that is just accepted ... To me, that's the kind of thing that people can do in a very natural, unselfconscious way that's going to make more difference over time than all of the ACT-UP demonstrations are ever going to achieve.

CONVERSATION WITH THE AUTHOR,
FEBRUARY 7, 1992

13

On the Firing Line

While Peter had taken advantage of his role as a TV columnist to comment on general issues like sexuality and homophobia, he'd had no occasion to comment on or interpret misleading news reports. This silence ended, however, when he was confronted by a campaign that challenged his own philosophy as a physician with AIDS.

The driving force behind the U.S. campaign to impose mandatory AIDS testing on all health care workers was a 23-year-old woman named Kimberly Bergalis, a Florida resident who developed AIDS in 1989 after having a tooth pulled two years earlier. Bergalis, one of at least five patients believed to have been infected by a dentist, David Acer, was the first known case of a patient who had contracted HIV during a medical procedure.[1]

Outraged by the lack of support from local and state medical authorities — who initially refused to believe that Kimberly was infected by her dentist — Bergalis and her family sued Acer's estate and accepted a $1 million settlement after his death in 1990. A year later the Bergalises were back in the headlines with a campaign to invoke mandatory testing of all health care workers performing invasive procedures. As their crusade picked up steam in the American media, the debate spilled over into the Canadian press.

When Peter decided to continue practising medicine following his AIDS diagnosis in 1986 he had weighed the options carefully, consulting his own physician and the AIDS care team at St. Paul's, as well as medical school colleagues. He had never expected that HIV-positive caregivers would become a focus of such intense media scrutiny.

According to Phil Sestak, the issue was a matter of scientific knowledge, not controversy; as long as Peter — or any other HIV-positive health worker — was competent and took all precautions against exposing his blood to patients, there should be no reason to restrict him. Peter was advised against performing any invasive procedures in which he could cut himself and expose a patient to HIV. "Assisting in an operating room would be difficult and quite iffy. I would have recommended him not to do that. And high risk obstetrics, where he's delivering babies and he could contaminate the mother's and the baby's blood at the same time," Sestak said. So Peter avoided doing obstetrics and surgical assists despite the fact that no studies of HIV-positive orthopedic surgeons or obstetricians had shown increased risk in HIV transmission.

In one of his first diaries Peter told viewers that he continued practising medicine after he had AIDS, and he suffered no backlash as a result. But when the Bergalis campaign for mandatory testing intensified in the summer of 1991, he made his case more forcefully.

Recently the whole issue of health care workers being tested and having this information [HIV status] available has come up because of a case that's happened in the States. It seems that there's a dentist in Florida who may have infected as many as five of his patients with HIV. Now, this is the only such case of a health care worker apparently passing along the infection to patients in all of North America and Western Europe. And if this were to happen as an accident — to have five patients in one practice so affected — the odds against this are so staggeringly large as to make it almost impossible. What's the other possibility?

Sadly, it seems that there's a strong likelihood he may have infected them intentionally. A hard thing to prove. But no one's discussing this; instead, there's been this incredible leap of logic to the point where they're talking about mandatory testing of all health care workers. Now, if you looked at what were to happen in that scenario, then health care workers would be demanding that their patients be tested, and if someone were found to be positive, then a health care worker who was negative might not want to look after them because if they were potentially to become infected, it would jeopardize their livelihood. The scenario goes on, and it could be quite a catastrophe.

If you are concerned about becoming infected with HIV through a dental or surgical procedure, you needn't be. If you were to look at all of the things that would be potentially fatal complications of surgery or dentistry, HIV infection would be so far down the list as to be completely inconsequential. As a matter of fact, you'd be at a far greater risk of any of those things just getting in your car and driving to your doctor's appointment. Unfortunately, with HIV, all sense of rationality and proportion go right out the window, even amongst health care professionals. We shouldn't be talking about mandatory testing for HIV, we should be talking about mandatory education of health care workers — then we wouldn't even be discussing this whole issue.[2]

In the United States, the Centers for Disease Control (CDC) were backing away from mandatory-testing legislation as a result of opposition from state and local health officials, medical societies, and PWA advocates. Such legislation, these groups argued, would unfairly destroy careers while wasting millions of dollars that would be better spent on prevention and care. In Vancouver the local health officer agreed. Mandatory testing, said Dr. John Blatherwick, "will force the people you are looking for underground, and you'll do lots of tests on healthy people. You offer them help — you don't take away their livelihood."[3]

Despite these arguments, Kimberly and her parents, George and Anna Bergalis, arrived in Washington, D.C., on September 26, 1991, to present their case for mandatory testing before Congress. Eyebrows were raised in the gay community when they enlisted the support of right-wing senator William Dannemeyer — a Republican from California who was known for his opposition to gay rights legislation.

The Bergalis bill, tabled by Dannemeyer in a closed hearing of the House Subcommittee on Health and the Environment, called for mandatory testing of all health care workers known to perform invasive procedures.

With so much at stake, Bob Young almost forgot how strongly he had opposed Peter's decision to go on television the previous year, and how he had cited the Bergalis case as a reason for his son not to go public. When Peter announced he would be facing off against the parents of Kimberly Bergalis on CBC's national Newsworld channel, Bob gave Peter his blessing.

It was an explosive confrontation. George and Anna Bergalis had taken their daughter's cause to the American people on every major U.S. talk show. While Kimberly returned home to Florida to rest, her parents met Dr. Peter at Newsworld's Toronto studios for the October 19 *On the Line* phone-in show. The Bergalises weren't interested in Peter's background, credentials, or education; all they needed to know was that he was a doctor with AIDS who opposed mandatory testing. With abrasive host Patrick Conlon, a couple of angry suburban parents, and a sensational "question of the day" ("Should all health care workers be tested for the AIDS virus?"), Peter was immediately put on the defensive.

George Bergalis, city finance director for the small Florida town of Fort Pierce, opened with a passionate defence of mandatory testing and an indictment of doctors with AIDS who continue to practise. Asserting his daughter's right to know about the possible risk to her health, he explained how the medical profession, government, and health authorities — including the CDC in Atlanta — had conspired to avoid accountability for the dentist's actions.

"Voluntarism in the U.S. is what caused this to happen to Kimberly and other Kimberly Bergalises," opined George. By initially refusing to acknowledge that Kimberly had been infected by her dentist, he said, the CDC had only "protect[ed] the interests" of the American Medical Association and the American Dental Association. The Bergalises cited the U.S. military's 1985 decision to invoke mandatory testing of all personnel as proof that a precedent had been set and that all other institutions needed only follow suit.[4]

"For a doctor who knows they have an active case of AIDS to continue practising ... they are a coward," said George, glaring in Peter's direction. "It's immoral — it's worse than any felony anyone could commit." The middle-aged man sat only a few feet away from Peter, but his body language suggested he would have been more comfortable had the homosexual doctor with AIDS joined the discussion from a faraway studio.

George and Anna may have had little interest in AIDS before their daughter's diagnosis, but they had certainly done their homework since that time, and Patrick Conlon gave them ample air time to vent their rage. Still, Peter did manage to make a few points. For one thing, he reiterated that David Acer was the only medical worker in the world known to have infected a patient. Hepatitis B, which killed between 200 to 300 health care workers a year in the U.S., was of far greater risk in the hospital setting. In terms of AIDS, said Peter, the use of universal precautions ensured that "the mechanics of a health care worker infecting a patient are extremely difficult." (In fact, 57 other health care professionals in the U.S. had told authorities they were HIV positive. Not one of their 19,000 patients had tested positive by June 1993.[5])

This calm, measured argument only enraged Anna Bergalis more. "Everybody talks about instruments and universal precautions," she said. "Nobody talks about the active, open, draining lesions that that man [David Acer] had in his mouth and on his chest. What are you supposed to do, put the whole man in a glove? Is that what you're supposed to do, Dr. Peters [sic]? When 90 percent of your HIV-positive patients have lesions and more than one type of lesion ... "

Peter interrupted. "I don't know where you're getting that figure from. I've been looking after HIV-positive patients for four years and ... "

"I got that from a book from the University of Miami bookstore when I took my daughter down to the clinic at the University of Miami, and I took her at five o'clock every morning twice a week for almost a year, and they have no cure ... "

George, defending his wife's outburst, explained how the Bergalis family had been thrown into a situation it never invited when their daughter became ill. "One thing we have done since 1989 is we've learned about AIDS. We have learned about how it's transmitted, about how people look, and about how they react and are controlled by the virus."

> CONLON: And you believe what you're told, I guess?
> GEORGE: Not what we're told. What we read. What we get from talking to people —
> ANNA (shouting): We're getting active, open experience!
> GEORGE: The statistics ...
> CONLON: Because I'm looking at two different sets of information here, and I'm confused as hell ... .
> GEORGE: All you need to believe is one thing: Is your life important? And if it is, and you're willing to go to Dr. Peter and have him perform an exposure-prone procedure on you, then God bless you.
> ANNA: God help you.
> GEORGE: And we'll send you a sympathy card when we hear about your demise.

In one of his more memorable non sequiturs, George concluded, "We're not trying to promote hysteria, but if it takes hysteria in a certain person or people in order to alleviate their fears, then they have a right to do that."

The Bergalises showed little patience with callers who disagreed with them. Each time a viewer — often a health care worker — suggested that mandatory testing would drive people with AIDS underground, George countered with brash, American chauvinism: Canada was clearly "behind the times" in AIDS awareness and should catch up to the U.S. in learning how to protect itself. (This despite the U.S. medical establishment's decision not to invoke mandatory testing, for much the same reason that Canada had not implemented it.)

Peter's suggestion that David Acer may have intentionally infected Kimberly only confirmed Anna's worst fear that "some people who are mad at the world" could easily use their positions as trusted professionals to take revenge on an innocent public. Although Acer was the only documented health care worker to have transmitted the virus to patients, Anna Bergalis was convinced that if one person did it, anyone can do it.

To this logic Peter wryly observed how strange it was that people get "exceptionally outraged" about AIDS, "and yet, if someone can take an assault rifle to the local strip mall and shoot up 30 people, it doesn't incite the same degree of horror." This was a reference to the Bergalises' home state of Florida, where gun-related deaths had reached epidemic proportions long before AIDS became an issue. Peter's remark was completely lost on Anna, who could only wince in confusion at the irony of a man she clearly considered one of an evil minority who deserve their fate.

"Actually, the mother wouldn't even sit next to me," Peter recalled a few weeks later in an interview. "I was the enemy, decidedly ... The people who watched it said it was so obvious. The body language, particularly of the mother, was so full of malevolence. I got the impression that she's on the edge, that she could easily be tipped over into something, I don't know what."[6]

Peter was disturbed by the Bergalises' preoccupation with mandatory testing as a key AIDS issue. Their lack of involvement with AIDS education before their daughter's diagnosis was puzzling, given that Anna worked as a public health nurse in a sexually transmitted diseases clinic. Would she have campaigned so hard for a mandatory testing law if most people with AIDS were heterosexual, Peter wondered? Did the Bergalises even support the human rights of gay men with AIDS? If so, why would they enlist the help of someone like William Dannemeyer, who had consistently opposed gay rights legislation? Was their current campaign merely a way of taking revenge on homosexuals for the apparent crime of one gay man against their daughter?

During her appearance on Capitol Hill, the ailing Kimberly raised suspicion among gay PWAs when she told reporters, "[I have] done nothing wrong and yet I'm being made to suffer like this." George Bergalis, describing his daughter's role as "God's messenger on earth," urged Congress to treat AIDS as a disease "rather than a civil rights issue."

David Barr, representing the Gay Men's Health Crisis of New

York City, reminded reporters that 180,000 Americans had already been diagnosed with AIDS, and 120,000 of these PWAs had died — more than twice the number of casualties in the Vietnam war. Yet, he added, no other AIDS case had received as much attention as Kimberly Bergalis. "We are not enemies, even though we are represented as such," said Barr. "We are dying from the same neglect."[7]

Kimberly Bergalis had already left the senate chamber when Barr spoke these words, but it's doubtful they would have had much effect. AIDS politics, as Peter's encounter with Kimberly's parents later demonstrated, were still polarized between "innocent" and "guilty" victims — with the "guilty," who contracted AIDS through sexual practices or drug habits, allegedly deserving their illness. Mandatory testing would fade from the public agenda in the wake of Kimberly's death, but the memory of her bitter campaign lingered on.[8]

14

The Reluctant Activist

After his October trip to Toronto for *On the Line*, Peter and his sister Nancy travelled to Amsterdam for an AIDS conference. Peter met representatives from developing countries where AIDS demographics remained far different from those in North America; in these countries the rates of infection for women and children were much higher. However, as he told AIDS Diary viewers on October 23, some trends in those countries were disturbingly familiar.

It seemed in a lot of cases, these people related that their governments were ignoring or denying what was happening. And when I thought about it, I thought well, that's not really different than what happened in North America. AIDS was first identified in 1981, but it was 1985 before the president of the United States ever said the word AIDS in public. [In 1989] we had the fifth International AIDS Conference in Montreal, but we didn't have a national AIDS policy in Canada. Locally, it wasn't until November of 1990 that funds came through to provide an outreach nurse to provide education for the gay community.

When you look at what's happening in a third world country, it's sort of what's happening or what happened in North America but on a much larger scale. There was an expectation that there might be 40 million cases of HIV infection worldwide by the year 2000. At this conference, they were talking about three countries accounting for that number by the year 2000. That's India, Nigeria and Brazil — countries that have totally ignored what's happening. And it's gotten to the point where they can't ignore it any longer.[1]

Shortly after his discussion of government leadership in AIDS awareness, Peter was one of the few members of the Vancouver AIDS community to be invited to the November 5 swearing-in ceremony of British Columbia's recently elected New Democratic Party government. On the next day's diary he acknowledged how "exciting and flattering" it was to be invited.

If I could be counted as a representative of the AIDS community, I think it's the first time that our provincial government has recognized this group and included us. The last government certainly didn't show much support or cooperation with some of the community-based organizations such as AIDS Vancouver and the Persons with AIDS Society, especially considering that a lot of the work that they were doing was work that should have been the responsibility of the government — they just weren't doing it.

For example, the last government's big AIDS education effort, this 90-second video that cost about $160,000 to produce and no one ever saw it. It was deemed to be immoral — the world's longest condom commercial.

There's two reasons, I think, why this new government is going to be sensitive and helpful for people with AIDS. One of them is that I think that they're more sensitive to gay and lesbian issues in general. In Mike Harcourt's address yesterday, he alluded to the hope that there would be a decrease in discrimination based on the colour of one's skin, one's sexual orientation, or other ethnic or cultural differences. That, coupled with his commitment to improve and keep strong our health care system, makes me hopeful that things for people with AIDS are going to improve greatly in this province.

I've never really been a great follower of any particular party. I always would vote more for the individual than for a party, but in this case, having been marginalized very much by the previous governments in this province, I sort of feel that for once, I'm going to be included.[2]

With governments providing little or no leadership in education, treatment, or the race to find a cure, people with AIDS had to seek their own solutions from the very beginning. Starting with New York's Gay Men's Health Crisis in 1981, most major cities in North America had a Persons With AIDS (PWA) coalition or society by the mid-1980s. These groups focussed on lobbying for drug access, better housing, disability benefits, and basic human rights for people with AIDS, in addition to running food banks and other essential services. Initially they could count on very little government funding, so had to survive on the goodwill of the gay community and on constant AIDS fundraising drives. The efforts of these groups were supplemented by organizations formed to educate and raise awareness (in Vancouver this function had been fulfilled admirably by AIDS Vancouver since 1983) and by PWA groups that targeted women and minorities with concerns not specific to the gay community (i.e. IV drug users and various ethnic communities).

It was generally considered unwise to establish a competing organization, one whose services either duplicated those offered by other community groups or whose fundraising mandate was vague. But such a group, the Foundation for Immune Diseases, formed in Vancouver in the late 1980s. Comprised mostly of local physicians and other concerned professionals, the group was initially conceived to raise research funds for St. Paul's doctors. It was ultimately defeated by its own identity crisis. Despite its exclusive purpose of raising money for AIDS research, the group decided not to use the "A" word in its title because it was afraid it might not get support.

Peter, one of the board members, was frustrated by the group's approach, especially its decision to hire a fundraiser whose salary ate up valuable funds. When FID disbanded in 1991, he was much less enthusiastic about getting involved with other AIDS organizations. When AIDS Vancouver asked him to be on its board of directors, he declined. In a later diary, he explained his reluctance.

I haven't become involved with any specific AIDS-related groups for a number of reasons. One of them is that I have zero tolerance for politics and bureaucracy. Another and perhaps the main reason is that although a lot of these groups do good work, they don't necessarily get along and I don't really understand the reasons for the discord.[3]

Peter's critique of internal squabbling was not well-received by the AIDS community. As someone who had limited experience in community-based organizations, his criticism of the "discord" seemed rather naive, said Tom Mountford, vice-president and support committee chair for the Vancouver PWA Society. "By saying 'I won't be political. I refuse to get involved in the politics or the bureaucracy' — that's hiding your head in the sand," Mountford contended. "I felt the same way when I joined this organization, but you can't get away from it. You can't belong or have any part in an organization like this and not be political." Given that most of the community's gains had been achieved through vigorous politics and relentless lobbying of bureaucrats, he said, Peter's refusal to engage in "politics and bureaucracy" only trivialized the genuine achievements of AIDS activists.[4]

Others were disturbed by the exclusive manner in which he approached AIDS awareness. Once Peter received his public platform, they said, he didn't share it with anyone. "It used to make me angry that he would not spend more time collaborating with other AIDS activists," PWA Society president Arn Schilder recalled after his death. "And I thought it was rather hurtful and exclusive not sharing [his] experience — and probably isolated him even more."

Peter never responded to this kind of criticism. He felt that the assumption that every public person with AIDS should be part of a coalition undervalued his efforts. Sure, his weekly diary was not about to create a bushel of new drug treatments, nor could Peter solve the PWA housing problem by going on television. But he was making more straight people aware of AIDS, and front-line organizations were probably receiving more money as a result. He was contributing to the growing public perception that AIDS was important and that straight people should pay attention — even if the majority of PWAs were gay. So why should he feel guilty just because he wasn't sitting on some committee?[5]

For the most part, local AIDS organizations embraced Peter's efforts. To AIDS Vancouver he was an indispensable resource who opened doors previously closed to its speaker's bureau by addressing corporations such as the BC Telephone Company and business fraternities as far away as Toronto. Was this not a valid form of activism? The PWA Society couldn't really complain either, given that Peter provided valuable promotion for the walkathon on the diaries and took frequent phone referrals from members with CMV retinitis, many of whom depended on Peter as the only gay man they knew who was coping with blindness.

But there was a lingering skepticism surrounding Peter's relationship to the organized AIDS community. Some of his gay critics couldn't let go of the image they had of Peter from pre-AIDS Diary days. There were many gay men who had watched as he reinvented himself from Peter Young the North Vancouver schoolboy to Peter Jepson-Young, medical professional; then, following his blindness, Peter Jepson-Young the party animal became Saint Peter, AIDS ambassador. For people who had watched him all these years, it was hard not to look at Dr. Peter and see a shameless opportunist.

This was certainly Oraf's impression. Oraf, a towering, leather-clad, bohemian performance artist who had lived in Vancouver for twenty years and had seen the best and worst of the city's night life, had been the court photographer at many of the upscale parties attended by Vancouver's yuppie gay set in the late 70s and early 80s. It was during 1981 that Oraf first encountered Peter Young.

With characteristic venom — and a small dose of class anger — Oraf recalled Peter's milieu as a collection of "coffee table gays," men whose apartments resembled a feature spread in *Architectural Digest* magazine, whose sexuality was only visible on weekends — and then only visible to the young and gorgeous who belonged to the same economic class as themselves. These men played all the right games on the corporate success ladder and didn't make waves politically.

Peter was representative of this circle. With his gym-toned body, stylish clothing, and easy charm he exuded the confident air of an Ivy League jock. Oraf and many future AIDS activists bumped into the attractive young student at bars like Faces, the Playpen, the Gandydancer, and Buddies, but he would never talk to them when they approached him. Oraf thought that, in his case, this was because Peter considered him too poor, too political, and not "genetically correct" enough to fit in. One longtime member of the PWA Society described Peter as "a complete snot" who didn't bother getting to know someone "unless they fit his idea of youth, beauty and privilege. You know, if you wore Polo and went to Palm Springs, then you were alright."

To Oraf, the advances in gay liberation following the Stonewall riots in 1969 were like winning a war, but the aftermath in the 1970s was a ten-year sexual looting spree following the victory.[6] What bothered him from the perspective of the 1990s was not that Peter had joined the "looting" (how could he or anyone else have known what the health consequences would be?) but that he wasn't willing to acknowledge his own actions once the spree was over, and made no reference to them on the diaries. Instead of examining the 70s and early 80s in all of their hedonistic madness, he said, Peter was approaching AIDS Diary with complete piety and sanctimony, allowing himself to be portrayed as a saint. When Oraf encountered him at a party one night in 1991, the now-blind Peter — surrounded by an adoring flock who focussed all their attention on him — seemed startled at the sound of Oraf's voice, as if the artist were some Dickensian Ghost of Excess Past.

Rooke Ovalle had a much different view of Peter's transformation. As anatomy professor at UBC's School of Medicine, Ovalle's initial contact with Peter was limited to the lecture hall in which Peter's demeanour — like that of most other students — was generally earnest and respectful. They met in a gay bar for the first time in June 1985, just after Peter graduated and shortly before he departed for his internship in Ottawa. For Peter, the shock of meeting his anatomy professor in a place so far beyond the rational confines of the university was almost too much. Here was Dr. Ovalle, a rather bookish fellow with horn-rimmed glasses and a shy manner, standing with a drink in his hand and appreciating the scenery. Just like he was. Slightly embarrassed by the revelation, Peter chatted with his professor but maintained the formality he had shown in the classroom. He wasn't about to discuss gay things with a prof.

Two years later, Ovalle was reintroduced to Peter by a mutual friend. Ovalle was shopping in a supermarket when the young man came in and told him he wanted him to meet a friend.

"What's his name?"

"Peter Jepson-Young."

"Oh, I know him. He was a student of mine," Ovalle said. "I haven't seen him in a couple of years."

"Did you know he has AIDS?"

When the two walked out to the young man's maroon-coloured Jaguar, Peter said hello and was polite and reserved — just like the last time.

When Ovalle saw him again, another two years later, it was at a Hallowe'en party at Graceland, a post-modern dance club in downtown Vancouver. Ovalle walked in alone, dressed in street clothes, to find Peter decked out as a creature from outer space: short, dumpy, and rather silly looking, with large tentacles. While the other partiers revelled in the madness, Peter maintained his facade of politeness and gentility.

"Jesus," Ovalle thought. "This guy doesn't like me."

In late summer 1990, however, Ovalle encountered a different Peter when he spotted him across the floor in a busy sportswear boutique. Ovalle didn't bother trying to get his attention — he didn't see the point, given Peter's distance in all their previous encounters — but when Peter recognized him, Ovalle was surprised by his enthusiasm. "Hi!" Peter exclaimed, crossing the floor to greet him.

Although he had never said a word to Ovalle about his illness, he turned to the topic of AIDS almost immediately, asking his former professor what was being taught in the UBC curriculum about it. Within weeks of that meeting Peter was addressing first-year students, accompanied by either Ovalle or Michael Myers.

He also struck up a friendship with Ovalle, and his former professor got to know the Peter who was able to laugh at himself, who enjoyed long walks and was entirely at peace with the world. It was as if,
having become blind, he didn't need to keep up appearances anymore. He could just be himself.

❖

P eter never did discuss his earlier social life with reporters or
on the diaries. He likely decided that, despite its relevance to
his journey with AIDS, such gossip was nobody's business
but his own. As well, he knew a description of his earlier behaviour
would reinforce the stereotypes of promiscuity and hedonism that are
used by homophobic columnists to discredit the gay movement.[7]

At the same time, he also rejected the notion that his comfortable
lifestyle and his position as a doctor isolated him from the experiences
of most people with AIDS. "In some respects one could argue that
here's someone who is white anglo-saxon protestant, middle class,
educated and the only thing he's got going against him is that he's
gay," Peter said during a later interview. "Well I'm sorry but in our
society that's like the biggest thing that can go against you. I could be
everything that I am and straight and Jewish, or Chinese or whatever,
and it would not be so universally reviled as the fact that I'm gay.
And that undoes all of the rest, in many respects."

At the same time, he was anxious not to blame his sexuality for all
his misfortunes.

I think there's a lot of people out there who use their sexuality as an excuse
for why they had a difficult time in the world — like maybe why they haven't
succeeded, or whatever — and it becomes very easy to do that. I mean,
there's people who'll say "Oh, I didn't get that job because I'm fat." Or "I
have trouble at my work because I'm gay." It's not "I have trouble at my work
because I'm an obnoxious creep," [but] "I have trouble at my work because
I'm gay." It doesn't have anything to do with the fact that [they] might not
have been qualified, or [are] not particularly good at that. But the reason that
they've been turned down is that there is something that is, to some degree,

socially unacceptable. And a lot of people use that as an excuse, and a lot of those people are very angry and they focus on their sexuality. I mean, certainly you can be alienated for being homosexual, but you can't necessarily put down everything negative that's happened to you [as being] a result of your sexuality.[8]

For Peter, the only answer to his critics was to keep doing what he did best: informing the general public. In the fall of 1991 one topic he had no hesitation addressing was the recent series of reports that straight people were not as much at risk for AIDS as scientists had earlier feared. This belief, outlined in Michael Fumento's 1990 book *The Myth of Heterosexual AIDS*, was not only damaging because it was wrong, said Peter, it was harmful because it was presented in a way that encouraged heterosexuals to ignore the plight of gay people suffering with the disease and created a homophobia of indifference.

Following coverage of these reports, including a *Globe and Mail* article which argued that heterosexuals have about a three-in-a-million chance each year of contracting AIDS, Peter went ballistic. It wasn't the numbers that were important — everyone knew that the rate of HIV infection remained much lower among North American heterosexuals than homosexuals — it was the likelihood that Fumento's book and the *Globe* article would result in complacency among straight people, that they would feel no need to educate themselves about AIDS, thus putting themselves more at risk. In one of his angriest diaries, Peter rattled off a variety of statistics while dismissing such attitudes as "arrogant and stupid."

We have a vaccine against HIV infection. That vaccine is education. It's the best we've got right now, but getting that message out to the general public has been difficult, and it's made more difficult sometimes.

Recently, a report that came out of Hamilton, Ontario said that HIV infection was really of very little concern to the straight population, that basically there was this "big lie" perpetuated about the risk for HIV, and why was all this money being spent on education? Perhaps the most galling thing that came out of this report was the contention that it was of little concern because there was low chance of a woman giving it to a man. What does that tell the women of this country — that they're not worth educating how to protect themselves? Sure, the epidemic has been fairly stable in Canada; still, about 95 percent of people with HIV infection are gay men. That was true in the States eight years ago; it's not today. Gay men perhaps only account for 65 percent of people with HIV infection, and the pattern of infection is changing in countries all over the world, and there's no reason to believe that we should be immune to that here in Canada.

Last year, a test of all the newborn babies in Montreal showed that one out of 400 was HIV positive. In New York City during the same time, the figure was one out of 33. We could have learned a lot about this epidemic and prevented a lot of infection if we'd been watching what had been happening in the States and other countries previously. If we don't start to do that now, we're going to be in for a big surprise.

Just because you're white, middle class and straight doesn't mean that you're protected from this disease. HIV knows no boundaries — political, geographic, social or economic. It doesn't discriminate against who it infects. So to sit back and think that you're protected just by who you are and what you do is arrogant and very stupid.[9]

Peter gave another angry commentatary on events in the news eight months later when, in Diary 90 (June 3, 1992), he delivered a scathing indictment of populist U.S. presidential candidate Ross Perot. Perot had just announced that he would not have a homosexual in his cabinet and did not believe that gays and lesbians should serve in the military.

Sixty years ago, he could have come out and said he wouldn't knowingly have a Jew in his cabinet, and that would have been acceptable. Thirty years ago, he could have come out and said he wouldn't have a woman, or a Negro in his cabinet, and that would have been acceptable. Today he can come out and say he wouldn't have a homosexual in his cabinet, and no one says anything.

Now the interesting thing is the way he worded it. He wouldn't "knowingly" have a homosexual in his cabinet. What does that mean? If he were to have a man or a woman in his cabinet who was clever and competent and did their job well, and then he were to discover that they were homosexual, what would the effect be? Does that negate that person? Does that negate all of their abilities?

... I guess this is indicative of the way we blindly accept a lot of prejudice. And homophobia is the last bastion for bigotry ... The message that he's really getting out there is, maybe he wouldn't have a Jew or a woman in his cabinet [either], "but I can't say that anymore. But I can say I wouldn't have a homosexual and people will accept that." Well it's not acceptable, because that unthinking kind of bigotry affects all of us.

Peter's attack on Perot, like his criticism of bigotry and homophobia in general, was laced with the sarcasm and zeal typical of the recently converted, of someone who had come to gay activism later than many people his age and was still working through his anger. But while Perot's comment would have surprised no one in the gay community, Peter's response was entirely appropriate for a general television audience which routinely hears these homophobic remarks and passes them off as facts of life. It is unlikely that Peter would have gotten away with such editorializing when he first began AIDS Diary, but now that he had gained the trust of so many viewers his power was that much greater. They knew him well enough to appreciate his anger when he expressed it.

It was forceful diaries like these that demonstrated where Peter's true activist qualities lay. He didn't need to be part of an organized group to combat homophobia with AIDS education. The public response to AIDS Diary was a persuasive argument that all involved in the struggle against AIDS could fulfill different functions in pursuit of the same goal.

15

Season of Protest

Peter's October 1991 warning against heterosexual complacency about AIDS seemed like prophecy a month later when basketball star Magic Johnson announced on November 7 that he was HIV positive. The revelation was a chilling reinforcement of Peter's argument that "HIV knows no boundaries" and "doesn't discriminate against who it infects." It also sparked a media frenzy of AIDS coverage that would keep him busy, both on the diaries and in interviews, for the next month.

Media fascination with Johnson's method of infection was widespread. In the first week following his announcement, Johnson appeared on U.S. talk shows where he was forced to deny that he was gay or had had a single homosexual encounter. In Vancouver, *Province* columnist Bob Stall suggested that Johnson could not presume to be an AIDS spokesman unless he was willing to explain how he and AIDS "became acquainted." Peter was disgusted by this kind of nudge-nudge, wink-wink mentality. "Basically what Stall was saying was, 'Come clean and tell us that you're queer,' but he didn't have the guts to ask it," Peter told a reporter. "I came very close to phoning him up and telling him he was an asshole. Then I thought, 'No, I'll just do it on television instead'."[1]

By the time he got together with Paperny to tape the diary, Peter had couched his reprimand in a fairly even tone.

Magic Johnson announced the other day that he's HIV infected. It's a terrible tragedy, he's a brilliant athlete and had a fantastic career ahead of him. But that doesn't make his HIV infection any more tragic than anyone else's.

The other thing people have been bantering about is, "How did he get it?" It's not enough that he has come forward with this very personal problem in a very public way, and perhaps allowing for the opportunities for education and informing people about this problem; people seem to want the dirty details. Magic Johnson is a special person, but I don't think there's anything particularly special about his HIV infection or how he got it. He got it in the same way that two million or more other North Americans have become HIV infected; either through unprotected sex or through needle sharing.

A lot of people ... seem to think that there's going to be something about his infection that perhaps he can pass along so that other people can avoid it. You could spend hours titillating yourself with the possibilities of how he became infected. It doesn't really matter. The point is, he's infected and he's doing the best with it that he can. And I think that we're all going to benefit from his [going] public with this.

There was a lot of options that he could have used for retiring from basketball — remember, it was a "watermelon diet" that killed Liberace.[2] I think a lot of people want the reassurance that one of the day's greatest athletes isn't a junkie or, worse yet, a fag.

In interviews, Peter directed some of his criticism at Johnson himself, who appeared to be playing into the media's homophobia. While it was commendable that he was offering his time and efforts to AIDS education, said Peter, Johnson implied that it was "outside the realm of possibility that he could be a great basketball star *and* a homosexual." Instead of simply stating that he was straight but reminding his interviewers that sexuality is irrelevant, "he almost made it laughable to conceive that a basketball star might be gay."

Peter would have had his hands full had he responded to every instance of media homophobia and AIDS that month; the week following Johnson's announcement, British film director Tony Richardson died, followed the next day by Canadian figure skater Robert McCall, and Queen lead singer Freddie Mercury on November 24. The publicity surrounding McCall's death raised the spectre of homophobia in the figure skating world — many insiders feared the disclosure that a prominent male figure skater was infected with AIDS would further stigmatize a sport already associated with stereotypes of the feminized male — while the tabloids responded to Mercury's death with a flurry of sensational coverage describing the flamboyant singer's decadent lifestyle, as if to suggest he deserved his fate. But Peter had more serious issues to address much closer to home.

Late in November a twenty-year-old Nanaimo prostitute with HIV was charged with two counts of "aggravated sexual assault" after two men came forward to police and said she had not informed them of her HIV status when she had sex with them. Although the men remained unnamed, the Vancouver *Province* reported the woman's name in a front-page article on November 30, warning readers that an HIV villain was on the loose. The willingness of the press to victimize the woman disturbed Peter greatly and he wanted to do a diary on this case, but after discussing it with Nancy and Lionel in Nanaimo he decided not to. The case was still before the court and the woman had briefly gone missing. Publicity would unfairly affect her trial.[3]

Peter had no such hesitation about a similar human rights issue that came to his attention during this time. About one week before news broke of the Nanaimo prostitute, he received a call from a nurse he knew at Vancouver General Hospital. She had just been speaking with a distraught young man who had come in for his HIV test result. The reason for the man's distress was not that he had tested positive — he was only confirming what another doctor had told him years earlier — but that he had been forced to go underground for several weeks to avoid a media witch hunt that threatened to destroy his private life. The nurse gave Peter his telephone number and Peter called him the next day. The following week he told the man's story on Diary 65 (November 27, 1991).

Confidentiality is perhaps the most sacred aspect of the physician-patient relationship, and I've been very glad that the people I've entrusted my care to have respected this. But it doesn't always happen that way.

Recently there's been a much-publicized case of a woman who was allegedly infected with HIV through artificial insemination, and there's been an unwitting casualty in the media circus that has surrounded this particular event. That is the man who donated the sperm that allegedly infected this woman. Now, he set out to donate something that was going to benefit someone else, and did so on the understanding that there would be complete anonymity between himself and the person to receive his sperm. Instead, it set up a chain of nightmarish events ...

The man was Eric Kyle, a 34-year-old arts production manager who had recently been named in the press as the sperm donor in the case of Kobe ter Neuzen. Ter Neuzen had just won a landmark $883,000 malpractice suit against her doctor, Gerald Korn, six years after she contracted HIV through a sperm donation from his clinic — allegedly a donation of Kyle. When ter Neuzen decided to take Korn to court in 1986, her lawyer obtained a court order that forced Korn to reveal the name of the sperm donor. The lawyer then added Kyle's name to the action beside Korn, the principal defendant. Kyle had not known this at the time, nor was he notified that anyone had been infected by his sperm.

He had known since the summer of 1985 that he was HIV positive, however. At that time, Korn had asked all his sperm donors to submit to a voluntary AIDS test[4] and Kyle, who had no reason to suspect his would turn out positive, complied. He was stunned when he received an "angry, accusatory" phone call from Korn with the news that he was, in fact, HIV positive. He was further devastated by the manner in which Korn informed him. Kyle says that Korn offered no sympathy or advice on counselling, but instead complained aloud about the possible implications for his practice.

Kyle had heard nothing more from Korn in the next six years, and he no longer donated sperm, but on November 4, 1991, he returned to his downtown Vancouver apartment to find two frantic messages on his answering machine, from his sister and father. He immediately

called his sister, who told him that he had been named as the ter
Neuzen sperm donor on BCTV's six o'clock broadcast.[5] In another
hour the story would be repeated on the night final broadcast, then
picked up by the global press. Kyle, realizing he had been robbed of
his right to privacy, asked a friend to contact BCTV news on his behalf. The friend was told by night final anchor Linden Soles that the
media had every right to report Kyle's name, since he had already
been listed in a court action.[6]

The next day his name appeared in both Vancouver dailies and the
Globe and Mail; within a week the story reached countries as far away
as Zimbabwe and Lithuania.[7] His private life was now subject to total
disclosure in the media, regardless of accuracy. Some reports left the
impression that Kyle knew of his HIV status before he donated; others suggested that he was nowhere to be found and presumed dead
from AIDS. In fact, he remained in good health.

The media coverage alone would have been enough to force anyone into hiding but there was a more urgent reason for Kyle to seek
refuge. On Sunday November 10 he was told by the lawyer he had
contacted through legal aid that Kobe ter Neuzen's lawyer wanted
Kyle to take the stand in court.

Despite his lawyer's advice that he honour the request, Kyle and
his friends were unconvinced that a court appearance would be beneficial. There was no doubt he would be ruthlessly cross-examined and
that his role in the affair would be reduced to that of a pawn for either
side of the lawsuit. On the advice of his friends, and the second opinion of a local human rights lawyer, he decided to hide out in a neutral
location, a safe house, until the trial was completed. He stayed with
two different friends for a period of ten days, venturing back to his
apartment only twice during that period.

For Kyle it was a Kafkaesque nightmare. After giving up his identity
and his home, he had to face the breakup of a long-term relationship.
One night as he and his lover tried to settle their differences in private by meeting at his apartment, the two men were interrupted by a
loud knock at the door. Realizing it was likely a process server with a
summons to appear in court, Kyle suddenly felt like a caged animal.
One move would have signalled he was home, so he and his lover sat

motionless for 45 minutes, waiting for the intruder to leave before they finally returned to Kyle's safe house.

Now that the trial was over, he told Peter, he was finally able to return to his own home without fear of harassment from legal authorities. But what else might happen to him? Would the press continue to pursue his story? One reporter from the Vancouver *Sun* had left a sympathetic note under his front door but Kyle was unfamiliar with the reporter and had no reason to suspect that the *Sun* would play the story with any more compassion than the *Province* had. (One Vancouver *Province* article of November 15, 1991, was headlined "AIDS sperm donor had deadly secret.") He didn't respond to the message.

His only hope of a media advocate, it appeared, lay with the AIDS diarist. After meeting over lunch, Kyle was immediately assured that Peter would pre-empt the next diary segment he had planned in order to address his situation.

Kyle's choice for a media spokesman was a wise one. As a gay man with AIDS, Peter could empathize with the man's crisis, and its human rights implications, more than most members of the media. But Peter had a far more personal reason for jumping to Kyle's defence, a reason he would not reveal on AIDS Diary. One of the first things he and Kyle discussed over lunch, Kyle recalled, was that Peter himself had made several sperm donations to Gerald Korn when the doctor was soliciting for his clinic at the UBC School of Medicine in the early 1980s. While Peter had refused to be tested and never knew he had AIDS until 1986, he now realized that there was every chance his sperm could have infected someone. In that case, he wondered, what made him any different from Eric Kyle? Would he have suffered the same treatment from Dr. Korn had he submitted an AIDS test? And if the information were made known now, how would he be treated by the media and the public?

E ric Kyle's story was clear proof to Peter that he had been hopelessly naive earlier that year when he told a group of UBC students they had nothing to fear about taking an HIV test. He had been on campus during a safer sex health promotion week and had spoken on the pros and cons of HIV testing — what it meant to test positive, where to get a test, and what level of confidentiality one could expect. In most practices he had worked, he told them, confidentiality was a given. The blood was drawn in the office by a physician, the forms were filled in so the patient's name remained anonymous — "using either the patient's initials or fabricated initials and the patient's birth date" — and the results were usually known only to the physician and the patient. Usually the form was destroyed instead of being entered on a patient chart. Given these standard procedures, he said, it made a great deal of sense to take the test. (He didn't tell them that he had consistently refused to take one himself before he was diagnosed.) "It's too bad that the social stigma surrounding AIDS is so strong and people are so concerned about what's going to happen if someone finds out they're HIV positive that it's maybe keeping a lot of people from being tested," he concluded, summarizing the talk in Diary 26 (January 26, 1991). "It's very important to be tested. It could be very beneficial and in general it's something that only you and your physician need know."

Kyle recalled signing a written agreement of confidentiality provided by Korn. However, there was no way of proving this because — as Korn revealed in court — Kyle's records had somehow gone missing in the period following the revelation of his HIV status.

Several days after their first meeting, Kyle came to Peter's apartment to meet him and Sue Ridout, who was producing AIDS Diary while Paperny was away. Kyle appealed to Ridout for more balanced coverage of the case; in recounting his story, he reminded her of the CBC's mistaken assumption that he was "nowhere to be found and presumed dead from the disease." Ridout was struck by the respect Kyle showed to Peter and was sufficiently moved by his story that she respected his wish not to be interviewed for a more extensive piece. Later she admitted to Peter that the *Evening News* had come very close to showing an eight-by-ten photo of Kyle during one of its broadcasts.

(Kyle had done an open audition for CBC casting in the early 1980s, and the corporation still had the photo on file.) Peter was relieved that she had decided not to use the photograph, and he reminded her that such an action would have been a highly unethical and blatant invasion of privacy.

On November 27, Diary 65 went on the air with Peter expressing his outrage at the system's failure to protect Kyle. The injustice of ter Neuzen's predicament had been extensively covered in the media throughout the two-week trial; Peter now provided the first media recognition that the sperm donor had rights too.

Certainly, there is no medical or legal precedent for someone who has donated blood, or semen, or organs to be named if there's been consequences to the recipient. If there have been, it's a result of a screw-up in the system, and not the responsibility of the donor. But because this involves HIV, it takes it out of the realm of the ordinary and someone decided that it was important that he be identified. This decision has been shattering to his life. He has been persecuted and subjected to a bunch of ruthless, sensationalistic, and unsubstantiated media reports about him.

Now, a doctor who does a misdeed can be held responsible and answerable for his actions. But a judge who has released a name such as this will not be accountable.[8] Our lawmakers have effectively insulated themselves from accountability. This man's human rights have been violated grossly and it doesn't appear that he has any recourse. This Sunday, December 1, is World AIDS Day, and the focus locally is AIDS as a human rights issue. We need look no further than our own backyard to find out that the system, in this case, has failed miserably.

Peter knew only too well what it meant to be public property but, unlike Kyle, he was fortunate to have had a choice in the matter. He also could decide which aspects of his life he would and would not make public. Although Peter did not reveal his own history with Dr. Korn's donor clinic to anyone other than Kyle, he was speaking for himself as much as for Kyle when he criticized the breach of confidentiality. As he told a reporter a few months later when asked about the case, "If I'm able to personalize a story where I, say, take another person's story and use it as a focal point for a diary, and I can in some way relate that back to myself, then that's okay. And David [Paperny] hasn't discouraged me from taking any political stands, because some of the diaries have been fairly political."[9]

One Richmond viewer was outraged that Peter would even consider defending the sperm donor.

> How dare you feel pity for the donor of sperm ... What kind of a life do you think the woman he infected thru his Dr(?) She suddenly has a very short life to look forward to & I can imagine how pleasant that will be for her as you should know.
>
> I am so discusted [sic] with you, who are so obviously able to live at least in material comfort. I am so angry at your misguided sympathy. Why you are giving everybody, thru TV, advise [sic] when you couldn't avoid Aids yourself.[10]

Kyle, meanwhile, received a note from the very person with whom he was never supposed to have had contact. These words, handwritten on a simple greeting card, finally brought an end to the climate of hysteria and accusation Kyle had experienced through the media.

> Dear Eric:
> I want to be sure that you know how sorry I am that your name was mentioned in the media. I had no idea that it would.
>
> I now know that you exist, and can only imagine how it has interfered in your life to have private things made public without warning. Had you come to the trial, I would have had support there for you from our local organization.
>
> I have no grudge or ill will against you. As far as I am concerned, you are one of us — PWAs — and I support you in whatever way you have chosen to deal with your life and your illness.
> Sincere best wishes,
> Kobe[11]

16

Voices Denied

T he same month Peter was speaking out against human rights violations of people living with AIDS, he met a man who was having a private struggle with another powerful social institution. Hugh Dundas was a Catholic priest who had much more in common with Peter than an interest in books, travel, and philosophy. His career, like Peter's, had only just begun when he learned he had AIDS; two weeks after he was ordained in 1989, Dundas was told he had tested HIV positive.

Unlike Peter, who could take whatever public stance he wanted without fear of reprisal from the medical establishment, the 32-year-old priest's public actions were governed by a centuries-old institution that has consistently shunned openly gay men while stifling the slightest expression of dissent. Dundas — an Anglican convert who was totally dedicated to Catholic teachings — did not want to take any action that would harm his church. Instead of being appointed to his first parish, where he would have said public mass and administered sacraments, the young priest was informed by Vancouver archbishop James Carney that he would not receive an assignment. His ministry would be limited to private consultations and official church business, such as reviewing cases at the diocesan marriage tribunal.

By fall 1991, however, he was craving more contact with lay people in the community. He also wanted to share his experience of living with AIDS. Dundas felt that visiting patients — especially other PWAs — at St. Paul's would allow him to provide comfort to the ill while adding meaning to his own life. With the death of Carney and the arrival of his apparently liberal successor, Adam Exner, in 1991, Dundas saw an opening. Within a day of his first inquiry, Exner approved his request to do pastoral work at St. Paul's. Dundas enjoyed his work with HIV-positive patients, and his compassionate presence was vital in a Catholic-owned hospital which had seen its share of homophobic interference by church officials.[1] He also discovered from this work that there were many lessons he could share about living with AIDS in the community at large. While he knew the church had made up its mind about a parish assignment, he didn't stop looking for other options.

One day, Dundas was visiting a close friend — another gay Catholic priest — when the man asked him how many people he knew who were openly and proudly gay. Dundas pondered the question. He knew several gay men, of course, but most of them were closeted church members like himself.[2]

"Not many," he answered. "Why?"

His friend told him that the better acquainted Dundas became with someone proud of his homosexuality, the better he would feel about his own. It was a matter of self esteem, he said. When Dundas told him that he was somewhat acquainted with Dr. Peter — they had recently met in the waiting room at the Infectious Diseases Clinic — his friend encouraged him to cultivate the relationship. Peter would be an excellent companion, he said, because he was educated, witty, fun-loving, and completely at peace with who he was. And he had demonstrated that he could remain a functioning professional despite having AIDS.

Dundas agreed, and he and Peter soon developed an easy friendship. They took many long walks with Harvey, talking endlessly about architecture, philosophy, and issues of life and death, and Peter enjoyed being driven around the city by Dundas — driven so fast, apparently, that Dundas once temporarily lost his license.

While Dundas recognized that Peter was clearly not a religious person in the traditional sense, he did have a personal spirituality that was very attractive. Hugh told Peter how impressed he had been with AIDS Diary — particularly the segment where Peter recited his "Affirmation" — and he commended him for his frankness in discussing the many physical and psychological challenges posed by the illness. When Peter asked him why he couldn't fulfill a similar function by discussing the spiritual challenges of AIDS in public, Dundas was enthusiastic about the idea. He had already joined a national task force on AIDS, and had met many fascinating people when he attended a meeting in Ottawa; now, perhaps, he was ready to go public with his illness. Shortly after their discussion, in the fall of 1991, Peter introduced him to David Paperny.

"Hugh's story came flowing out," Paperny recalled, "and I gave him the option right then to come to me if he wasn't getting any satisfaction from the church — using the threat of coming to the media as leverage with the church. The invitation was always open from CBC to talk." Senior producer Sue Ridout concurred, "I remember us all saying 'We have a tremendous appetite for that if you can get him to talk.' Probably, if Hugh Dundas had said 'I'll talk but I'll only talk with Peter — you can shoot me talking with Peter,' my feeling is that we would have said 'Sure.'"

But Dundas never did get on television, either alone or with Peter. When he first approached Exner, he asked for permission to join the national advisory task force on AIDS. (He had already attended the Ottawa meeting without the church's permission.) He mentioned that he had opportunities to do public speaking on AIDS, but he wasn't specific about the venue. Exner said he would get back to him with a decision, but no answer was forthcoming. Dundas went back to Exner a second time and used the television idea as leverage to approve his involvement on the task force. The next day Exner told him he could go on the task force but said nothing about the television idea. It was Dundas himself who shied away from going public, said the friend who had first encouraged him to meet Peter; "Hugh eventually dropped the TV idea" when reminded of the possible repercussions to his family, the church, and himself. "He felt that there was a lot of criticism of the church already and he didn't want to add to that."

But Curtis Metzger, an Anglican chaplain for palliative care at Vancouver General Hospital, recalled a different version of the story. According to Metzger, who visited Dundas during one of his rounds at VGH, Exner had made it clear he would not approve of the young priest's appearance on television. "When the church said 'No' Hugh was really frustrated, because there was a hopeful sign that he could do this," said Metzger. "He was feeling shut down by the church, and incredulous that they couldn't see the good of what he was proposing. Hugh would have talked about the issues of HIV globally and personally. That's probably what worried the church; what was he going to say about them — about how awful they'd been — and would he talk about being gay?"[3]

Whatever the case, Dundas asked Peter not to encourage him any further to go public with his illness. Like many other gay Catholic priests, Dundas found the possibility of ostracism by the Vatican too high a price to pay for defying the powers-that-be. He quietly continued his work with AIDS patients at St. Paul's Hospital until he was too sick to carry on. When he died in the summer of 1993, a front-page obituary in the Vancouver *Sun* did not even mention AIDS. (The church only confirmed the cause of his death the following October, when questioned by *Sun* religion reporter Douglas Todd.)

Archbishop James Carney had died in 1990, but his influence was still evident three years later when one church official justified Carney's decision to bar Dundas from regular ministry. Father Greg Smith of the Vancouver archdiocese suggested that, by remaining silent about having AIDS, Dundas had chosen the more spiritually "authentic" path. "Let's put it this way. I think his quiet acceptance of the illness was a lesson for many of us that may not have been the same had it been in the public eye," Smith told the Vancouver *Sun* in October 1993. "By virtue of it being so private, it was very authentic. Sometimes when you become a public figure, you wonder what your motives are." Smith defended Carney's decision to ban Dundas from public masses by citing "the congregation's general distress. In those early days, the whole thing was less clear to us than it is now."[4]

Smith's logic was puzzling in a number of ways. First, it would have been impossible for parishioners to learn a lesson about Dundas' "quiet acceptance of his illness," had a Vancouver *Sun* reporter not forced a confession out of the archdiocese several months after his death. Second, 1989 could hardly be considered the "early days" of the epidemic. AIDS had been in the news for eight years, and methods of infection had been common knowledge for at least five. Finally, the congregation's potential "distress" seemed the best reason of all for Dundas to go public about his illness. As AIDS Diary had shown, education tends to be a strong antidote to distress.

W hile Peter could do nothing to act on Hugh's behalf — and he was reluctant to bash the Catholic church — he was finding that there were many other people with AIDS who could use his help. The more involved in AIDS education he became, the more people he met from the AIDS community whose voices were rarely heard in the mainstream media. At the B.C. AIDS Conference in November 1991 he spoke with an HIV-infected IV drug user who enlightened him about some of the problems facing that group of PWAs. Despite the high number of infections that were prevented by Vancouver's needle exchange program — about 50,000 needles a month were being exchanged — the continuing discrimination against IV drug users put more people at risk, Peter was told. On December 4 he tried to make sense of this problem in a diary.

We have as a society some very strong feelings governing substance abuse and IV drug use, and I don't really know where they come from. But sometimes because of our inabilities to see beyond the stereotypes and other negative feelings we have about this group, we're not able to address a lot of concerns that affect this group and one of them is HIV infection.

For example, there's many ways that we fan the flames of the HIV epidemic in this particular group. Several years ago, a law was brought in in the eastern U.S. that made it illegal to carry injection drug paraphernalia unless you had a prescription or some other medical certificate. So someone who was using drugs wouldn't want to have their own stuff in case they were caught by the police. They'd be thrown in jail just for having a syringe. So instead of going into a drug store and buying a sterile syringe for eighteen cents, they'd go to what's called a "shooting gallery," pay four bucks to rent a syringe, and then that syringe would get passed on to the next person. Is it any surprise then, that in New York City AIDS is the number one killer of both men and women in the age group of 25 to 44? ...

I certainly don't condone IV drug use, but I don't see that we should be condemning those people. It's not bad enough to be a junkie — you've got to be a junkie with AIDS. Adding HIV to all that despair only makes life that much worse. If the best thing that's going to happen in your day is going to come out of a needle, who is anyone to judge?[5]

Peter's discussion of IV drug use was just one indication of his expanding role as AIDS diarist. The higher his profile became, the more he realized how lucky he was in comparison to many other PWAs and the more responsibility he felt to talk about those less fortunate. The "human face" of HIV had been changing for some time (more women, natives, and babies were testing positive), and the vicious cycle of urban poverty and IV drug use was creating a whole new wave of people with AIDS which had nothing in common with educated, middle class, gay white men — the first wave of the AIDS epidemic, to which he belonged.

Peter had addressed this trend back in March.

It's because of this second wave that AIDS is becoming known as a disease of poverty. This is because it's affecting particularly the urban poor. In the States, Hispanics and blacks, groups where there is a high incidence of intravenous drug use. It's also happening in Canada, affecting a large number of street people and particularly young native people and young native women.

There's another side to AIDS being a disease of poverty. Perhaps you were white and middle class when this diagnosis was made. But this may lead to a downward spiral for a number of reasons. First of all, someone with AIDS may be too ill to work, and they may not have the backup protection of a disability plan or other sorts of insurance, as is the case with me.

In some cases, AIDS may lead to a disability such as blindness, which for me has left me unable to work at this point, because I can't get paid to do counselling in British Columbia, and as a blind physician I don't really see what else I can do. There's also a very high cost to this disease in terms of drugs and other forms of treatment. I spend about $400 a month on medications aside from AZT.

It's frightening to think; the people who were affected in the first wave of AIDS were to a large degree ignored by society, the powers that be. But then many of those people were well-educated and had resources to draw upon in order to improve their own situations. I guess perhaps I should consider myself lucky to be a part of that wave. But the people affected in the second wave don't have those resources — they often don't have the education, they don't have access to medical care and so on. It's pretty frightening. What's going to become of these people?[6]

IV drug users, the urban poor, and Catholic priests with AIDS were just a few of the people affected by HIV who voices are often denied a public forum in which to discuss their experiences. Peter, who had been criticized from the beginning by gay activists who felt he did not sufficiently represent the less privileged, could not possibly be all things to all people. But he realized that with the only first-person platform to talk about AIDS on television, he had a perfect opportunity to at least describe these experiences to viewers.

17

'No one has ownership
of this disease'

O
ne of the more unexpected results of AIDS Diary was how
Peter discussion of various drug therapy alternatives led to a
dialogue with his viewers. People with AIDS and other
illnesses who had for so long relied on the single, unalterable opinion
of one doctor were refreshed by Peter's homespun maxim that "as
long as it's not doing you any harm, if you believe in it, it's probably
going to do you some good." As a result, he received several requests
for advice on treatment, plus a few letters from viewers offering their
own organic or pharmaceutical solutions.

Many correspondents were eager to prove their motives were sincere ("Please believe me — I'm not just some quack trying to sell you
a product," wrote one. "You could very well think I am a nutcase trying to cash in on someone who is very sick, [but] I'm not," wrote another.) Most of them were interested in Peter's KS treatment. One
letter implored him to support American chemist Dr. Linus Pauling's
controversial theory of using massive doses of vitamin C to treat
AIDS-related cancer; another, from a Seventh Day Adventist, sug-

gested red clover leaf tea. One doctor with experience in complementary medicine recommended mistletoe, which he had prescribed to his own patients with cancer.

> Since my research and personal use has indicated positive results with mistletoe, and no side effects, it seems to back up the numerous scientific papers indicating that mistletoe has definite stimulatory effects on the immune system ... Other studies in animals have shown enlargement of the thymus with mistletoe.
>
> I have not seen any studies on mistletoe being used on people who are HIV positive but restoring the immune system equilibrium with mistletoe therapy would surely benefit them ...[1]

Another dedicated viewer included a handwritten, 200-word excerpt from an article in the March/April issue of the new age magazine *Body Mind and Spirit*, which chronicled six cases of people with AIDS who allegedly tested negative after using homeopathic treatments.

> According to a report in "Internal Medicine World Report" (April 15-30, 1990), six HIV-infected patients tested negative for the HIV virus after being treated with two homeopathic drugs [Composium and Engystol]. The treatment reportedly worked on patients recently diagnosed with HIV & who had not taken AZT or any other anti-viral drug.[2]

This second letter was not very useful to Peter, given that he had pumped himself full of toxic medications for the last five and a half years. And for all his open-mindedness about herbal remedies, Peter remained dedicated to the pharmaceutical regimen he began when he was hospitalized with PCP in 1986. More recently, despite a gradual deterioration in his health, he believed that the chemotherapy he had begun the previous spring was actually improving his condition. Friends had assumed his hair would fall out and that the medication would leave him constantly nauseated, but his treatment was not particularly toxic and his tolerance level was high. The chemotherapy had actually improved his physical appearance, particularly around his eyes where the KS patches had faded considerably, and Peter took this as a sign of progress.

He did occasionally express doubts about the long-term effects of combining his drug therapies, as he revealed to viewers in Diary 67 (December 11, 1991).

> I sometimes wonder how much of this stuff I can take. I'm starting to feel a bit like a human toxic waste dump, and I wonder how much my body can tolerate pollution with all of these different types of quite harmful medications. But I guess I shouldn't really worry about it too much. The other day I was in a shop and a woman who worked in there asked if she could see my hands. She explained that she was a palmist and she wanted to have a look at my palms. So she says "You've got an incredibly long life line. I don't care what the doctors are telling you, you're going to be around for a long time." So, who am I to argue with her?

But not all the treatments he sought were available. After his first bout with PCP in 1986 he was lucky enough to fit all the right criteria for AZT treatment, but for several of the new drugs being studied at the end of 1991, test patients had to have at least 50 T (helper) cells. At last count, Peter had ten.

> There's drugs out there that I could be benefitting from but at this point I might not have access to because I don't meet these criteria. Everyone wants their study to look good, and it looks bad if someone kicks off during the course of your study. It might have nothing to do with the drug itself; it may just have to do with other health problems. And certainly the lower number of helper cells that you have, the greater number of health problems. But nonetheless, I feel like I'm being written off as a bad risk; that there's something out there that I might be benefitting from, but I just can't get included in having access to it.

Peter's discussion of drug politics was most powerful when he used the diaries to dismiss the hypocrisy and opportunism of AIDS profiteers. At the end of 1991 articles about a drug called acyclovir began appearing in North American newspapers. Acyclovir was an anti-herpes drug which, used in conjunction with other drugs like AZT, had long been a potent therapy in combatting HIV. The problem with the news reports was that they hailed the effectiveness of this drug as a new discovery. In the wake of this coverage, Peter received a number of excited phone calls — one of them from his mother — wondering if he'd heard about acyclovir. Given that he had been using the drug for about five years and knew of others who had been using it as well, Peter decided the news coverage was worth investigating.

> So I talked to one of the pharmacists that I see at St. Paul's Hospital, and I said "Am I missing something here? Is there something new?" And she said "Well no, there isn't, it's the information that we've had all along." And she admitted that maybe she was being cynical — that the drug company stock wasn't doing so well and so they released this study to the press, so it comes out as if this is all new information. And I guess the idea is that people not in the know who are prospective investors see that this company owns the rights to AZT and acyclovir, and these offer sort of an "AIDS cure," and so therefore it might be a good investment.
>
> I guess what sort of annoys me is that although it's a good drug, it's a real manipulation of the market, and it's also a real manipulation of those people who have friends or relatives affected by HIV. They get a sense of false hope and false expectation that something new is on the horizon when there's really nothing new at all.[3]

Finally, there was the constant swirl of controversy surrounding AZT, the first drug approved for AIDS treatment. Early in 1992 Burroughs Wellcome — the American multinational corporation that originally marketed AZT for AIDS treatment in 1986 — complained to St. Paul's Hospital when it learned that the hospital had begun purchasing a generic version of the drug from a Canadian company that was selling it at about two-thirds the Burroughs Wellcome cost.

> AZT was invented in the early sixties as an anti-cancer drug. But it wasn't successful for that ... [Burroughs Wellcome], however, recognized that it maybe had some anti-AIDS potential. They pulled this drug off the shelf,

invested a relatively small amount of money in getting it licenced, and since that time have made well over a billion dollars on the sale of AZT worldwide.

So why is it that this Canadian company can come along and manufacture this drug at about two-thirds the cost? It can't be because the original company is paying off years of expensive research and testing. Basically, they have a group of people by the neck — people with a serious illness who are willing to pay what they can in order to find something that will potentially help. The cost for AZT has been prohibitive in rich western nations. It's totally out of sight for people in the third world, and this is where HIV is spreading unchecked. Frankly, I think St. Paul's should be applauded for getting this drug to as many people as they can at the lowest cost that they can. This should be the goal. Not profits.[4]

For all his criticism of Burroughs Wellcome, however, Peter was not about to write off AZT altogether. As he had stated in Diary 11 (October 24, 1990), AZT could not kill the virus and was not a cure for AIDS, but because it stopped HIV from spreading and was thought to prevent further damage to the immune system, he believed it could prolong life.

When I started on this medication we didn't know a whole lot about it and the dose at that time was twelve pills a day. There were a lot of nasty side effects with that dose but I was very lucky. I was able to tolerate it. I've stayed on that medication over the past four years and over those four years we've gained a lot more knowledge about the drug so now the maximum dose is five pills a day and there's a lot less side effects with that dose.

There still are a lot of people, however, who [are not] able to tolerate AZT.

Longtime AIDS survivor and singer Michael Callen was one of those people. During his July 1991 visit to Vancouver to promote his book, *Surviving AIDS*, he dismissed AZT as a toxic poison which only quickens the destruction of the immune system. When asked about these comments by a reporter, Peter dismissed Callen for not having the medical knowledge to back up his claims. "People don't always listen to everything they hear — they pick up bits and pieces," he told the Toronto gay publication, *Xtra*. "And I think there can be a danger picking up bits and pieces from Michael Callen, because I can just see people going in to their doctor and saying 'I'm not taking these drugs' or 'I'm not doing this, because Michael Callen doesn't, and he's lived for nine years.' I think what happens is that someone finds out they're HIV positive and they don't really know a lot about it — and maybe their doctor doesn't even know a lot about it — and so they go off somewhere like PWA and they get hooked up with a peer counsellor who says, 'Oh God, AZT will kill you. Don't go on that stuff, it's poison.' They may be sharing personal anecdotes, or they may be spouting something they've read in Michael Callen's book or whatever, [but] they're not really in a position to make that kind of assessment. [When] someone is presented with, 'Here's the pros and here's the cons, you make up your own mind,' that's the ideal situation."[5]

here was another health care philosophy, held by many individuals in AIDS activist groups, which Peter could never endorse: the belief that decision-making and support in AIDS groups should be limited to those who are HIV positive. He had always resisted this rigid model of self-advocacy but had never commented on it publicly, and to this point in the series he had never used the diaries to criticize the work of frontline AIDS advocacy groups. His silence ended, however, when his sister Nancy became embroiled in a political squabble over her role in a Nanaimo support group for PWAs and their caregivers.

Nancy Hennessy's short-lived experience with AIDS activism began early in 1991 when she started the Mid-Island AIDS Network. She had previously completed a counselling course with Nanaimo Family Life, and in her work with a volunteer counselling program had encountered a number of people suffering from HIV-related illnesses. She realized there was great need for support services in a town like Nanaimo, a smaller, more conservative community where resources were less available than in a city like Vancouver. She decided, based on her own counselling experience, to provide these services herself.

After consulting the Vancouver PWA Society, AIDS Vancouver,

and AIDS Vancouver Island, she received a grant for $5000 from the local public health unit to set up a downtown office in February 1991. Then she started two groups (one for PWAs, the other for their families, friends, and lovers) and offered one-on-one counselling. Confidentiality was especially vital to people's involvement, since many of those who were infected were still closeted sexually. Others simply wanted more information about methods of transmission but weren't willing to visit the office. "I remember one call from a businessman wanting to know if his pneumonia symptoms were caused by the prostitutes whose services he had used while on the road," Nancy said later.

The project quickly fell apart. The grant money ran out in December, volunteers suffered from burnout, and accusations were made about Nancy's motivation in starting the support group. One PWA wondered if, as an HIV-negative person, she was not simply exploiting her brother's fame to take advantage of people with AIDS. By the spring of 1992 she was accused by two activists of embezzling the group's funds. A seven-page letter to the public health unit outlined the allegation, but nothing ever came of it and Hennessy continued to seek donations. The office eventually shut down in July. Far from siphoning the group's cash, Nancy and her husband Lionel were out of pocket by the time the office closed.

Peter had watched his sister's difficulties for several weeks before he spoke out in Diary 77 (February 26, 1992), delivering a stern lecture calling for PWA groups to accept a more active role for straight and non-infected people.

One thing I've heard is that some people with HIV and AIDS feel that only other people with HIV and AIDS are able to care for them or support them. And it's not the case. There's a lot of people who are willing and able to get involved with this type of work. Just because they're not affected personally doesn't mean they're not able to do this.

For example, my sister started a support group on Vancouver Island to provide services for people with HIV and their families in smaller communities where these things weren't available. Every now and then she runs into roadblocks because, well for example, some people feel that because she doesn't have HIV herself, what right does she have to be involved in all of this? There's a lot of these smaller organizations that are struggling to get going, and perhaps some people don't find out about them because other people don't feel they're legitimate.

No one has ownership of this disease; unfortunately, it belongs to all of us. And the only way that we're going to conquer this is if there's cooperation.

Network 92, the first AIDS conference on Vancouver Island, took place in June, just one month before Nancy's support group office closed. The conference's purpose was to introduce the various groups serving the Island AIDS community and to discuss the unique problems facing people with HIV in small towns or rural communities. Dr. Peter was asked to present the keynote address.

The final topic of Peter's speech — the AIDS community's "ownership" of support and care strategies — caused the biggest controversy at that weekend's conference. In large urban centres such as New York, he began, it was understandable — often desirable — for gay people with AIDS to seek help only in the HIV-positive gay community. "But in a small community," he went on, "you have limited resources. You have to accept the help that's offered." He then made a veiled reference to the activists who had spurned his sister's efforts. "The people that are getting involved in this are [doing it] because they want to get involved in this. It may not be obvious why they're getting involved, but that's not really the point. The point is that a helping hand is being extended, and it's very important to take that helping hand and encourage that kind of behaviour."

The next morning during the plenary session, one of the activists who had opposed Nancy's involvement stood up and told the moderator that people who weren't infected shouldn't be involved in support services because they didn't understand what it was like to live with AIDS. The room fell silent as the man — a towering figure with an intimidating presence — addressed the crowd. Peter was fuming; he was in a lot of discomfort from pain that morning, but the activist's blatant dismissal of his keynote address was more than he could stand. Just before the lunch break he asked to speak for a few moments.

"If it weren't for non-infected people, I wouldn't be alive today," he said, to a hushed crowd. "It's a total insult to many of the people who have come from all over the Island to judge their commitment by whether or not they're HIV positive." The next day, at the end of the conference, the man approached Peter and apologized.

AIDS Vancouver Island executive director Dale Weston, recalling the incident, said the difficulties Nancy faced are not uncommon among non-profit service organizations. When a person of seemingly privileged background is seen to be holding the purse strings and making all the decisions for a group of people already disempowered by illness and social prejudice, resentment can surface very quickly. Nancy — a white, middle-class, heterosexual woman — was a convenient scapegoat in the political tug-of-war over representation. "If you now look at the people who were projecting their anger toward Nancy," recalled Weston, "they were none of those things she was. They were not middle-class, they were infected, they did not have a loving supporting family around them, they did not have the community profile, they did not have the community support that Nancy had. So the anger came from heavy doses of jealousy. That's the real frustration. Nancy was faulted for being a very good person."

In telling his viewers three months earlier that "no one has ownership of this disease," Peter was defending the right of all people to get involved in AIDS support and services, regardless of their HIV status. While self-advocacy might be the ideal model, it couldn't be the rule in every community. And if HIV-negative, straight caregivers were willing to truly sacrifice themselves to help people with AIDS, who was anyone to judge?

O f all the controversial territory Peter would cover on AIDS Diary, perhaps no other issue was as emotionally charged as the euthanasia debate. Peter had always supported the right of terminally ill patients to assume some control over the method of their death. Although it was an unpopular position for a doctor to take, this sometimes meant supporting passive euthanasia. "I [find] it especially difficult to justify the heroic measures sometimes taken to try and prolong the lives of 80 and 90-year-old people who don't know where they are or probably even who they are," he had written to Shirley during his internship at Ottawa General Hospital in 1986.

Residents and interns tend to want to do anything and everything they can to save a life — whereas a GP who's known a patient for 30 years knows when their time has come. Also there's the whole legal shit — you can let someone quietly slip away with pneumonia or heart failure, but if it ever gets to court and it's demonstrated that everything wasn't done to save someone then it's big trouble. Apparently this is more of a North American phenomenon — in Britain, it's common practice to let old debilitated people slip away with pneumonia and other ailments without having slammed them with every antibiotic in the book.[6]

The question of death with dignity became more urgent for Peter when he became ill less than a year after writing that letter. He didn't address the issue publicly until four years later, around the time he began taping AIDS Diary in 1990.

On August 14, 1990, David Lewis, a high-profile member of the Vancouver PWA Society, told the Vancouver media that his pain was becoming unbearable and that he intended to take his own life with a drug overdose. He refused to disclose what day that would be, although he confirmed it would be before September 1. Lewis, a 38-year-old psychologist and longtime gay rights activist, had already attracted international attention when he revealed in July that he had helped eight friends with AIDS kill themselves by drug overdose in the past nine years. After going public with his own intentions, Lewis's personal crusade for euthanasia became a death watch as the media covered his every move. On August 24 he closed off his home to reporters, surrounded himself with family and friends, and changed an intravenous drip from a saline solution to a powerful sleeping potion. He died that day.

Peter never mentioned Lewis by name, but during the first of his two videotaped interviews with UBC psychiatrist Michael Myers several weeks after the activist's death, he supported Lewis's decision to commit suicide. "For someone facing a prolonged illness, I feel that it's a very comforting thing for them to know they can choose to escape from it," he said.[7]

In a subsequent diary he suggested that such a solution would not be out of the question once his own time was up.

When I got out of hospital and was facing a lot of unknowns, there existed the possibility that I was going to become very ill and debilitated. I derived a certain amount of comfort from the image of being able to take an overdose in the company of loved ones, family, and so on. Now things of course have gone very well and in general I'm pretty healthy ... at some point though, I still derive some comfort from this image of being able to choose when I want to leave if things get to be too much. We all live in individual ways and we all die in individual ways. No one judges us for taking control over our lives and I don't think anyone can judge us over taking some control over how we die.[8]

In spite of his support for the rights of those who choose assisted suicide, Peter did not foresee choosing active euthanasia for himself. In discussing the David Lewis case with his cancer specialist, Dr. Karen Gelmon, Peter realized that only he would know when his time was up — and that time continued to be pushed further into the future. Because of his zest for life, he couldn't imagine making the choice David Lewis had made; there was, quite frankly, too much fun to be had. Surely even as his health was failing he would find *some* thread of joy that would make him want to stay alive, surrounded by loved ones, just a bit longer.

Peter believed that the degree of comfort and care available made all the difference in whether a person with AIDS would be willing to live longer. This fact came home to him when he was talking to his own physician, Phil Sestak, in mid-November 1991. At one point Sestak had nearly 400 patients who were HIV infected; in the early days of the epidemic some of those patients — faced with an uncertain end and an illness that was destroying their bodies — opted for suicide. But since the palliative care unit had opened at St. Paul's Hospital in 1989 there had been no suicides, no AIDS patients on that unit had asked for active euthanasia, and only a couple of terminally ill patients with other sicknesses had. Sestak felt, and pointed out to Peter, that the difference between euthanasia and palliative care as options for terminally ill AIDS patients was crucial.

When Peter talked about this on Diary 64 (November 20, 1991), viewers noted that his definition of euthanasia neatly avoided any morally loaded words such as "assisted suicide" or "mercy killing."

Palliative care refers to keeping the terminally ill patient comfortable; there's no medical intervention beyond pain control. It provides a setting where the physical and psychological pain for people at the end of their lives has been removed. Many patients die in acute care beds simply because we have no other place to put them. I've been in acute care beds before, and I know for sure: that's not a place I would like to die.

Euthanasia refers to a good death, an easy death. It's something that we all have a right to. And perhaps providing the facilities for people to die either in their own homes or in a comfortable setting in a hospice or a palliative care unit is all the euthanasia that we need to provide.

His discussion of death with dignity did much to advance public discussion of euthanasia. He wasn't about to advocate the legalization of doctor-assisted suicide, but by adding his voice to this debate he might ease the conscience of those health care professionals who felt they had no choice but to respect the wishes of their dying patients.

Whether it was a choice of euthanasia or palliative care, drugs or herbal remedies, infected or non-infected caregivers, Peter insisted that all patients had a right to be informed of their options and the right to choose the therapy or medication they preferred. Peter would, after all, expect the same treatment for himself.

PART 4

Crossroads

If I have managed to reach out and educate people, to touch them and perhaps change their viewpoint about people with AIDS and gay people; if I've been able to do that with people who ordinarily wouldn't have any knowing exposure to someone who was gay or who had AIDS, then I think that will be my greatest contribution.

FROM A BEDSIDE INTERVIEW AT
ST. PAUL'S HOSPITAL, OCTOBER 1992

18

Taking Stock

By the beginning of 1992, Peter's stature as an AIDS celebrity merited a four-page feature in the January issue of upscale, glossy *Vancouver* magazine. The article recounted Peter's childhood and the discovery of his illness, and listed his vital statistics in a breathless parody of the *Teen Beat* genre of celebrity profile. ("He is a Gemini ... He has one sister, who is a year and a half older. They are very close. He has brown hair and brown eyes. He is five-foot-seven, 163 pounds ... He wears an earring in his left ear.") Readers learned what Peter found attractive in a man ("intelligence and a sense of humour") and what types he found sexy (Hollywood leading men like Tom Hanks, Steve Martin and Harrison Ford).[1]

The article generated several letters. One correspondent, East Vancouver resident Sharon Mackin, was remarkably candid about Peter's role in her life. Her reaction to the diaries typified the response of many other viewers.

I know some gay people — mostly women, but do not personally know anyone who has AIDS — except you. I feel I *do* know you personally. Though you have never met me, so the "friendship" is one-way, I feel you have been more frank and intimate with me about your life and concerns than many people I count as friends and relatives. My relationship to you has altered my relationship to the disease AIDS.

The turning point for me was the night you came on and you looked bad. You were blind, your legs and face were swollen, and your skin was blotchy. I realized then that up until that night I had not really taken you seriously. You looked so healthy, I guess I didn't believe in my heart of hearts that you had AIDS. That night I believed it, and I first began to think of the possibility of you dying. It was a shock. It was not the feeling I have when I read in the paper that a celebrity has died of AIDS. This was not removed. It was my friend, Peter, and I was shocked and saddened.

Both the *Vancouver* article and Sharon Mackin's concern for Peter's health raised a fundamental question that more people had been asking of late: how long would the diaries continue? David Paperny admitted there was much discomfort and denial around the question of when to stop shooting. "I worry about what would happen if his health does deteriorate," he told the magazine writer. "As a friend, I want to protect him. I worry that my job as a producer — wanting to get as much from him as possible to present to the audience — will be in conflict with my friendship with him." Paperny made it clear that the decision rested with Peter; the series would go "as far as Peter wants to take it," he said, "as long as he's physically able to do it." But the question of where the series was going would confront Paperny long before Peter's physical ability to continue became an issue.

By spring 1992 there was much debate in the CBC newsroom about the direction of AIDS Diary. Much of it was prompted by a series of segments devoted largely to gay and other sexuality issues. The final segment of this group of diaries, which aired on March 18, was Peter's response to an AIDS Vancouver public awareness campaign. A safer sex poster — with the slogan "Gay, Bisexual or Straight. It doesn't matter who we are. We all have choices — safer choices" and a photo depicting an appropriately broad spectrum of gay and bisexual men — was to appear on BC Transit buses around the Lower Mainland. It was a fairly tame ad; indeed, the fully clad models looked more like they were promoting Levis than safer sex. But officials at BC Transit saw things differently. They had received several complaints from bus passengers disturbed to see the words "gay" and "bisexual" in public.

While this kind of objection was predictable, to Peter it was a disturbing reminder of how much education had yet to be done. Attempts to keep gays and lesbians invisible, he told viewers in Diary 80, were the most damaging form of anti-gay prejudice.

> If someone comes up to me and says "All faggots should be rounded up and shot," it's easy to respond to that — it's such blatant bigotry. But the homophobia of exclusion is silent and therefore very difficult to respond to, because basically [it means] we don't exist. If gay men and lesbians were represented in television, movies and advertisements as much as they are in the rest of society, then posters like this wouldn't be a problem. It wouldn't be unusual. We would just be represented as we are, a smaller part of a greater whole.
>
> Now, this particular education campaign that AIDS Vancouver is doing is trying to target some different groups. This poster is geared towards gay and bisexual men. They're trying to reach as many people as possible; not all gay and bisexual men hang out in gay bars. They should have access to information like this in public places, such as riding on a bus.

It was one of Peter's typically measured, articulate diaries, but it was the third week in a row he had talked about sexuality and this worried a few people at the CBC. Kevin Evans was particularly concerned. The news anchor's difficulty with the series had always been concealed on-air by his objective style. But lately, he told the producers back in the newsroom, Peter's diary had become repetitive. Perhaps having said all there was to say about methods of HIV transmission and the daily struggles of living with AIDS, Peter was merely recycling used material. In recent weeks he had recited the "Affirmation" poem for the second time, introduced Harvey for a third time, and castigated homophobia at every possible turn.

This wasn't the first time the status of AIDS Diary had been questioned. Throughout the first year there were regular meetings in which the scope and direction of the series was reviewed. The initial concern was that Peter too often crossed the boundary of "objective" journalism by presenting his personal opinion on highly charged political issues.

But AIDS Diary was never intended to be objective. As David Paperny had argued from the beginning, it was clearly separate from the rest of the program in much the same way an op-ed page or columnist is set off from the "hard news" in a newspaper. There was also no precedent with which to compare Peter's role as a regular contributor who addressed his *Evening News* audience in the first person. Additionally, no other station even approached the level of depth on medical, health, and social issues that Peter offered with his unique series on AIDS.

Gradually, there was less pressure on Paperny to rein Peter in. For the first few weeks of the series, producers closely monitored Peter's every word; the more viewers began to trust him and feel he had a contribution to make to AIDS awareness, the more the newsroom was willing to support Peter and the more licence it was willing to grant him as the weeks went by.

At the same time, Paperny and Ridout were constantly looking for new ways to make the diaries more interesting to the viewer. They both agreed, for example, that too many diaries consisted of only a single shot in which Peter looked passively into the camera. While this approach, recommended by Paul Wynne's producer, had proved most effective in the earlier diaries when the viewing audience was first getting acquainted with Peter, it now depended on an especially strong monologue to keep viewers' attention. To add more vigour to the segments, Paperny occasionally added "B-reel" footage — background clips and other images which, when combined with Peter's voiceover, made the segments more visually appealing than a simple, one-shot monologue.

A year and a half into the series, however, it appeared to Evans and a few others in the newsroom that no degree of production enhancement would make a difference. The diaries had been an excellent addition to the AIDS education field, Evans argued, but how much more could really be said? And what was Paperny going to do once Peter's health began to deteriorate? Evans was only the most vocal on the news team with this position; others shared his view that the series should, at least, be scaled down. A number of *Evening News* staff members liked Peter but felt that the diaries weren't consistently strong from one week to the next, and were often repetitious. Perhaps, they suggested, Paperny should just wait for the really good segments and run them once or twice a month. (Paperny recalled later that much of the newsroom impatience with the diaries may have been due more to short attention spans than genuine discomfort with Peter's health. Like most current affairs producers working beside a news team, Paperny faced the classic tug-of-war for air time with news hounds in pursuit of new material. "TV news is a fickle medium," he explained. "It jumps around the world, from subject to subject, with great ease. For some people in our business, to see our show coming back to the same person all the time would make them want to say 'Let's move on.'")

Evans called an open meeting of producers to address the issues. About a dozen members of the *Evening News* production team took part, and CBC regional director John Kennedy, the ultimate authority for all programming at the station, sat in.

"I was really concerned about the line between journalism and voyeurism," Evans recalled. "I didn't think we'd be doing our audience any favours, and Peter and his family any favours, nor the CBC any favours, by turning this into a death watch." Indeed, some people in the newsroom who were not involved in the decision-making had already approached Ridout and Paperny, asking when it would all be over. Evans felt uneasy about entrusting the decision of when to end the series to Peter, given that no one could rule out the possibility of dementia setting in as his health failed. He argued that the CBC should maintain some editorial input on how to wind down the series.

Then there was the gay issue. Despite the host of themes Peter had explored in more than 75 diaries already aired, Evans still felt that the diaries were too often a platform for gay rights. "When the subject of sexual orientation is relevant to the mission of AIDS education," he said, "that's fine. Fair enough. But when it becomes gratuitous — when it appears as though we're advocating a gay lifestyle — then I think we've crossed the line."

Paperny was disturbed by Evans's choice of words. "What do you mean by 'advocating'?" he asked. Evans explained that many viewers still believed that homosexuality was a matter of personal choice, and that gays and lesbians not only want others to tolerate their lifestyle choice, but to adopt it. While he himself did not subscribe to that view, Evans explained, he just wasn't sure the *Evening News* was the appropriate venue to address the issue one way or the other.

It was pretty much the standard industry argument for journalistic objectivity, but Paperny and Ridout countered with a question: Wasn't it considered part of CBC's mandate as a public broadcaster to explore issues more critically than its rival private broadcasters? It was Paperny's current affairs mandate to produce challenging television on controversial social issues. Peter, by attacking homophobia at every available opportunity, had fulfilled that role admirably. Paperny told Evans once again that the series title, "AIDS Diary," implied that its subject was talking about his own life and was therefore entitled to comment on issues from a personal perspective.

Paperny added, as he had at the beginning of the series, that it was impossible to discuss AIDS issues in the context of Peter's life without addressing homosexuality; Peter, as a gay man, offered a more authentic perspective of homosexuality than any straight liberal could have offered. His reaction to various gay issues — regardless of their relevance to his illness — provided valuable insight. Paperny believed that Evans's objection — far from representing the interests of viewers — further politicized the issue of news coverage. Rendering gay issues invisible would cast the CBC's reputation as cutting edge television in doubt; by presenting the issues up front, the CBC wasn't necessarily endorsing one position or another, simply reflecting Peter's reality.

Evans countered that no other minority group or issue had been given the kind of platform that Peter enjoyed. Was this fair? As news anchor — the final connection to the viewing audience — he found it hard to justify that gay rights were the only special interest which received full editorial licence from the CBC. If other groups were offered this kind of platform, he'd have no objection. Furthermore, he resented the implication that because he had concerns and was asking questions about the series — as he would of any other project — he must necessarily be homophobic or anti-homosexual. Paperny and others, he found, had assumed such ownership of AIDS Diary since 1990 that they quickly became defensive at the slightest criticism. Evans dismissed the notion he was homophobic by citing his extensive television experience covering gay issues for various stations in Canada.[2]

Despite the force of his arguments, Evans finally conceded the most practical, bottom-line reason for leaving AIDS Diary the way it was: audience response. The bond developed between Peter and his audience had elevated AIDS Diary to the point that, for many, Wednesdays had become the most anticipated newscast of the week. (In the final year of the series, diaries were repeated on the Sunday night broadcast as well.) If gay rights had truly overshadowed everything else then someone must not have told the cancer and heart disease patients, blind people, and others with disabilities — most of them straight — who gained so much inspiration from the diaries. And many other viewers, regardless of their health, simply watched the series because they liked what Peter was doing.

Thus, Paperny argued, the corporation should recognize that Peter was on a unique "journey" in television broadcasting and should be given as much room as possible to complete it. Regional director John Kennedy agreed, casting his vote of confidence. By the end of the meeting, the senior production team renewed its commitment to the series: AIDS Diary would continue on a weekly basis until Peter no longer felt he could go before the camera.

Some of Paperny's colleagues still felt that a policy should be developed for dealing with Peter's ultimate decline: to what extent would the cameras intrude as he moved closer to death? Would a CBC crew be allowed into his room at St. Paul's if his condition worsened? Would the *Evening News* even want to venture that far into his illness?

For Peter, discussing the matter with Paperny after the meeting, there was no answer to that final question. He hadn't much thought about when he was going to die, but it wasn't likely to happen at St. Paul's Hospital — he wanted to die at home.

Peter also disagreed with the argument that the diaries had become

repetitious. While some of the themes may have been the same —
blindness, sexuality, education — he always managed to find new
ways to explore the issues. His zest for life and his ability to explore
new activities despite his illness allowed him to produce *human* diaries of more personal interest than the basic AIDS diary or gay diary.

I n dealing with blindness, for example, he was never at loss for
an idea. Diary 73 (January 29, 1992) opened with Peter delicately
fingering the keys of a piano as his teacher stands beside him.

The day that I found out I was going to lose the vision that I had left, I
decided that I wanted to start to play the piano again. It was something that
I'd done as a child, but I hadn't taken lessons since I'd finished high school
and hadn't really had access to a piano. So on the way home from the
hospital I stopped into a piano place and made arrangements for a rental,
went out and bought some music and then started to plunk away. It was a lot
of fun and very rewarding but I didn't get particularly good at it, and then the
vision that I had started dwindling away to the point that I couldn't read the
music anymore.

[PETER SPEAKS DIRECTLY TO THE CAMERA] Well then, I still had this piano
and I had this crazy idea that because I'd gone blind I would have suddenly
acquired an ability to pick pieces out by ear, and I discovered that that wasn't
so at all. So I thought about taking piano lessons but I really wasn't sure what
the options were. I knew there was Braille music but that sounded rather
difficult. So I didn't really do much for a year, but about two months ago I
finally decided to make the move and start taking lessons again.

[HIS MONOLOGUE CONTINUES AS A VOICEOVER WHILE THE SCENE SHOWS
HIS TEACHER AT ANOTHER PIANO PLAYING CHORDS WHILE PETER MIMICS
THEM ON HIS PIANO.] And now what we do is my teacher reads out the notes
onto tape, we tape the lessons and then I can go over them again and again
at home ... [AS HIS TEACHER DESCRIBES HIS INTUITIVE APPROACH TO
PLAYING, PETER PLAYS THE OPENING CHORDS OF CHOPIN'S PRELUDE NO. 15.]

PETER: It's a really different feeling than reading music. I'm not
intimidated by the music, I'm not intimidated by the number of sharps or

flats or difficult chords that are coming up. So I really feel that I'd be able to play whatever I want to at the rate that we're doing it by just going through a piece, and by feeling it much more than I used to.

Toward the end of March, Peter was asked to speak at an AIDS Vancouver benefit held at a local art gallery. The invitation reminded him of how long it had been since he had painted. (He had considered himself an accomplished amateur while a UBC undergraduate.) He also realized that there was a lot more to art than the final product of a canvas. "There's a lot of art to the way that we live our lives, stuff that isn't captured any permanent way, but you can certainly enjoy it as it's happening," he reflected. "I guess it's something that AIDS has really made clear for me: time isn't indefinite, so you've got to make as much art in your life as you can and take advantage of all the situations that come along." So Peter decided to paint something for the event and auction it off for AIDS dollars. Diary 81, broadcast on March 25, shows him sitting on his bathroom floor with paints scattered all around him, working on his painting and rinsing brushes in the toilet.

I used to play around with paints when I could see but I was never very good at it. Now that I'm blind, I've got an excuse if I'm not a wonderful artist. So I got a hold of some art supplies — kindly donated — and a friend came over and I ... started to paint.

[PETER SPEAKS TO HIS FRIEND] So I'm just going to blow it dry and then I'll put on some other colours. [HE FLUSHES THE TOILET AND LAUGHS]

The toilet provided a good place for water to be changed quickly and easily without having to get up and move. I got my hands into it a lot. It's a lot easier to use your hands when you can't see the canvas, because then you can tell what parts are wet and what parts aren't covered with paint, and — actually, what ended up being covered mostly with paint was me.

[TO FRIEND] I'm going to be just using one colour now so ... I'll just use the jar now. [HE ADDS A YELLOW STRIP BESIDE A GREEN FLOWER ON A RED BACKGROUND, CREATING A VAN GOGH EFFECT] Does that look anything like a banana?

The whole process was a lot of fun, and I ended up with two canvases that

I took along to this benefit, auctioned them off and made some money for
AIDS Vancouver. It ... made me realize that maybe there is an opportunity
for a blind artist to make a living.[3]

Peter was also breaking new ground on the speaking circuit. In addition to the standard medical conventions — he addressed a group
of ophthalmologists on CMV retinitis in February and an international conference of family practitioners in May — he also took his
message to a couple of communities that badly required AIDS education but didn't get a lot of attention from governments: rural B.C. natives and the prison population.

When Peter was asked to address a group of native youth counsellor trainees, he jumped at the chance. He saw it as an opportunity to
build bridges with different AIDS communities. "Native people are at
high risk for HIV, particularly young native women," he told viewers
in Diary 74 (February 5, 1992). "I think what happens is that young
native people come to the big city and they may end up in the poverty
mill of the inner city life — on the street, or using intravenous drugs.
And then these people return to their small communities and take
HIV infection with them."

The diary showed a classroom session in which the young trainees
flashed cards with words like "kissing," "fantasy," "masturbation,"
and "vaginal intercourse."

I talked to them about HIV and AIDS, gave them some basic information for
themselves, but also how to convey this information to the kids they're going
to be working with. Part of this involved using a safer sex game where
different activities were described, and then I would get these people to
organize these activities into high risk, low risk and no risk activities ...

Perhaps one of the difficulties in getting this information out there is that
a lot of native people in rural communities don't perceive themselves to be at
risk. They're far away from the big bad city, and therefore they're far away
from this problem. But perhaps one of the participants in the conference
summed it up the best when he said: "We've learned our lesson in the past
from other illnesses such as smallpox and measles. We don't want HIV to
become another one of those that is going to decimate our people."

Peter understood the sentiment behind the last statement. Although he had never been much of a conspiracy theorist, he had seen first hand how illness could decimate a minority population while governments stood by and did nothing. Ten diaries later, in discussing some of the darker possibilities of the AIDS crisis, he explored the notion

> that there's a concerted effort on the part of government and other officials to suppress a cure, because this would allow AIDS to take its natural course. A kind of homosexual genocide — that AIDS would get rid of a lot of gay men from society and in some people's view would solve a problem ... Maybe there's some credence in it, who knows? It was four years into the AIDS epidemic before Ronald Reagan ever acknowledged that it existed, and by this time thousands of people had died. It makes you wonder.[4]

During a trip to Nanaimo in May, Peter addressed a group of inmates at the minimum security Nanaimo Correctional Centre. "The only difference between this audience and many of the other audiences I've spoken to is that these people are living in a very restricted, artificial environment," he explained in Diary 88 (May 20, 1992). But that wasn't the only difference; while there were no mass murderers among this group of about a dozen inmates, it was a hardened, chain-smoking, tattooed bunch of street-wise men that Peter encountered that day.

"The air was thick with prison machismo," recalled CBC reporter Ian Gill, who produced this diary. "I was prepared for all sorts of juvenile sniggering and nudging each other, but was surprised by how well-behaved they were and the connection [Peter] made with them. They turned it into a practical discussion for themselves."

By this time Peter was quite comfortable speaking to groups of all sizes and demographics. Since he was unable to see these men, who sat only a few feet in front of his chair as Harvey lay by his side, there was nothing to intimidate him. The inmates, for their part, found the whole experience exotic. Instead of the standard public health presentation, which usually consisted of some bureaucrat lecturing at them, they got to hear a TV celebrity who appeared to be pretty hip as well.

"He did his standard talk but it was laced with a couple of swear words," recalled Gill. "He was very measured with them, and funny. And Harvey did his usual steal-the-show thing." Any speaker would have squirmed at the prospect of discussing sex in prisons, but Peter managed to make his point with subtlety.

[TO GROUP] I want to keep this really informal today. Basically, I'm here to talk about HIV and AIDS. In an institution like this, it's important to have a way to protect yourself. I understand that in the provincial system, they haven't made condoms available yet, they haven't made bleach available yet. They have in the federal system as of December. Prior to that, a lot of corrections officials had the attitude like many parents do, that if you make these things available, you're giving them the green light to say, you know, "Go ahead boys, let's do it. You know, here's some condoms, here's some bleach to clean your needles." It means acknowledging that these things happen on the inside. And they happen, but a lot of people don't like to think that they happen, would rather ignore it.

You cannot get this infection by casual contact, even in the circumstances where you know someone bites someone else. HIV has never been spread that way.

INMATE: Say if you hit the guy, you cut your hand over on his teeth, and then he was bleeding from his cheek, and then you hit him in the cheek again and you ground your fist right on your cut right into his cheek, could you get it that way? Cause you're almost grinding his blood into your blood.

PETER: There might be a very low chance, but you're looking at maybe one infection out of millions. You know, the chance of getting struck by lightning would be a lot greater. So I don't think you really need to worry about that. I mean ... [LAUGHS] there's probably a greater chance that you're going to get killed in the fight than, you know ...

[VOICEOVER] I guess I have to wonder to some degree what I was doing here today, talking to a group of people who aren't able to protect themselves. I hope at some point that provincial corrections recognizes that sex and drugs do happen on the inside, and allow prisoners access to condoms and bleach, so that they can protect themselves. Failing that, some of the information that I've given them today will hopefully be useful when they get out of here. AIDS applies to both sides of the fence.

INMATE: [AS HE PATS HARVEY] You show a hell of a lot of guts to come out here.

PETER: Well thank you.

Peter had shown that there were still many important issues to share with his viewers, and he was finding innovative ways to present them. However, within weeks of his trip to the Nanaimo Correctional Centre it became apparent that time was the critical factor in his ability to continue.

19

Long-Term Survivor

S hortly after his 35th birthday in June 1992, Peter was told that he had become the longest-surviving AIDS patient in British Columbia. "Basically that means that someone who had AIDS longer than I have just died," he told viewers on June 17. "It's a rather dubious distinction when you think about it: on one hand, I've beaten all the odds; on the other hand, I've survived all these other people."

One of those people was Jay Wadsworth, the CNIB mobility instructor who had been so helpful when Peter was losing his vision. Ironically, Peter had to comfort Wadsworth in the last few months of his life as he developed cytomegalovirus retinitis, the same AIDS infection that had robbed Peter of his eyesight. Wadsworth's death was an especially hard blow as he had done so much to help Peter overcome depression and regain his independence after going blind.

There were many other losses to deal with as well. There was his ex-lover Brian, bitter until the very end about his fate; there was Rod, a young Canadian Forces soldier who became ill before he was able to find the new life he sought after leaving the prairies; and there was Fred, a friend from New York City he had met in 1987 while living with Marc. Peter tried to reach him at Christmas and left several messages, only to receive a call from another friend telling him that Fred had just died.

It came as a total shock to me. I knew he'd been having some health problems, but I had no idea that he was that sick. I met him four years ago, and at that time he was very fit and strong. But his lover had died a year previous to that, and I don't think he'd ever really recovered from that loss. And when he started to have health problems himself, I think all the fight was gone. It's not that uncommon. AIDS is one of those illnesses where it's often the sick looking after the dying. And if you lose someone who's meant a great deal to you and then you face your own illness, there's often nothing left for yourself.[1]

Fred's death reminded Peter why some of his own friends — particularly those from out of town who couldn't monitor his progress by watching the weekly diary — grew so anxious when he didn't speak to them or return their calls for several weeks. The death of so many friends in such a short time had a sobering effect on Peter. "I can't help thinking that there's an hourglass out there with my name on it, and I'm not sure how much time is left," he said. "I guess all I can hope for is that I keep beating the odds."

Peter's lengthy odyssey was taking its toll on some of his older friendships. While many of his friends were willing to stay by his side no matter what the circumstances, others found his illness harder to endure than he did.

In one of his earliest diaries, Peter had told viewers how his first hospital stay in 1986 affected his priorities. With blindness, Peter's lifestyle changed far more dramatically than it had in the period following his initial illness. Since mid-1989 he had not been able to pursue the fast-paced, urban gay life he did before — driving from restaurant to theatre, picking up friends, going out to nightclubs, flying to sunny vacation spots, and doing several activities in one day. Peter had made dozens of friends through this kind of lifestyle, but now there were many of them he couldn't see anymore, literally or otherwise.

One of the first friends he cut loose was a constant partying and travel companion. Marty, a strikingly handsome young man who had known Peter since his UBC days, resented Peter's accusations of superficiality. ("He is bright and he can be quite funny but I always feel there is a barrier up that I can't quite penetrate," Peter wrote Flora Hillier, describing Marty. "There is a side to him which I really don't trust ... He can be very manipulative and controlling ... ")

Another friend, who had nursed Peter during and shortly after his hospitalization in 1986, began to disapprove of the "Dr. Peter" persona. He thought that Peter came across as too earnest on television, too eager to please, and that Peter was entirely the wrong role model to represent people with AIDS. Fed up with the adulation Peter was receiving and the way he savoured it, he broke off the friendship. Peter was devastated. He was indebted to this friend for having remained by his side in the early days of his illness and believed he shouldn't have been so final about ending the friendship.

Ross Murray soon found that he had to retreat, too. He admitted that Peter's illness was often harder on him than it was on Peter. While Peter resolved to push on and live his life no matter what, Murray was having emotional difficulty with his friend's illness and needed time to adjust to his many losses; at the same time, he felt that Peter had too many expectations of him, and he felt that the diaries had replaced one group of acquaintances with another: the hangers-on, the AIDS celebrity groupies and others who built Peter up as a saint. He thought Peter was abandoning many of his earlier friends in favour of those who didn't question or challenge him. Early in 1992, he and Peter decided they needed some distance.

"Peter was like a flower in the sun," Murray recalled. "He moved toward those friends where the light was strongest." When he was healthy and independent that meant people he could party and travel with. When he was ill, Murray suggested, the "brightest" people were those willing to attend to his every need. Before long, a large gap separated Peter's two groups of friends: those who knew him before he had AIDS and those who knew him after. Murray's own reappearance toward the end of Peter's life caused some friction with members of the latter group.

For one of those, Chris Tyrell, it seemed as though too many people had given up on Peter just when he needed them most. "If I was a Martian looking down on Earth and someone asked me to describe AIDS, I'd say 'Well, you lose weight and your friends change'," he recalled.

Tyrell's comment was a harsh critique of Peter's friends, but also a challenge to the gay community at large. He believed it was impossible to appreciate what it means to be gay in the 1990s without being a personal caregiver to someone who is dying of AIDS. "Listen, as far as I'm concerned, if you're minus the AIDS experience, then you're not a gay person." It is only by caring for one's sick friends — washing them, dressing them, helping them with treatment, taking them out in public — that healthy gay men discover what it means to be truly vulnerable. The way Peter confronted AIDS had inspired Tyrell and his partner, Steve Schilling, with a sense of pride and well being they had never known before. It wasn't so much that Peter allayed their fears about death and dying; it was more that he had taught them how to live.

Peter insisted on enjoying life to the maximum, no matter what doctor's orders were. If that meant hauling along his various medicines for an outing, so be it. On one camping trip to Galiano, where a group of friends stayed in a small trailer, Peter handed Tyrell a glass and asked him to mix a strange, milky fluid for him.

"What's that?" Tyrell asked.

"Oh, it's my ddI," Peter told him. "I haven't taken it yet today."

Tyrell shook his head in wonder and mixed the life-sustaining fluid.

Entertaining at home was not quite so casual. For the simplest occasion Peter would set the atmosphere with overdressed tables, candelabras, and classical music. He and Andy were notoriously slow as hosts — friends called them "Fiddle and Faddle"; they usually started preparing dinner so late that Peter would have to sustain his guests on a diet of cheese and crackers while Andy went to the store to buy some forgotten ingredient. When the gourmet meal finally arrived hours later, however, it was usually excellent.

Similarly, picnic lunches were like scenes from *Brideshead Revisited*: wicker baskets, white linen napkins and champagne with the finest cheese and paté and the freshest strawberries and cream that the local market had to offer.

Peter's enjoyment of such pleasures was essential to his well being at this time. But while he may have been encouraged by the "longest living survivor" announcement, his chances for a lengthy life appeared to be getting slimmer. Weeks before the announcement, on May 25, he was hospitalized for the second time with *Pneumocystis carinii* pneumonia, the same illness that nearly killed him when he was first diagnosed with AIDS. Although his face was ashen and covered with KS lesions, and the cataracts in his eyes had whited out almost completely, he still went on television with an optimistic message.

The first bout was very serious — I almost didn't make it out of hospital. This time it's much less so, partly because of the medication to prevent it, partly because I was aware of the signs and symptoms of it, so that when I was suspicious of it I went for treatment and started getting treatment at home with pills. Now something went wrong and yesterday I had extremely high fevers and nausea. I wasn't able to keep anything down and I got quite dehydrated, so I landed in here. Not my favourite place, but I felt much better once I got here.

There's always the fear that there's something else going on. Just because you've got one illness doesn't mean you can't get another, and this is the reality for many people with AIDS. In many respects I've been lucky; the things I've had to deal with have come one at a time. For many of my friends they've come one on top of another — kind of an avalanche effect. And I was afraid yesterday that that's what was happening ...

But once I got in here I had a chance to talk to my doctor, got hooked up to some intravenous fluids and so on. I felt much better, much safer. And then when I woke up this morning with no fever and an appetite again, I felt infinitely better. Feeling the way I did yesterday, I can certainly understand how a long drawn-out illness would make one just want to say "Bye-bye, it's too much trouble to stick around." The way I'm feeling today, I've got a lot more fight in me.[3]

Despite his determination, however, pain was becoming a regular part of his life. And for the first time since he began taping the diaries, the physical evidence of that pain was becoming all too visible to viewers. In Diary 91 (June 10, 1992), taped at his apartment, Peter's bare legs revealed how dramatically the Kaposi's sarcoma was spreading. His left thigh was swollen to a size half as big again as his right one, and the difference in colour between the two legs was striking. The tumour of small blood vessels had "overgrown in a tangle," Peter explained, making it difficult to bend or straighten his leg, or to walk.

The presence of so much pain was weakening his resolve to avoid painkillers, a solution he had always resisted prescribing as a doctor because of the addictive properties of painkilling drugs. By June he was taking two Tylenol 3 tablets (containing 60 mg of codeine) every six hours. Although his decision to increase the dosage was understandable, he felt the need to justify it medically to his viewers. It was clear that his experience as a patient was affecting his philosophy as a doctor.

> On several occasions I've come across well-meaning physicians who have been cutting back on the pain medications for a terminally ill patient. And when you ask them why, their response is "Oh well, I wouldn't want them to become addicted." Well so what if they become addicted?! When I think about it in terms of myself, I'm not concerned that I'm going to be doing any physical harm by taking these medications — I'm already poisoning myself with x number of other pills. I'm not concerned that the use of these is going to undermine my moral fibre. Maybe on some level I'm concerned that I'll become an addict. But at this point, that should be the least of my worries.[4]

By this time, Peter had been waiting several weeks to begin radiation therapy for his KS. Although the delay was not life-threatening, it was an annoying and painful inconvenience. In Diary 94 (July 4, 1992) he wondered, if his AIDS-related cancer brought him to the brink of death, would he still have to wait for the treatment?

This expensive equipment is sitting there, and the reason people have to wait for it is because it's only being operated from nine to five, Monday to Friday. I don't know at what level decisions like this are made, but there's no reason why these machines couldn't be working twenty-four hours a day. It would relieve a great deal of anxiety for patients and it perhaps in the long run could save the system some money. If I were called up tomorrow and told that I had to go in at two o'clock in the morning for radiation therapy, I'd be there with bells on.

By the end of June, with the radiation equipment still unavailable, Peter arranged for another session of chemotherapy and left for one more trip abroad. On June 30 he flew to England with Maggie Johnston, his former guide dog trainer from Ottawa. They travelled to York, the Lake District, and the seaside towns of Whitby and Salt-burn, and spent several nights at Maggie's father's pub in Northum-berland, where Peter enjoyed Scotch, pub food, and the various dialects and accents of northeast England. They travelled further north to Edinburgh, Scotland, and visited a number of art galleries with Maggie's brother. In Yorkminster they attended choral perform-ances and visited the set of *Brideshead Revisited*, Peter's favourite Brit-ish television program, where he was nearly thrown off the premises when he sat down at a grand piano and began plunking away at the keys. It was like being a kid again. Only once during the trip was Peter's energy so low that he was forced to spend a day in bed with a high fe-ver. "We read trashy English tabloids and watched television," he re-called later. "That fell on day ten after my chemotherapy, so it really wasn't a big surprise. I often get fevers on that day. So I just laid low and the next morning I was fine."[5]

Back in Vancouver Peter had a unique opportunity to be a "pseudo-parent" when he looked after his nine-year-old niece for two weeks while she attended an art camp at Granville Island. As Diary 97 (July 22, 1992) opened, he was standing in the kitchen preparing lunch with Nancy's daughter. The time with his niece had given him a new appreciation of what it meant to be a father, he told viewers. With scenes of Peter and his niece playing cards and sorting out his compact disc collection, this was the AIDS diarist at his most charming.

There's a lot of things that you don't think about. This person is quite dependent on you in a lot of ways — you've got to feed them, keep them clean, get them to bed, amuse them. All kinds of different things that are difficult enough some times to do for yourself. But, regardless of how you're feeling yourself, you've got to be there for this other person. I really understand now what it means to be a parent, particularly a single parent, and how difficult that must be if you've got more than one to look after.

Now, our relationship is perhaps a bit different than that of the average adult and child, because I'm dependent on her to a certain degree. [With my] being blind, she can be my eyes, and so I might be dependent on her in other ways. It's been a big adjustment for her, dealing with my illness. As she's gotten older, different aspects of my health have failed, I've lost my vision.

It's really great to have the opportunities to spend some time alone with her, so that we get to know each other and appreciate each other. It's very special.

It was one of his only regrets, he later told Michael Myers, that he would never get to see his niece and nephews grow up.

This was also one of the last diaries that wasn't devoted in some way to the ravaging effects of AIDS.

20

Dying with Dignity

O ne morning early in August, Peter was returning home from a walk with Harvey when he heard the telephone ringing in his second-floor apartment. He rushed upstairs to answer but could barely speak when he picked it up. The loss of breath was eerily reminiscent of the last few days before he was hospitalized in 1986, when his lung capacity was reduced to nearly nothing. This wasn't the only problem Peter had noticed recently. His voice was beginning to sound hoarse and he was having difficulty swallowing. The prognosis, he told viewers on August 5, was not good.

I finally discussed it with one of my doctors. He took a peek down my throat and noticed that the tissues were very very swollen. Then I had a CAT scan of my neck, and they've discovered that I have Kaposi's sarcoma in my larynx, or voice box, and the area around it. Basically what that means is that this AIDS-related cancer has spread to the upper part of my airway. The tissues around that have become swollen, and essentially the tube going into my lungs has become increasingly narrower and narrower. The reason that I've been more short of breath is simply because there's not that much space to move air through. So with any exertion these days, I'm just knocked for a loop.

Now, I went into the cancer clinic yesterday and was all measured up for this special plastic mould, so that when I go in for the radiation therapy it'll be delivered to exactly the same spot each time. And that starts next week. In the meantime, however, I've been totally amazed at how much and how quickly things can change from day to day. I'm so limited in what I can do right now for the simple reason that I just can't move enough air.

By this time the Kaposi's sarcoma lesions had spread beyond control, leaving large splotches on Peter's face. If he was able to remain somewhat blasé about his condition, his viewers certainly weren't. "I know what's going to happen to him, and I don't want to see it anymore," one woman told Paperny over the phone, suggesting that the *Evening News* was exploiting Peter by continuing to tape the diaries well beyond the point of dignity. By the end of the conversation, however, she insisted that she loved Peter and that she didn't want the series to end.

Paperny had grown accustomed to this kind of response. Many viewers had been comfortable with Peter's presence on television as long as his illness remained invisible — as long as the unpleasant realities of AIDS remained an abstraction. Once the KS lesions began spreading on his face, arms, and legs, however, the truth could no longer be ignored: that friendly, unthreatening man who had gained their trust and affection over two years was finally, unmistakably, dying.

In Peter's 100th diary the following week (August 12), the scratchiness and wheezing that had recently become noticeable in his voice was even more pronounced, and under the harsh TV lights he did not look like a man who would live much longer. "Three weeks ago I was water skiing at Shawnigan Lake," he began, his voice cracking over a scene of a still photograph showing him leaning on a dock, preparing to be pulled away by the power boat. Succeeding photographs showed him falling, then getting up again. "Some people felt it couldn't be done, but I did get up and I had a lot of fun." The radiation treatments, he added, were proving to be helpful.

The doctor told me that any decrease in the swelling at the entrance to my lungs is going to make it a lot easier for me to breathe. Because the volume of air you move through a space is related exponentially to the width of that space, any increase in the width is going to make quite a big increase in the volume of air. Now, how much easier it's going to make my breathing is difficult to say at this point. The full results may not be for ten or eleven weeks, and there may be some limitations on what I'm able to do, but we're just going to have to wait and see what those limitations are.

Kevin Evans wasn't fooled by Peter's optimism. Sitting opposite Jay Wortman in a live interview to mark the 100th episode on August 12, Evans implied that Peter should consider ending the series because of his declining health. Wortman was taken aback. "I think Kevin had a bit of an agenda and he kind of blindsided me with it," he recalled. "His first question was something like: 'Where do you think this is going to go?' It was a real challenge, like 'Look at how awful this is.' The implication was that this is bad and we should put a stop to it. I basically said it would go where Peter chose to take it, and that the media's responsibility now was to respect his wishes."

In honour of the 100th diary, the Toronto *Globe and Mail* ran a major article on Peter the following week. This was Peter's first exposure in Canada's so-called national newspaper in the two years he had been shooting AIDS Diary. Perhaps indicative of the *Globe*'s influence, the telephones were buzzing at the CBC's network offices in Toronto only hours after that day's edition hit the streets. Less than a week after the *Globe* article appeared, the network commissioned Paperny to produce a one-hour documentary to be broadcast in early November. This announcement, along with the network's decision to provide a $38,000 budget for the project, was a major psychological boost for Peter. For the next two months Peter could afford to devote most of his time to the project, with a camera crew recording more of his life. Paperny later speculated that Peter's excitement at the prospect of working on one final documentary may have been the strongest factor in his survival past the summer months.[1]

On the August 19 diary Peter was shown in bed, hooked up to an oxygen tank. He was acutely short of breath and was suffering dramatic side effects from the radiation. His voice was reduced to a small squeak, his throat was sore, he couldn't swallow anything without difficulty, and his need for oxygen was becoming more constant. Only the use of nasal tubes attached to the oxygen tank allowed him to deliver this diary.

I woke up on Sunday morning feeling quite restless because I was short of breath. I hooked up to the oxygen that I had at home, but that really didn't help. Lying here doing nothing, even with the oxygen on, I was still short of breath. I was really working hard to breathe, really pulling. I got a true sense of what it must be like to have a bad asthma attack. And I started getting scared. I told my sister that this was happening, and that I wanted to call the specialist about where I should go. At the same time it was discovered that the oxygen tank was a quarter full. That meant only another fifteen or twenty minutes. That's when things started getting a little panicky.

It was decided that I should go into St. Paul's emergency. And the oxygen tank ran out literally as we arrived at the door. I had this vision of having to have an emergency tracheotomy right there in the waiting room but that wasn't to happen. I don't think I've ever been so glad to step into a hospital before. There they have this endless supply of oxygen. Once I got there, they gave me a high dose of cortisone, which helped relieve the swelling in my throat and made it easier for me to breathe.

Now, there's always potential side effects to different medical therapies. I was told that something like this could happen. But the way it happened wasn't like the way it was supposed to have happened. And it was pretty scary. I've had some pretty nasty side effects, and some things have happened to me that — not meaning to sound paranoid — haven't happened to other people, generally. This time I was lucky.

By late August Peter had stopped taking anti-viral medication and was switching from radiation therapy to a drug called etoposide for the KS in his right hand and left foot. Karen Gelmon, his cancer specialist, was concerned about the extent of KS in his lungs and by how quickly it had developed in his right hand, just over the course of the previous week.

Despite his worsening health, however, he insisted that the next diary be shot outdoors. After helping him get dressed, Paperny brought Peter to a peaceful sunny pond in Queen Elizabeth Park. Seated under a tree, Peter told viewers about his use of etoposide. "We decided that because of the speed at which things were progressing, we'd have to change the therapy, so I switched to a new chemotherapy agent — one that I take at night time every day for a couple of weeks. It carries a high risk of losing my hair, but considering the potential benefits of it, it's really not something to be that concerned about."

The KS blotches on his face were plainly visible from several feet away before the camera moved in for the closeup. It was less than two years since he had told viewers that "AIDS is not a focus in my life," but now there was no denying the power of multiplying cancerous cells. Peter, looking resigned about his situation, paused between sentences as he waited to catch his breath.

I used to have difficulty believing in cancer. I imagine that sounds ridiculous but even when I was in medical school, I had difficulty with the concept of a bunch of cells growing out of control having the ability to make someone very sick and possibly even kill them. I thought that in most cases of someone with cancer, their heart and other organs would be functioning quite well. So how did these out of control cells have the ability to strangle out life?

Well, personally I'm starting to experience exactly what it means to have those cells growing out of control. And I'm getting a sense of the impact that those cancer cells can have on a person's life and their quality of life. The Kaposi's sarcoma that I have ... has started growing very quickly in the last little while. Perhaps it's not growing any faster than it had before, but because the total number of cells has increased, every time that number of cells doubles, there's just that much more to battle. And it's gotten to the point where it's outstripped the efforts that we've made to keep it under control.

By this point the simple act of talking or crossing a room was taking his breath away. He felt pain in his scrotum, arm, foot, and throat, and now his KS pressure sores were discharging fluids. After switching from pills to liquid morphine to reduce his anxiety, pain, and shortness of breath, Peter had a home care nurse treat his open sores. Early in September Phil Sestak arranged for a stool to be put in the shower and grab bars for the toilet.

❖

For much of that month Peter's health appeared to stabilize. He suffered from occasional fatigue and low-grade fevers in the first week but his energy was generally high.

He was feeling especially playful the night he was to speak at a benefit for the Vancouver Meals Society, an organization that delivers hot meals to people who are homebound with AIDS. He was supposed to deliver his standard "AIDS 101" speech — describing methods of transmission, advocating safer sex, criticizing homophobia — but Peter thought this approach might be a bit too sombre for what was otherwise an entertainment event. After all, his talk would be preceded by a folk band, a juggler, a poet and a modern dance troupe, so why not join the act himself?

"Andy, would you get me the duvet cover?" he asked his partner before going out the door with Harvey.

"What for?"

"Well, if I told you what for you probably wouldn't approve. So just get it, won't you?"

It was a fairly inspired work of performance art that had occurred to Peter only moments before leaving for the benefit. The result, an "interpretive dance" routine captured by a CBC camera for Diary 103, showed two assistants pulling a duvet cover over his entire body as he began describing the biological process of HIV infection. Typical of the dark, Monty Pythonesque humour he had always loved, Peter's routine was a *tour de force*: the ailing AIDS diarist spoofed the stale sobriety of medical demonstrations by masquerading as a writhing HIV organism. His routine stunned the capacity audience at the Vancouver East Cultural Centre, which was not quite sure how to react to a dying man hamming it up even as he struggled for breath. The clapping was sporadic at first, and the footage revealed many uncomfortable smiles in the audience. But Peter's tone reassured everyone and by the end of his routine, the entire crowd was on its feet.

[PETER SPEAKS FROM INSIDE THE CLOSED BAG] It's really dusty in here ... Um

... HIV infection. I will now represent the HIV virus. [SHOTS ALTERNATE BETWEEN THE CROWD RESPONSE OF LAUGHTER AND APPLAUSE, AND PETER, WHO IS NOW LYING ON THE FLOOR OF THE STAGE LIKE A LATE-SIXTIES YOKO ONO, COMPLETELY ENCLOSED IN HIS "BAG." HIS BREATHING GROWS HEAVY WITH THE LACK OF OXYGEN] Now, once inside the body, it finds these other cells. These are cells that help fight off infection, and they kind of worm around like this [HE ROLLS AROUND IN THE BAG, WRITHING TO AND FRO] ... And, the virus is really attracted to them and it ... it binds onto them ... and the cell says "Come on inside!" ... So the virus comes inside, and there's all this hanky-panky that goes on [HE BEGINS KICKING OUT HIS ARMS AND LEGS, SIMULATING A WILD SESSION OF INTERCOURSE] ... in the production of new viruses. So, basically ... [HE STOPS AND SITS UP IN THE BAG, GRADUALLY PULLING HIS WAY OUT OF IT] ... the best way to avoid this kind of thing is to climb inside your duvet cover and you'll be protected. [LOUD ROUND OF APPLAUSE, FOLLOWED BY STANDING OVATION]

Even as he broke up a benefit show audience with his humour, however, Peter was quietly preparing for the end. On September 7 he talked about his final medical arrangements with Andy and Phil Sestak. He wanted to die at home if possible, and would only request palliative care at St. Paul's Hospital if his symptoms got too bad; he only wanted medical intervention if it would maintain or improve his quality of life.

He also had to think of his legal affairs. Preparing a will was not something Peter had thought much about during his illness; most of his energy had been devoted to living longer. Only when he was hospitalized again with PCP the previous spring did the reality finally sink in. "After having AIDS for five and a half years, I hadn't had a will. That was kind of goofy — I just kept putting it off," he told viewers on September 9. He also began discussing the details of his living will with Nancy, and with Richard and Debbie Bebb — two medical school friends he had previously recruited to supervise his last days of medical care. Peter and Andy invited the Hennessys and the Bebbs over for dinner to talk about what he wanted.

The dinner, taped by Paperny for the CBC documentary, was a memorable scene. At one point, as Nancy and Lionel discussed the arrangements for Peter's death with Richard and Debbie Bebb, Andy broke in with an earnest reminder of how important it was to respect Peter's wishes. What was it that *he* wanted? Peter, realizing the scene had taken on a much too earnest tone, leaned back in his chair. "Ultimately, I want to be in my own bed," he mused. "Preferably a large, four-poster bed with a dozen down cushions and a red velvet bedspread. Sort of like Ebenezer Scrooge, with hundreds of weeping relatives." Ever the perfect dinner host, he broke up the room once again.

Peter knew he was fortunate to have as much support as he did. Recently he had spoken to a friend whose lover was dying of AIDS. As often happens with PWAs, the dying man's mother had removed Peter's friend from the will and obtained a restraining order that prevented his having access to his lover, despite the fact that his partner needed his support. "The reason this can happen is that the mother's relationship with the son is quite sanctified in law," Peter explained in Diary 104 (September 9, 1992). "The relationship between the two men has no basis, it is not at all recognized in law and there's no basis there for a partner to protect their rights in a situation such as this."

September 14, 1992

Inside the 125-year-old St. Peter's Church in Quamichan, near the south Vancouver Island town of Duncan, Peter recognized the familiar wooden scent and creaking floorboards of a chapel he had visited as a child. "It's funny that I'm so attached to this place, because I never believed in organized religion," he told the chaplain, Logan McMenamie, in a private moment. "Well," replied McMenamie, "don't throw everything out, because it has some saving graces."

"I wasn't talking about you," said Peter. As a result of his recent reconciliation with the church, Peter requested that communion be served at his funeral. The Eucharist, he said, would be a sign of thanksgiving and a symbolic meal to be shared by family and friends.

Escorted by McMenamie, with Bob and Shirley, Paperny, and a

CBC camera crew close by, Peter then walked the grounds of the church toward the spot where he planned to be buried, enjoying the fresh air of the Cowichan Valley he recalled from his youth. When they arrived at the spot, everyone grew silent as Peter bent over and took a few moments to feel the turf. "Oh, this won't do. This won't do at all," he said, getting up. "Why not?" someone asked. "It's too close to the oak tree," he grinned. "Six years of toxic medication is going to kill that tree for sure."

In the next week Peter's voice grew progressively hoarser and the yeast infection built up in his throat so much that Sestak ordered special lozenges for him. By September 20 he required marijuana pills to treat the nausea that caused his poor appetite. And five days later an ulcer was discovered in the swallowing area of his throat. When Sestak made a house call on September 27 he saw that the oxygen level in Peter's blood was so depressed that he was becoming nauseous whenever he walked without an oxygen tank. Lindsay Lawson and Sestak decided to put him on continuous oxygen and increase the dose of morphine.

"My lungs are functioning so badly that there isn't enough oxygen in room air to really allow me to do much," Peter told viewers from his sister's home in Nanaimo. "Even with the oxygen, I'm still very limited in what I can do. It's very frustrating when you've got two arms and two legs that are working, you've got lots of things that you want to be doing, but you just can't, 'cause your lungs don't allow you to. When I had pneumonia six years ago, it was simply a case of taking antibiotics. The pneumonia cleared up. I could breathe again. It's not as simple as that anymore; I may be stuck with this."[2]

Earlier on September 27, Peter had had to leave the sixth annual Walk for AIDS without taking the ten-kilometre stroll around the Stanley Park seawall — he was feeling too nauseous to do it. For the second consecutive year he delivered the keynote speech, but this time he sounded much less confident as he acknowledged the passing of yet another milestone in his AIDS odyssey: the sixth anniversary of his diagnosis. After the brief speech he left the stage and asked to be brought home. Three days later he learned that another infection, cytomegalovirus — the same infection that ravaged his eyesight — had spread to his throat and rectum.

As Peter's health failed he tended to concentrate on physical and medical information in his diaries, but Paperny had the impression that there was still unfinished business, something Peter needed to get off his chest before he died. When Paperny asked what was going through his mind as he approached death, Peter told him he was still frustrated by the fact he never felt safe enough to come out to his parents when he was a teenager. Bob and Shirley's homophobia had caused him a great deal of pain, and he felt that they still didn't understand why this was the case. Paperny was struck by Peter's comment; it was clear that his resentment, and the anger he had denied viewers for so long, was only now rising to the surface as he approached the end of his life.

Ironically, Peter's defiant moment occurred with the full participation of his own mother. In the first and only time either of his parents were featured in a diary, the September 16 segment began with Shirley and Peter sitting at his dining room table as Shirley described family photographs to him.

SHIRLEY: And there's one with your Dad, my goodness in '61 your Dad is 30 years old there. [THE CAMERA SHOWS A PHOTO OF BOB YOUNG WITH PREPUBESCENT PETER AND NANCY, AND THE FAMILY DOG] And there's Amos and Nancy and yourself. And you're kind of sitting at the side and you've got your [SHIRLEY BRINGS PETER'S HAND TO HIS FACE], you're holding your chin up, I don't know if you remember — you remember seeing that picture? That's really cute.

PETER: Where, where were we?

SHIRLEY: You look like Opie from the *Andy Griffiths Show.*

PETER [LAUGHS]: Where were we?

SHIRLEY: In Stanley Park.

PETER: Oh.

SHIRLEY: And there's one here of you in about Grade 11, lovely, wearing the hairstyle of the times [SHIRLEY LOOKS AT HER SON LOVINGLY], which is quite long, I'm sure not as long as you wanted it to be at the time ... [AN OVERHEAD SHOT REVEALS SHIRLEY FLIPPING THROUGH UBC GRAD PHOTOS] We've got some of your grad, medical grad ...

For the next scene, Paperny sat off camera and interviewed Shirley. She had no idea of her son's agenda when she agreed to be taped, and she thought he was asleep while they shot the scene. But Peter, lying on the living room sofa a few feet away, was listening to every word.

Whatever Peter is doing, he's happy doing. He took music, he was in Cubs and Scouts and swimming, he was a lifeguard, skied extremely well, always had a happy circle of friends around. To us it just seemed like a young man with a purpose, he's going to become a medical doctor. And naturally our hopes and dreams were that some day he would marry and give us grandchildren. That wasn't to be. Instead, we just got a super special son.

Later, in a clip that was never used, Shirley told Paperny that she wished Peter had told her earlier that he was gay, because she and Bob would have been more understanding once he became ill. After wrapping the scene, Shirley got up to leave for a few minutes on an errand. Peter waited until his mother had left the apartment, then bounced up from the couch, full of anger, and told Paperny to get the camera rolling. Shirley had come off far too innocent and clean-handed in the interview, he said. He felt she had ignored the question of his sexuality for 29 years because she never wanted to know he was gay, yet now she was making it sound like it was all his problem. Why didn't she acknowledge that there was real distance between them? Why didn't she talk about how difficult it was to deal with? Once Peter had calmed down, Paperny arranged the shot and the AIDS diarist was much more restrained in his commentary.

Realities can be different for everyone. There was the reality of who I was for my parents and the reality of who I was for me. And that meant growing up gay. Not an easy thing. I knew that I was attracted to men from a very young age. Actually a couple of years before my peers began discovering sexuality. So I couldn't discuss it with them; I couldn't discuss it with my family. When my friends started talking about women — girls — I thought "Well, this is all well and good but I'm not that interested." I couldn't relate.

I thought maybe this was some kind of phase that I was going through. So I decided that maybe I could convert myself. So I'd drag out my Dad's *Playboy* magazines and thumb through them, looking at the pictures. When I discovered that I was spending more time looking at the fully clothed Marlboro Man than I was looking at the completely naked female centrefold, I realized that's not what I was interested in, and it wasn't something that I was going to be able to change. So I put that all away, and decided that this was something that was going to have to be on hold.

My mother gave me a copy of *Ann Landers Talks to Teenagers About Sex.* There was a chapter in there on homosexuality. I can't remember the gist of most of it. I do remember the last line, however. It went something like this: "Well just thank God that you're normal." And I thought: "Who has she written this for?" It was just devastating. I wonder how many children of the fifties read that very line and were completely crushed, as I was.[3]

Peter hadn't said as much as he wanted to, but Bob and Shirley were struck by his diary when they saw it a few days later. In all those years he had never said a word about the Ann Landers book, and now he was complaining about it on television. "Typical," Bob smiled.

That same month, Peter sat down for his second videotaped interview with Michael Myers, the UBC psychiatry professor with whom he had taped an interview about living with AIDS two years earlier. That discussion had been dominated by Peter's optimistic outlook; in this interview he talked more about death and dying. "If someone said to me that 'you're going to die on December 25 at nine o'clock in the morning, but between now and then you will have perfectly good health and no limitation on what you can do,' I don't think I'd be an unhappy person at all," he told Myers. "But I could be here a year from that date and in the intervening year be incredibly limited in what I'm able to do and achieve, and I might not be so happy.

"Spiritually I feel prepared. I think I feel ready. I don't feel that there's any great existential questions that I haven't had answered for me. I'm 35 and it's maybe half of my three score and ten, but it's been a full half. There are two things that I regret as being fore-shortened: seeing my nieces and nephews grow up and the comple-tion of that cycle, and the continuing fulfillment of the relationship that I'm in." He had met Andy two years ago, he added — about the same time he did his first interview with Myers — "and in that two years, we've developed a really phenomenal, very complete and re-warding relationship. I kind of feel ripped off that that isn't going to be 25, 30 years. We've gone through a lot together in two years, prob-ably much more so than an average couple would do."

On October 15, the Open Learning Agency — a local college spe-cializing in distance education — held an extraordinary convocation of the board to present Peter with an honourary Doctor of Laws de-gree. Peter's acceptance speech showed signs that his odyssey was nearing its end. He required assistance as Harvey led him to the po-dium, and he had trouble finishing his sentences. "Today adds an-other dimension to the ... I guess the appreciation that is out there by honouring us with this very important honour ... as far as providing an educational service," he said. "And it just really, I think, nicely rounds it out for me, as far as where we've been able to head and the completeness with which a project like this can be done in such a simple fashion, and still get a message out there that is taken seriously and appreciated. So, I'd like to thank you very much."

By this time, media attention was entirely focussed on Peter's deter-iorating health. He looked awful. How were his spirits? reporters asked. Had he given up the fight? And if he did decide to let go, would he die the same way that David Lewis did — would he take his own life? "Dr. Peter's under a fair bit of scrutiny," Peter understated in an interview with the Vancouver *Sun* published October 31. "If there was any question about the cause of my death, it would prob-ably become known very quickly. I don't have any problem with be-ing given an increasing dose of morphine until such a time as I stop breathing."

21

Border Crossings

Despite his condition, Peter insisted on spending the Canadian Thanksgiving weekend on the Oregon coast. With oxygen tank in tow he left for the trip on October 16 accompanied by Andy, Nancy, Richard and Debbie Bebb, and two other friends. For Peter, this trip across the border was a final act of defiance. No matter how much this illness took away from him, no matter how many losses he experienced, he would prove that AIDS could not stop him from enjoying life. Staying at a friend's cabin not far from the ocean, he spent the entire weekend indoors, reminiscing with his companions and enjoying the warmth of the fireplace.

When the group returned from the trip on October 19, however, Peter was much shorter of breath, even when sitting in bed. He was vomiting and couldn't control his bowels. While Hiscox arranged for more home care nurses and rearranged the apartment for wheelchair access, Peter was once again admitted to St. Paul's. He was too sick for a bronchoscopy but was presumed to have PCP in addition to Kaposi's sarcoma. On October 21, with his pain out of control, his oxygen was doubled and his morphine increased. He finally agreed to rent a wheelchair and a commode, while an occupational therapist came in to install guard rails in the apartment. On October 23, the day Peter was released from hospital, he was taken to pick up his wheelchair. Five days later his morphine dose was increased again as he was having more vomiting, was still incontinent, and had ongoing fevers.

In October, AIDS Diary missed a week because of Peter's health. It was a sensitive issue for David Paperny. He wanted to leave the decision in Peter's hands but both he and Peter were afraid to stop the series because that would be an admission that his life was over. They agreed to leave their arrangement open-ended. "Even that week we took off, we didn't know he'd be back but we didn't want to pull the plug on him," said Paperny.

During a visit on October 27, Paperny and a cameraman left their equipment in the van while they talked to Peter about his condition. As Paperny's wife Audrey, the designated caregiver for that day,[1] attended to Peter's needs, the producer tried to convince him to keep the diaries going.

"Peter was insisting he didn't want to do a diary," Paperny recalled. "He was feeling lousy, he said he had nothing to say, he couldn't muster up any great thoughts, he was terribly weak. And I simply said 'Look, just tell us how you feel — people want to know. Even though you're feeling lousy and you've nothing to say except to tell how you're doing, for people out there [who are] very, very worried about you and want to know, then that's fine.' So he said he'd try it, so we went back and got the camera and set it up."

When the diary aired the following day, Peter looked worse than he had at any time in the previous two years.

> I was in hospital for five days last week ... another touch of pneumonia. Since I've been home, I've still had some pretty bad days ... I'm needing more oxygen than I did before, even just to lie around. And particularly when I've got a fever.
>
> The fevers — we've been trying to figure out what's been going on there for quite some time, and haven't found any answers. So they just have to be tolerated when they happen. But when they happen it's not very easy to tolerate ... It's difficult to cope with sometimes ... You never know what your day is going to be like. You might wake up with no fever, and it looks like

everything is going to be fine. Two hours later, you might be burning up, and in my circumstances that makes a huge difference in what I can do, how much I can move around ... It's getting to be a real struggle.[2]

When the diary was complete, it occurred to Paperny that this was the first time Peter had admitted to himself — let alone his TV audience and the people in his bedroom that day — that his odyssey was nearly over.

On Monday November 2, a new weekly current affairs program called *Witness* debuted with an hour-long documentary titled, simply, "Dr. Peter." Produced and directed by Paperny, the program was an impressive catalogue of Peter's most memorable diaries, combined with studio footage of the AIDS diarist reflecting on the past two years. The juxtaposition of the thin, tanned, and beautiful Peter of 1990 with the puffy, gray-skinned Peter of 1992 made for graphically dramatic television. Here the handsome Peter is proudly taking his new guide dog, Harvey, for a walk; there the depressed and heavily sedated Peter is lying in a hospital bed, wondering how much time he has left. Peter is shown skiing, learning to play the piano, arranging his will over a dinner with friends, and, finally, visiting his grave site in Duncan.

Throughout the condensed package of diaries, Peter's narrative tone remains determined, even as he realizes his time is up. In his closing comment he addresses the question most often asked of him: how long can the diaries go on? "The only end point I can see is that at which I no longer have the physical or emotional strength to do the diaries. And who can predict when that time will come?"

On November 3 Peter's spirits were high and he was confident enough to attend the annual B.C. AIDS Conference to deliver a speech. First, though, he decided to tape a diary in time for the next evening's broadcast. Dressed in a black turtleneck shirt with a gold necklace, and with oxygen tubes attached to his nostrils, Peter spoke with less effort and appeared in much better condition than he had in the previous diary.

As things progress and change with my illness, I have to progress and change as well in my expectations. One thing that I was resistant to — one thing amongst many, I guess — was the concept of having to use a wheelchair. I don't know why but I thought that this was a real step away from independence, and something that was ... irreversible. A step that was taken that you couldn't go backwards on, and I guess there's a certain amount of fear in allowing that to happen.

I didn't necessarily want to be banging around the apartment, I mean, particularly since I'm not really in any position to drive myself involves getting someone else to push me around and find out where I'm going to go. But I've come to realize in the last couple of weeks that I don't have a whole lot of choice. And as a matter of fact, when I came home from hospital the other day, we stopped and picked up a wheelchair on the way and ... what a relief. It made a huge difference in just getting around the apartment. But it's also become a necessity for getting out of here.

I've got a speaking engagement this afternoon and I'm going to have to go out. This involves going down a flight of stairs in my building. Now I can't go down in the wheelchair obviously but I do need to be carried down there in some capacity. And then once I get outside, I've got the freedom of the wheels.[3]

The camera kept rolling as Peter was taken out of his apartment by Jack Forbes, head of B.C. Children's Hospital's HIV pediatric care unit, and Michael Rekart of the provincial health department, with Nancy Hennessy following close behind. The final scene showed Rekart rolling Peter down the aisle toward the podium at the conference, with Harvey following close by. As the crowd rose in a standing ovation, Rekart recalled the conversation he had with Jay Wortman three years earlier, about the doctor with AIDS in their own clinic who was looking for something meaningful to do but didn't want his identity revealed. Now that same man was one of the most respected health educators in the province. The footage of Peter moving slowly toward the podium was the last glimpse viewers would have of the AIDS diarist. Diary 111 was the final installment, after more than two years, of a series that was only supposed to last a week.

In his untelevised speech, Peter addressed the issues of change and challenge, and of how he had to adjust to each new loss he experienced. Unlike the first five and a half years of his illness, he said, "the changes in the last six months have been coming very fast and have very much affected my ability to do things, have changed my expectations and put me on a different plane, I guess, as to where I'm at in the overall process of life and this illness."

> Change and challenge are two words that inspire a lot of people. But I can tell you right now that change and challenge are really shitty words [laughs]. You just get so damned tired of change, so damned tired of challenge; you just beg for some routine, for something that isn't going to change for a while, that you can just sit back and relax — take stock of things. Unfortunately, living with AIDS isn't like that ...

His talk was lucid and engaging; despite his exhausted physical appearance, Peter gave no indication of how close he was to death.

The following evening Phil Sestak dropped by for a house call. After increasing Peter's dose of morphine, he wanted to check his exercise tolerance. Peter attached his nasal prong, turned up the oxygen to six litres per minute (twice the normal concentration in air), and got up to take a few steps with his walker. He walked about two steps, turned around, and nearly collapsed. He was disoriented, confused, and frightened.

"Peter, you're really desaturating very quickly," Sestak told him calmly. "You have no oxygen reserve at all. You've only got enough [air] at the moment to keep you sitting comfortably. As soon as you try to exert yourself or do anything, you need to up your oxygen, and you need to recognize that you just don't have enough in your body to reach that point."

Peter listened quietly as he regained his composure. He didn't like what he was hearing, but he could no longer argue with the facts. The KS was irreversible and he was going to die very soon — within weeks, possibly even days. Sestak told him that, since it appeared he was going to die of respiratory failure, he should reconsider his decision to die at home. People who are in respiratory distress often become frightened and feel like they're drowning, he said. It's horrifying for both patient and caregivers.

But this was not what Peter wanted to hear. Was Sestak saying he had to go the hospital? What was the point of going to St. Paul's now? No drug was going to get him out of his bed, much less on a dance floor. And hospital hours were too structured; he wanted Andy to sleep beside him for every remaining night of his life. He wanted his friends and family to be near him, to talk to him, until the very end.

Sestak countered that it's difficult to manage a home death for respiratory failure unless the right amount of support services and people are in place. The death would be a burden on the caregivers and friends as much as the patient himself. But Peter was adamant: he would only go to hospital as a very last resort, if he felt his needs were beyond the capacity of his home care team. Andy agreed. If anything was crucial to Peter's — and his own — happiness, it was that the two remain together when the "final crossing" took place.

Sestak's hands were tied. He had great difficulty with Peter's decision, but he wanted to respect his wishes. And he had the additional stress of three other AIDS patients who were approaching the critical stages of their illnesses. "I really quickly recognized that I should get somebody else involved who's more expert in this than I was, who has way more expertise in managing terminal symptoms at home," he recalled. The next morning, November 5, he phoned Karen Gelmon at the cancer clinic and Dr. Jackie Fraser of St. Paul's palliative care unit, asking for their help with Peter's treatment. Fraser agreed to assess Peter, introduce shift nursing, and install a morphine pump for more efficient dosages. The following day Gelmon dropped by to reassure Peter: he needn't worry about dying at home as his quality of care would be excellent.

On Sunday November 8, Peter and Andy talked until 2 a.m. "You know, I don't know if I have the strength to go on," Peter told Andy. "Is it okay if I give up? Am I giving up?"

"Peter, it's okay and it's not giving up. If that's what you want to do, then I'll support you in that."

It was all he needed to hear. With a simple declaration of support from his partner, Peter decided to stop resisting the illness he had fought for six years. After spending so much time finding new ways to keep living, he could now concentrate, with no remorse, on dying.

On November 10 Peter told Andy and Nancy he didn't want visits from people who might encourage him to keep fighting. "Don't try to push me on," he told them. "I don't have the strength to explain why my time has come. It just has. I don't want anyone who's coming into this room to try and make me fight it." Fraser and Sestak arranged for a "Do not resuscitate" order, ensuring that no medical caregivers or paramedics would try to revive him if he suffered cardiac arrest or respiratory failure. Fraser put him on lorazepam to reduce his anxiety, and on November 11 she withdrew the IV fluids but continued dosages of morphine and lorazepam.

When his family arrived with a picnic lunch — it was Nancy's 37th birthday — he asked her to bring in the children so he could say goodbye to each one of them.

The following day, November 12, the morphine pump arrived and Peter was attached to it immediately. For the next three days he hovered comfortably in and out of consciousness.

I n those last few days, Peter's apartment was transformed into a sanctuary of friends, relatives, and caregivers. Food and drink were laid out in the dining room for visitors, candles were lit, and Beethoven piano sonatas played softly in Peter's bedroom. Maggie Johnston flew in from Ottawa at the end of October. It may not have been the "hundreds of grieving relatives" Peter had jokingly referred to months earlier, but the atmosphere was warm, almost festive. The presence of old friends, laughing and crying together just outside his bedroom, had a calming effect that allowed him to breathe more easily. And the humour he had always used to stay alive came back as he moved toward death.

"Nancy?"

"Yes Peter?"

"You remember when I broke my arm in Ottawa?"

"Yeah ... "

"And you remember how I told you that I had fallen off my bicycle?"

"Yeah ... "

"Well, that's not how I broke it ... ," he said, and went on to describe the incident in the Ottawa park.

E ver the doctor, Peter still had a few creative solutions for his own treatment. Tired of having to ask for help to pick up a drinking glass, he decided to have a portion of fresh water put into a saline drip so he could simply suck it out of the tube that was already in his mouth. "This is amazing," Jay Wortman said, coming out of his room. "The guy is close to death and he's still thinking of these ingenious feats of engineering to improve his comfort." On another visit, after spending a few hours with Peter, Wortman stopped at his door to say goodbye. "It's been grand, hasn't it?" he said, marvelling at the events of the last two years.

Peter sighed, turning to Wortman with a weary grin. "More like *grandiose*."

R ichard Bebb was talking with Maggie Johnston in Peter's bedroom when Peter suddenly blurted out, "All right, I've had enough of this shit. Let's get dressed and go to a movie. Only, don't invite Richard — I never liked him anyway." Bebb smiled and whispered in Peter's ear, "Listen, if you don't shut up I'm going to turn off the morphine." Peter woke up, startled and laughing, begging Bebb's forgiveness.

M ichael Simmonds was sitting in the bedroom when Peter began mumbling, "Where are the border crossings?" Simmonds was confused — what was he talking about? Peter persisted. "The border crossings? Where are they? How can I get through?"

"Oh," he finally replied. "The Peace Arch. Or Boundary Bay."

"And when are they open?"

Simmonds was stumped. "I'm sorry, Peter, I don't know."

"Well," Peter sighed, "when are the ferries crossing?" Later he spoke about parachutes, bus rides, and helicopters.

Jackie Fraser reminded Simmonds that when people are preparing to die — when they come to the point of acceptance — they'll go in and out of consciousness for days or weeks. They'll start to travel, to go on a journey, and they'll make preparations to embark on that journey, whether it's a walk, a bus ride, an airplane trip. There's usually a problem somewhere that prevents them from getting through. Instead of taking them too literally, friends should help them get through it.

T he plane's going," Peter said, "and we haven't got tickets." "That's okay Peter," responded Maggie Johnston, "the tickets are waiting for us at the airport."

"But what if you get there before me?"

"Don't worry, Peter. I'll wait."

On Saturday, with his condition worsening, family and friends took turns saying goodbye. By evening only a small group remained; Andy, Bob and Shirley, Nancy, Maggie, Richard, and Debbie all took a few moments alone with him. Earlier that day Peter had told his father he had no regrets about his life, but Bob could not respond. Now, facing his son for the last time, Bob told Peter he loved him. "I'm proud of you, Peter," he said. "I'm proud of your strength ... of how you've handled yourself, and what you've done these last two years. And," he added, "I'm sorry it took me so long to accept your sexuality."

Andy slept beside Peter throughout the night. Around 7 the next morning, he noticed a change in Peter's breathing and called the others into the room. Half an hour later on November 15, 1992, Peter quietly stopped breathing.

22

'The energy that is me will not be lost'

N ovember 24, 1992
John McKinstry, Peter's first boyfriend from 1977, felt like a stranger as he stood at the back of Christ Church Cathedral in downtown Vancouver. Unlike most AIDS memorials he had attended — he had buried at least 25 friends in the last decade — he could only identify about six gay men he knew among the crowd of 900 mourners at Peter's service. Looking over the aisles he saw a group of about a dozen blind people, all accompanied by guide dogs. There were throngs of pensioners, admiring high school students, and medical professionals, and in the front row, sharing the pews with Peter's family in full view of the CBC cameras, were the politicians.

"By his own example," said provincial Health Minister Elizabeth Cull, "Dr. Peter has shown how persons living with HIV/AIDS may do so with strength, courage, and dignity; and by so doing may break down society's barriers of homophobia, discrimination, and fear; and may unite communities and individuals in a common place of caring, understanding, and acceptance. Dr. Peter's work and commitment honour every British Columbian."

Neil Gray, the presiding Anglican priest whose respect for Peter had grown so much after their initial meeting at St. Paul's Hospital, saw Peter as a source of wisdom for the church. "The way Peter coped with disease, especially blindness, was a real reminder that there's nothing wrong with asking for help," said Gray. "We're encouraged to be strong, independent, to stand on our own two feet. We assume that if people can't do it on their own, that it's unnatural and weak. Peter's dignity when he had to ask for help was a real example to the church."

Such vulnerability, Gray added, was the embodiment of Christian values whether the church recognized it or not. "Whether it's baby Jesus in the manger or the vulnerability of Christ on the cross, the incarnation is God taking on our vulnerability, God setting aside his immunity. AIDS is something that can, if properly understood, really help the church to understand the way in which conventional understanding of power is challenged. Jesus helps us understand that power comes from vulnerability rather than striving to overcome that vulnerability. Peter realized that he didn't have to be strong."

Toward the end of the service Andy Hiscox walked to the podium accompanied by Peter's black Labrador guide dog, Harvey. "Peter was my very special friend, my partner and my lover," he said, coming out as a gay man for the first time in public. After thanking everyone who had supported Peter in the last two years of his life, Hiscox invited the congregation to join him in reciting the "Affirmation" that Peter had written shortly after his AIDS diagnosis.

As John McKinstry left the cathedral, contemplating the loss of his former lover, he noticed that the young woman in front of him was weeping uncontrollably. They were approaching the crosswalk on Georgia Street when the light changed to red and McKinstry stopped beside her. "How can you be so cold?" she asked him, shocked by his lack of any visible emotion.

McKinstry shrugged. "How can you be so hysterical?"

"Well, he was a great man — he did so much and now he's gone."

"Yeah, but did you know him?"

"Yes."

"How well?"

"I used to watch his diaries all the time."

The woman's response was not unusual; most of the 900 mourn-ers who had taken the afternoon off work to pay their last respects had only learned Peter's full name the previous week, through obitu-aries in the Vancouver Sun and Province, and the Toronto Globe and Mail. Peter's death was also mentioned in Time magazine, the New York Times, and Los Angeles Times. Unlike McKinstry, who had known him before he was "Dr. Peter," most people attending his memorial saw Pe-ter's death as the end of an intimate, one-way relationship that had gone on for two years.

The tributes hadn't stopped since the day after his death. On November 16, a special meeting of UBC medical students decided unanimously to have a plaque made in Peter's honour, to be placed in the lobby of the Medical School Alumni building on West Tenth Avenue. On the CBC Radio program *Almanac*, David Paperny joined Vancouver PWA Society president Brian Wade and AIDS Vancouver's education coordinator Rick Marchand, in summarizing Peter's contribution to AIDS awareness. "AIDS has always been very frightening to me," said Wade, then PWA president. "Over the last two years, seeing Dr. Peter on AIDS Diary gave me a lot of hope and removed that fear from me. Each diary I wondered what new thing he'd be doing — it was really exciting to see."

Marchand credited Peter for opening up the school system to allow better education by AIDS Vancouver. He reserved special praise for Peter's out-of-the-closet stance in schools. "We have this flip-flop that we do, where AIDS is affecting so many gay men but it's not a gay disease," said Marchand. "The [gay] movement struggles with trying to break through the homophobia and make sure the message gets through to the broader context. Dr. Peter broke through that."

Politicians were swift to respond, as well. At the provincial legislature in Victoria, Premier Mike Harcourt thanked Peter for providing British Columbians with "a rare glimpse of personal courage. For two years he challenged us to change our stereotypes, he challenged our attitudes and he challenged us to learn about the human costs of AIDS. Dr. Peter was also a physician who had hoped to dedicate his career to healing and to the prevention of suffering. Through his visionary segments on CBC and by sharing the last two years of his life with British Columbians, I believe he has fulfilled that goal."

Earlier that day in Canada's Parliament, Burnaby-Kingsway MP Svend Robinson — the country's only openly gay member of parliament — pointed out how Peter had "exemplified the remarkable caring, compassion and true family values of the gay community in fighting this epidemic."

On the same day, the B.C. Medical Association — which had done nothing to help him get a billing number for counselling — honoured Peter as "a remarkable man — an outstanding individual who brought honour to his chosen profession." The BCMA announced in December that it was establishing a $1000 bursary in Peter's name, to be awarded annually to a medical student at the University of British Columbia.

He was only one of about 1300 British Columbians to have died of AIDS when his illness finally overtook him, but Peter had burned his way into the public imagination like no other PWA before him. Indeed, "Dr. Peter" took on a life of his own through the mass distribution of his video legacy. While cassettes of the AIDS diaries were distributed in schools and translated into French, and Peter's ten-minute video *The Family Doctor's Role in HIV Management* was circulated by the College of Family Physicians of Canada, Michael Myers showed his two interview tapes with Peter at psychiatry conventions around North America.

Early in 1993 Home Box Office bought the rights to air the *Witness* documentary in the United States and flew David Paperny to New York for three weeks to edit the diary footage. The revised documentary, *The Broadcast Tapes of Dr. Peter*, aired in the U.S. on July 1, 1993, had several repeat showings, and was reviewed favourably in everything from the *Village Voice* and *People* magazine to leading newspapers across the U.S. The documentary was later broadcast in England and several other European countries, in Australia, and in parts of Asia. In January 1994 the film won three prizes at the Cable Ace Awards in Los Angeles. The awards, which honour excellence in cable television broadcasting in North America, chose *The Broadcast Tapes of Dr. Peter* for best documentary, best writer (Peter), and best host — beating out documentaries hosted by established Hollywood stars Katherine Hepburn and Glenn Close.

With so much success, it was only logical that HBO would put in a bid for an Academy Award. After the documentary was converted to film stock, all it took was a six-night run at a Pasadena movie house for *The Broadcast Tapes of Dr. Peter* to become eligible for an Oscar, and on February 9, 1994, it got the nomination. "I tried not to get myself too hyped up, too excited, because I didn't want to have expectations," said Paperny, who had told few people that the documentary was even submitted. As for Peter, he added, the AIDS diarist would have responded with characteristic pride: "Yahoo! We did it!"[1]

Although he would have been thrilled at this recognition from the TV and film communities, Peter had also been anxious that his legacy extend far beyond the television screen, that his name be used to help people living with AIDS. On November 10, 1992 — the same day he decided to stop fighting for his life — he asked Andy Hiscox and Nancy Hennessy to move up an announcement he had planned to make on World AIDS Day, December 1, establishing a new AIDS fund which would seek to provide "comfort care" for those PWAs who were less fortunate than himself.

"If all persons could be provided with the same degree of comfort care as I have been, then the Dr. Peter AIDS Foundation will have achieved that which government or society in general cannot provide," said Peter in a letter dictated to his sister. "There is no substitute for the ongoing involvement and support of caring people. Persons living with HIV and AIDS have needs greater than just survival." Peter's notion of "comfort care" would allow PWAs to live much more comfortable lives while fulfilling last wishes such as returning home, or visiting friends and family:

> As I have lived with AIDS during the last six years, I have been sustained by the love and support of so many people. In facing each new challenge, I have always been secure in this comfort care. There are, however, many people living with HIV and AIDS who do not have such good fortune ... Quality of life and well being are sometimes as simple as a trip to see family, a meal out with friends or being able to live the rest of one's life at home. You may be surprised to know that even these small goals are out of reach for many people living with the financial pressures of AIDS.[2]

In the press release two days later, Hennessy announced the Comfort Care Sponsor Program and the Dr. Peter Comfort Care Fund. The first was a plan to match long-term financial donors with people living with HIV or AIDS. The foundation, the sponsors, and the applicant would determine the appropriate program of comfort care. The Comfort Care Fund was the fundraising arm which would gather public donations for the program.

While donations to the fund began arriving almost immediately, there were grumblings from within the AIDS community about how that money would be spent. For one thing, the sponsor program description offered no indication which applicants would be eligible for "comfort care." For another, the fund's mandate to "fulfill short term needs" could possibly duplicate services already provided by the Vancouver PWA Society, AIDS Vancouver's Project Sustain, and the Positive Women's Network. Some activists also wondered why another AIDS foundation had been established without so much as a phone call to the Pacific AIDS Resource Centre (PARC); its member organizations could have provided much-needed advice on fundraising, allocation of funds, and other issues. Finally, the foundation's board of directors was composed entirely of Peter's inner circle. Apart from Nancy Hennessy, who had done work with the Nanaimo support group, only Jay Wortman had any long-term experience dealing directly with PWA organizations. The other directors were Andy Hiscox, David Paperny, and another friend, businessman Donald Hayes.

For most of 1993, donations piled up in a trust fund while foundation members took time to recover from Peter's death. Before developing a mission statement they had to solve one dilemma: how could they set up a system to meet individual needs of people with AIDS without soaking up valuable funds for office and administration expenses?

By summer the problem was solved. In February 1993 a group of AIDS service workers from the PARC had released a preliminary proposal for an integrated adult HIV daycare and treatment centre. The proposal stated that the increased longevity of people with AIDS had led to an increase in demand for hospital services. With the case load of AIDS patients at St. Paul's increasing tenfold in the past six years, the hospital was having to refuse patients or refer them to other hospitals with limited or no expertise in HIV treatment. The PARC proposal suggested a community-operated long-term daycare facility that would address the needs of people living with HIV, regardless of what stage they were facing in their illness. Approximately 40 places in adult daycare would be required.

When Jay Wortman phoned AIDS Vancouver the following July, he was only wondering whether the Dr. Peter AIDS Foundation would be eligible for federal grant money, to do its own needs assessment review. But his call was referred to Howard Engel, a member of PARC's board of directors, who promptly invited Wortman to their next meeting.

Before the end of the meeting both Dr. Peter AIDS Foundation members and the PARC board agreed that Peter's definition of "comfort care" could easily include many of the same ingredients as the PARC proposal on community-based HIV daycare. "The bells started going off for all of us," recalled PWA Society president Arn Schilder, one of the authors of the proposal. "This is where everybody could come together on common ground — [the Foundation] would actually be filling a void and not pulling away dollars from the AIDS community."

Wortman agreed. "It was exactly the right thing to do, because there was something they wanted and something we wanted." He felt the new idea was completely consistent with Peter's original vision. "I think Peter observed correctly that he had managed to maintain a rich quality of life during his illness, and not everybody had that, and that somehow his legacy would be able to add that to people's lives."

By the end of the year preliminary plans were in place for the Dr. Peter Day Centre, an ambitious project addressing the health and daily living needs of people with AIDS/HIV. The project was announced to the public on Oscar Night, March 21, 1994, timing that ensured the maximum public attention.

For Arn Schilder, the foundation's involvement with the centre served notice that Peter Jepson-Young had finally come home to the gay community. "The name has great value," said the longtime activist. "Face it: Peter was out of the closet, and he did it quite on his own. The final result is he's left a legacy that has the ability to make things happen even after his death, which is something that people [in the gay community] should not forget. This was his community, this is where he can demonstrate his belief structure. And I think he did give what he could, when he could."

It was the ultimate irony: after so much skepticism about Peter's involvement in the community, his activist critics were now, admittedly, "dancing on his bones," as Schilder put it: "He knew what the [PWA] Society would do with his name and image. He knew that it was a saleable product, and he knew that it had to be directed to something in AIDS and providing comfort to people living with HIV. So it's a bit of a gift at this point."

❖

A similar view of Peter's contribution was expressed by Chris Tyrell at a World AIDS Day function that Peter was hoping to attend before he died. Tyrell was taking in a "Day Without Art" event at the Vancouver Art Gallery on December 1, 1992, when he bumped into his old friend, Oraf. The artist stepped back and gave Tyrell his trademark glare. "I saw that piece you wrote about Dr. Peter," he said, referring to the warm tribute Tyrell had published in the Vancouver *Sun*. "It was all *too* kind of you. But I knew him before he had AIDS, and he wasn't such a saint, you know."

Tyrell smiled. "Well, that's the best part of the story, isn't it, Oraf? It just goes to show that there's hope for you and me."

Awards, Citations

○ Academy of Motion Pictures, Arts and Sciences (Oscar): *The Broadcast Tapes of Dr. Peter* received a nomination as best documentary feature.
○ ACE Award (American Cablevision): *The Broadcast Tapes of Dr. Peter* won in the category of best documentary, best writer, and best host.
○ Jack Webster Foundation Awards 1993: AIDS Diary's producer David Paperny was presented with a special jury award for excellence in broadcast journalism.
○ Honorary Doctorate of Laws from the Open Learning Agency
○ Province of British Columbia Exceptional Award of Merit
○ Canada 125 Commemorative Medal for outstanding Canadians
○ Commemorative Plaque from the UBC Medical Alumni
○ The James M. Robinson Memorial Prize (UBC) for significant contributions to public health
○ A Glass Sculpture tribute to Dr. Peter Jepson-Young from the Think AIDS Luncheon (UBC/St. Paul's AIDS Research Chair)
○ Communicator of the Year 1992 award from the International Association of Business Communicators
○ Treeplanting: the Ryan White Memorial AIDS Forest (The Jewish United Fund, Israel)
○ Honourary membership in the Rainbow Band (gay and lesbian orchestra) for Peter and Harvey

Author's Note

T he voice on the other end of the phone sounded slightly exhausted but playful. "Do you think it would be pretentious," an ailing Dr. Peter asked me on November 6, 1992, "if someone were to write my biography?" I wasn't fooled by his false modesty. "Don't be silly — it would be a great idea," I told him.

"Good," he said, "because I'd like you to write it." We were to meet the following week and begin taping interviews; the book would be an autobiography ghost-written by me.

But when I called Peter again the following Monday, it became clear that those interviews were never going to occur. "If I haven't phoned you by Wednesday," he sighed, "give me a call." By the time I finally reached Andy Hiscox by phone the following Saturday, November 14, Peter was hours away from death. At Andy's invitation, I went to the apartment in South Granville to spend a few moments by Peter's bedside.

We first met a year earlier when I was writing an article for the *Georgia Straight* on the media's homophobic AIDS coverage, but we hadn't spoken in more than eight months when I called him on November 6. I had left Vancouver the previous March to spend half a year living and writing in England, and we didn't keep in touch. He had been thinking of doing a book for several months, but I had no idea that he had chosen me to do it. I was honoured by his request, given that we had only known each other since the previous fall.

The first thing he asked me when I introduced myself on the phone in November 1991 was whether I had a brother named Robert. I did. It turned out that the two had briefly shared the same Grade 10 math class in Nanaimo, nineteen years earlier. Peter remembered Rob because he had a crush on him. "Do you look anything like him?" he asked me. "Yes, Peter," I lied. "Exactly like him." (In truth, the muscular Robert would have been far more to his taste.) Peter's strength of recall was impressive: the memory of a beautiful face hadn't faded in two decades. My brother, for his part, had no idea of Peter's lustful eye at the time, and when I told him about it later, Robert couldn't even recall the adolescent Peter Young of 1972. Only when I showed him Peter's school photo did he finally remember him, and he was stunned by the transformation: unable to reconcile the bright-eyed teenager with the puffy-faced AIDS diarist of 1991. Later I discovered that Peter had been confirmed an Anglican at a church only three blocks away from my childhood home, and that my own family probably had bank accounts at the branch managed by Peter's father.

Despite having seen many of the diaries, which I usually found informative, my impression of Peter before our first meeting was that he was completely isolated from the local AIDS community. Since moving to Vancouver's West End in 1989, I had been led to believe that the key people — both politically and in terms of media exposure — were the gay activists whose efforts had sprung from years of involvement in neighbourhood politics. As a resident of the gay ghetto myself, I quickly learned that the real "heroes" of our community were people like Kevin Brown, Greig Layne, David Lewis, Alex Kowalski, Pei H. Lim and Joe Ford, whose stories were passed on like legend after they died. On Davie and Bute streets, Brown in particular was remembered for his bold lobbying of the right wing, homophobic Social Credit government; he did this from a proudly defiant, out-of-the-closet gay position, and he did it long before AIDS became a chic issue in the mainstream press. Thus, my impressions of Dr. Peter were heavily influenced by the Kevin Brown standard.

Sitting with his guide dog Harvey in Barney's Cafe on Granville, he didn't strike me as any different from other people with AIDS I'd met; I was quickly impressed by his self-deprecating wit and his complete willingness to criticize public figures on the record. Truly a reporter's delight. After our first interview we developed an easy rapport based on our similarly middle-class backgrounds and our passion for eating: I marvelled at how easily a blind person could bake a three-cheese quiche to perfection, as Peter did when we met for a second interview. He also had a dark sense of humour and was a big fan of *Sodomite Invasion Review*, a gay literary journal to which I contributed. After his partner Andy read him selections from our third issue, Peter told me he wanted to contribute something for a later edition — a "sexy monologue" using the same narrative voice as the AIDS Diary, but with a twist. He would sign it Peter Jepson-Young, his real name, because most members of the public knew him as "Dr. Peter" and wouldn't realize they were the same person. We laughed over that one.

By the time I spoke to Peter on November 6, 1992, my opinion of his role in the AIDS community had changed considerably. The ghosts of Kevin Brown, David Lewis, and others may have lingered over the gay community, but Peter had been admitted to the mainstream public imagination like none of these men before him.

The reasons for this, in retrospect, seem embarrassingly superficial. The fact that Peter was white, middle class, conventionally masculine, and a doctor ensured that his discussion of AIDS would not alienate his largely white, middle-class viewers where a similar address from an explicitly political gay activist might have done. The fact that he was a doctor as well as a patient reassured his viewers that they were getting the goods on AIDS from a qualified "expert." And his most endearing qualities — his sense of humour, his optimism, and his resilience in the face of blindness and AIDS (some observers noted how Peter could describe his illness without showing any of the pain) — ensured that viewers came to like and trust him, where anger or suffering would have had them reaching for the channel changer. At least, that's what the powers-that-be at CBC would have us believe.

Ultimately, Peter's achievement was to build a bridge between gay and straight worlds. He recognized that gay men could not confront governments or change attitudes entirely in isolation; there had to be some sense of interaction with his viewers, some way of expressing his trust in them. This approach won many people to the cause of AIDS awareness and prevention, but it had its down side as well. There are still those among Peter's thousands of viewers, for example, who do not want to admit that their hero contracted AIDS through sex rather than immaculate conception. The same people would prefer not to know that Peter had a sex life at all; they would rather see his "gayness" as a matter of personal style and manners, completely divorced from bodily experience.

After an article I wrote about Peter was published in *Western Living* magazine, several friends of Bob and Shirley Young were upset by the description of Peter's pre-AIDS lifestyle. One of them, in a profoundly homophobic statement, said it destroyed the good work that Peter had done because it confirmed his own stereotypes of gay men. A couple from Calgary phoned Bob and Shirley to offer condolences, hoping they had recovered from the "vicious" article which could not possibly have been written by a friend of Peter's; a nurse who knows Shirley had difficulty believing the article was written by Peter's chosen biographer, since the article appeared to be so homophobic — she thought that the discussion of critical response to Peter was, in itself, homophobic. (This was rather amusing, since I have often been accused of gay chauvinism.)

These reactions prove just how much education still needs to be done. Does the ultimate value of Peter's work truly depend on whether straight people think he was a saint? I think not. Until straight people in North America come to terms with the impact of homophobia in all areas of society, I believe we will never fully understand why AIDS is still destroying so many lives, gay or otherwise.

Peter merely opened the door to that discussion.

❖

I n the year it took to produce this book, I depended on the time, resources and feedback of many people. Peter's family had the hardest job of all, sharing their memories, letters and photographs so soon after Peter's death. I am especially indebted to his partner, Andy Hiscox, who was always generous with time and resources, even as he grieved his loss; to his parents, Bob and Shirley Young, who showed considerable courage in confronting their own role in Peter's development; and to his sister and brother-in-law, Nancy and Lionel Hennessy, who cooperated at every stage of research.

Dr. Phil Sestak, despite a patient load of several hundred, managed to contribute not only a comprehensive account of Peter's medical history — a gesture that required official clearance from the B.C. College of Physicians and Surgeons — but also a wealth of information on AIDS itself, translating some of the more clinical details of HIV into plain English. Dr. Jay Wortman was also a key source, both in terms of his own role in the birth of AIDS Diary and as an observer of B.C. medical politics and the AIDS epidemic.

A very special thanks to David Paperny. Aside from giving me unlimited access to videotapes of the diaries and documentaries, leading me to other sources, and spending several hours over interviews and offering feedback at various stages of the writing, David showed considerable respect in recognizing our opposing functions as journalists: his job as AIDS Diary producer was to package and construct a man's life on television; my job as biographer was to get behind and deconstruct that same life. I think we both learned a lot about each other's work in the process; surely one of David's shrewdest moves was to videotape me in a similar "diarist" position as Peter's for a CBC news feature series on gay life in British Columbia. Although I had already done a television news story as a reporter, David knew that this project would give me the same sense of storytelling that Peter experienced.

In terms of the writing, special thanks should go to the Explorations Program of the Canada Council, which provided the grant that allowed me to write this book. I should also single out Rolf Maurer and Audrey McClellan at New Star, who believed in the book from the very beginning. Audrey, my editor, was exactly the calm voice of reason this project required; her patience and humour will always be an example to me. I'm also indebted to several writers, including Stan Persky, David Watmough, Kevin Griffin, Tom Sandborn, Anne Cameron, Alan Alvare, and the editor of *Sodomite Invasion Review*, Don Larventz, for advice, argument, and input. Others in the gay and lesbian community have cheered on this project, and I truly appreciate their support.

There are many friends in Vancouver and elsewhere who invited me for dinners and heard me talk endlessly about this project before I actually wrote it. To these people, I thank you for your endurance.

A final, special thanks should go to my poet friend and language cop for the last ten years, J. Marc Piché, and to *mon beau*, C.R., who remained upbeat in his encouragement despite losing his best friend, and two others, to AIDS. The two of you may share this book's dedication with my parents, Paul and Jeanine Gawthrop, without whom ...

> *Daniel Gawthrop*
> *Vancouver, B.C.*
> *Easter 1994*

Footnotes

Introduction

1. The Lions is a mountain peak north of Vancouver overlooking Howe Sound.

Chapter 1: Small Town Boy

1. *Anne Landers Talks to Teen-Agers About Sex.* Prentice-Hall, 1963.

2. During this time, Peter's concept of gay survival was similar to the "straight-looking, straight-acting" ethos that Kopay acknowledged in his book. This assimilationist approach would cause problems later in his life, as it did for Kopay. As co-author Perry Deane Young explained, Kopay "was caught in a lie between the masculine myth he so beautifully personified in public and the private reality of his life. His anxiety was so intense, he could actually feel the change about to happen ... He knew intuitively that he was about to make a move, but he did not know exactly when or how. He only knew it had to do with the lies he had been forced to live with." *The David Kopay Story: An Extraordinary Self-Revelation*, by David Kopay and Perry Deane Young. Arbor House, 1977.

3. Bob recalled one time when he invited a flamboyant — but straight — friend over for dinner. Peter, then 17, got angry at his father and pointed out the man's gay mannerisms. Bob later saw this as an early sign of Peter's inner conflict.

Chapter 2: Lifting the Mask

1. By 1993 the vast majority of the 250 men who tested positive from the sample of 770 men in the lymphadenopathy study had died.

2. Peter's conversations with Michael Myers, October 1990.

3. This condition was later described in the *Canadian Medical Association Journal* (vol. 140, pp. 173-174), in an article specifically relating to Peter's case.

253

Chapter 3: Freelancing

1. Despite an encouraging response from Chan, no medical jurisdiction in Canada had developed guidelines for physicians with HIV by early 1994.
2. Phil Sestak letter to Ava Hillier, March 23, 1990.
3. Peter Jepson-Young letter to Flora Hillier, March 4, 1989.
4. This creative visualization was an example of positive thinking that would have done Shirley Young proud. Peter had learned this method of healing from his mother, who he and his friends affectionately called "Space Age Shirl" for such homespun aphorisms as: "Now you just take that negativity and wrap it up in white light and send it away!"
5. Peter Jepson-Young journals, March 20, 1989 and March 30, 1989.

Chapter 4: Going Blind

1. Peter's conversations with Michael Myers, October 1990.
2. AIDS Diary 42, June 5, 1991.

Chapter 5: Going Public

1. The New York *Times*, July 6, 1990, p. A11.
2. The CBC would make an exception two years later when Peter was paid for his work on an hour-long documentary. The fact that the issue of payment never came up earlier was an indication, according to Paperny, of how the corporation brass never expected the AIDS Diary to become a long-lasting series. If Peter had asked to be paid, he added, the CBC would probably not have objected. He was, after all, preparing script ideas, consulting regularly with Paperny, and devoting several hours a week to taping the segments — the same kind of work many staff reporters perform.
3. Peter's conversations with Michael Myers, October 1990.
4. The case of the Florida dentist, David Acer, inspired a campaign for mandatory testing of all health care workers. His case and that of his most famous patient, Kimberly Bergalis, are discussed in more detail in Chapter 13.

Chapter 6: On the Air

1. The phrase "Sodomite invasion" was first coined in reference to the Gay Games by the Burnaby Christian Fellowship-sponsored *Life Gazette* (November 1988) as part of a smear campaign against openly gay Burnaby MP Svend Robinson. The front-page article blamed the influential Member of Parliament for the gay-friendly atmosphere that allowed such an event to occur. The journal argued that the presence of so many homosexuals in one place would result in a massive AIDS scourge and would corrupt all the Lower Mainland's children. "Sodomite Invasion" was later reclaimed by a local group of gay male writers for the title of its literary publication: *Sodomite Invasion Review*.
2. "Vancouverites should be proud that this event is being held in their city, for it is an important reaching out," the *Province* editorial read. "Almost a year ago, we called these games 'silly.' What's next? we asked. Bisexual games? Asexual games? What, we queried, does sexual orientation have to do with the high jump? Since then, we've been educated. We've learned that these games are intended to build bridges, strengthen community and bolster self-esteem ... It is not for us to question — so long as others are not being hurt — how the

homosexual community chooses to celebrate itself and to educate us, any more than it is our place to question how native Indians or blacks or women choose to define and refine themselves." Vancouver *Province*, July 31, 1990, p. 26.

3. Terry Fox, who lost a leg to cancer, became a Canadian hero in 1980-81 when he attempted a cross-country run to raise funds for cancer research. His media profile remains untarnished. Steve Fonyo, after completing the run that Fox was too ill to finish himself, was constantly dogged by an image of arrogance and opportunism. Following his run in 1985, his problems ranged from drunk driving charges to academic failure and career uncertainty.

4. His fear was not entirely unfounded. Within weeks of the series debut, Peter was leaving his apartment for a checkup at St. Paul's when he was stopped on 16th Avenue by a woman who had noticed his white cane as she drove by. She rolled down her car window: "Hey, aren't you that guy on TV?" Peter accepted her offer to drive him to the hospital and enjoyed talking with her children in the car. When he came out from his appointment, the woman was still waiting. She drove him back to his apartment, left her children in the car, and escorted him inside, where she began coming on to him. She only left when Peter told her his lover was returning at any minute.

Chapter 7: 'AIDS is not a focus in my life'

1. The message took a while to reach some of his friends. Joan, a 62-year-old friend of Peter, hadn't seen him for several months when she watched him announce in Diary 7 that he was going blind. Joan called up Flora Hillier in distress. "He looks so awful," she exclaimed. "Can't you get him off those bloody diaries? They're exploiting him."

"No they're not," Hillier replied. "He's fine."

2. Letter to Peter, March 4, 1992.

3. The tape was later reviewed favorably in the Washington, D.C., publication *Hospital and Community Psychiatry* (September 1992, vol. 43, no. 9). "Many of the concerns and learning points highlighted in this videotape," the review said, "are relevant to other chronic and life-threatening illnesses in which themes of loss, fear, denial, death and dying, and euthanasia challenge patients and health care professionals alike."

Peter consented to make this tape available to health care professionals. Inquiries should be directed to Dr. Michael Myers, c/o 405-2150 West Broadway, Vancouver, B.C. V6K 4L9.

Chapter 8: 'Being blind has been a real eye-opener'

1. Peter Jepson-Young's journal, August 6, 1987.

2. Vancouver *Sun*, December 10, 1990, p. C8.

Chapter 9: 'I've never bought into organized religion'

1. *North Shore News*, January 16, 1991.

2. AIDS Diary 22, January 9, 1991.

3. AIDS Diary 16, November 28, 1990.

4. AIDS Diary 28, February 20, 1991.

5. AIDS Diary 29, February 27, 1991.

6. AIDS Diary 78, March 11, 1992.

7. AIDS Diary 37, April 24, 1991. In retrospect, Bob and Shirley Young suggested the

more likely reason there was so little response to their son's joke was that the congregation was composed almost entirely of seniors, many of whom may have had hearing problems.

8. Cassette to Peter, November, 1992. The man did not, incidentally, reveal his position on female pornography.

9. Letter to Peter, July 30, 1991.

Chapter 10: The Mister Rogers Approach

1. New York *Times*, June 13, 1993, p. 30. The writer, Jeffrey Schmalz — one of the few daily newspaper reporters in the U.S. to write about his own journey with AIDS — died within months of writing this article, on November 6, 1993. His parting message was a desperate plea for more urgent action by the National Institutes of Health, the scientific establishment, and the gay community that was published in a posthumous article on November 28.

2. Peter was somewhat more forthcoming about ACT-UP in an interview for the Vancouver weekly *Georgia Straight* in November 1991. The activist organization, he said, was "an appropriate group in the States [where] you've got this society in which there's such an incredible disparity between rich and poor, there's no socialized medicine, there's no coverage for people [and] drug companies are basically using this to their advantage to make a quick buck. I think that ACT-UP has done a lot of good things in the States, particularly in the area of drug access." In Canada, he argued, more people "react to them with revulsion. Sadly, they play upon a lot of the misconceptions about AIDS [by] spitting on people or throwing ketchup as symbolic of blood. It's implying that we have the ability to infect you if you don't treat us properly, infect you in some casual contact way. And I think that's really negative." From the *Georgia Straight*, November 29-December 6, 1991, and conversations with the author.

3. AIDS Diary 47, July 17, 1991.

4. AIDS Diary 52, August 14, 1991.

5. Michael Myers letter to Kit Henderson, January 2, 1991.

6. C.B. Henderson letter to Michael Myers, February 5, 1991.

7. Peter Jepson-Young letter to Hedy Fry, April 9, 1991.

8. AIDS Diary 56, September 18, 1991.

Chapter 11: Taking It to the Schools

1. "Dr. Peter: A humble hero shares his story," by Barry Dumka, *Living Well*, Fall 1992.

2. AIDS Diary 79, March 11, 1992.

3. An example of the stereotypical judgments that were made is provided by Rick Waines, a hemophiliac and former president of the Vancouver PWA Society, who often addressed high school students on HIV issues. In one series he criticized the practice of putting people in "buckets": straight people who got the virus through blood transfusions were always put into the "acceptable" bucket, while gays, drug users, and prostitutes were put into the "disposable" bucket. Despite Waines's message that putting people in buckets, or categorizing them in any way, is wrong, the attractive, urbane young activist was asked in three of six presentations which "bucket" he belonged to. Reluctantly, he would answer that he was straight. Teachers later reported that some students returned to class after the talk and said, "He's lying. You can tell by the vest he's wearing."

4. AIDS Diary 45, June 26, 1991.

5. AIDS Diary 46, July 3, 1991.

6. AIDS Diary 39, May 15, 1991.

Chapter 12: The Fruits of Fame

1. In a later documentary, Andy appears in a group scene in which Peter is preparing his living will. Andy is referred to as "another friend."

2. AIDS Diary 44, June 19, 1991.

3. AIDS Diary 48, July 17, 1991.

4. Peter was lucky to enter the United States with no harassment from customs officials; under the terms of U.S. infectious disease control legislation, foreign residents with HIV were banned from entering the U.S. Presumably Peter's nondescript appearance and discreet storage of AZT pills in his overnight bag prevented him from blowing his cover. In any case, Peter had no problem getting across the border the many times he entered the U.S. after 1986. To the average customs official he probably looked like a slightly ailing, middle-aged blind man.

5. AIDS Diary 54, August 28, 1991.

Chapter 13: On the Firing Line

1. Acer told health officials he didn't believe he infected anyone, but did notify his patients of his illness just before he died on September 3, 1990.

2. AIDS Diary 49, July 24, 1991. Peter was not the only health care professional to suggest that the late David Acer may have intentionally infected his patients. Vancouver dentist John Hardie raised the possibility when he addressed a February 1991 meeting of the CDC. But the theory was not explored in the media until June 14, 1993, when the Florida Dental Association revealed that a sixth patient of Acer's, an 18-year-old woman, had recently tested positive while undergoing a routine examination for military service. "Unlike the five earlier patients," an Associated Press wire report said, "she had undergone no 'invasive' procedures such as root canals or extractions in routine visits to Acer that began when she was 13."

3. Vancouver *Province*, November 13, 1991, p. A5. As of December 1993, at least seven other doctors with AIDS had practised in B.C. before dying.

4. By 1985, the U.S. military was treating 195 patients officially diagnosed with AIDS or AIDS-related complex [ARC]. On October 24 of that year, Defense Secretary Caspar Weinberger ordered the largest screening program in the world, ultimately testing all 2.1 million active-duty personnel. By late 1987 at least 3336 military personnel had tested positive, including five colonels at West Point and a sergeant major who handled public affairs for the invasion of Grenada. Journalist Randy Shilts's account of gays and lesbians in the U.S. military, *Conduct Unbecoming: Gays and Lesbians in the U.S. Military* (St. Martin's Press, 1993), suggests that the Pentagon's chief concern in its decision to invoke mandatory testing was not the health of service personnel but, rather, damage control: it had to prevent the possible revelation that "gays were not only a crucial part of every branch of the military but in the possession of some of the most sensitive of military jobs."

5. New York *Times*, June 6, 1993, p. E1.

6. Conversations with the author, November 1991.

7. The New York *Times*, September 27, 1991, p. A1, A12. Jeffrey Leui, policy director of

the AIDS Action Council, was somewhat more blunt in his assessment of the Bergalis bill: "Her case is being used by some of the right wing forces to rekindle some of the fear that has always been lurking under the surface about AIDS."

8. Kimberly Bergalis died on December 8, 1991.

Chapter 14: *The Reluctant Activist*

1. AIDS Diary 61, October 23, 1991.

2. AIDS Diary 63, November 6, 1991. The former Social Credit government finally relented in 1988 when AIDS organizations and local health authorities received grants for support services. But there was a catch. "I was told 'You can have this money, but you must continue to criticize the provincial government'," says Vancouver health officer John Blatherwick. Socred health ministers "were authorizing grants that I could give to AIDS Vancouver for some pretty innovative street-type programs. But I was told by people in the ministry that I was not allowed to give them credit for it." In the twisted logic of Social Credit, it was acceptable to do the right thing — so long as the government was not seen by the voters to be supporting homosexuals.

As for the New Democrats, little had changed by 1994 as far as AIDS funding went, but the NDP government did amend the provincial Human Rights Code in 1992, as promised, to prohibit discrimination based on sexual orientation.

3. AIDS Diary 77, February 26, 1992. He could have added that involvement with AIDS groups demanded more time than he could give — his schedule of speaking engagements often took him out of town.

4. *Xtra*, May 1992, p. XS 23.

5. Schilder was ultimately willing to agree with this reasoning. "It was his path and his journey, and he's given something back to the community," the PWA president said in 1993. The legacy of AIDS Diary — which would include plans for an adult daycare centre for people with AIDS — was far more important than how its author expressed his community politics, Schilder said.

6. The series of riots that began on June 27, 1969, at the Stonewall Inn — a popular gay bar in New York City — is commonly considered the spark that ignited the modern gay liberation movement. A group of gays and lesbians, angered by continual police brutality and an aggressive campaign to shut down the city's gay bars in advance of the World's Fair, fought back with bricks and stones. Their protest forced the police campaign to end.

7. This criticism rarely considers how the sexual revolution of the 1960s and 1970s dominated the culture at large, and that there were and are many heterosexuals who could easily count their sexual partners in the hundreds.

8. Conversations with the author, February 7, 1992.

9. Diary 58, October 2, 1991.

Chapter 15: *Season of Protest*

1. *Georgia Straight*, November 29-December 6, 1991, p. 7.

2. Press reports shortly before Liberace's 1987 death from AIDS quoted the musician's publicist saying that Liberace's emaciated condition was due to a bizarre diet consisting mostly of fruit.

3. The following February charges against the prostitute were stayed. In the judge's ruling, HIV-positive prostitutes were declared a health problem, not a criminal matter. The revised Section 7 of the Health Act stated that criminal charges would only be laid against sexual "predators" or those considered to be deliberately trying to spread the virus.

4. Korn, like other sperm bank doctors, had learned through an article in the British medical journal *The Lancet*, that two Australian women had tested positive for HIV after receiving sperm donations. The revelation caused Korn to shut down his clinic until he had tested all his regular donors.

5. BCTV is the CTV network affiliate in Vancouver, and is CBC's main competition in B.C.'s Lower Mainland.

6. Soles, who later joined CNN, was a former CKVU television reporter in Vancouver who had won the prestigious Peabody Award for his 1988 documentary "AIDS and You." He was also one of the first broadcasters to submit a proposal to Jay Wortman when Peter was first looking for a television venue. Wortman and Peter both rejected Soles's idea, for a one-hour series of public service announcements from various people with AIDS, because they thought it was too sensational.

7. Kyle said he had two friends who were visiting these countries who learned of the story when they read his name in the local papers.

8. In fact, it was one of the lawyers, not the judge, who named Kyle in the action.

9. Conversations with the author, February 7, 1992.

10. Letter to Peter, November 27, 1991.

11. Christmas card to Eric Kyle from Kobe ter Neuzen, 1991. Kyle's troubles may not have ended with the conclusion of the case in 1991. On June 21, 1993, the B.C. Court of Appeal overturned the decision that awarded damages to Kobe ter Neuzen. A retrial date was pending and many of Peter's questions about the ethical and moral dilemmas posed by sperm donation remained unanswered.

Chapter 16: Voices Denied

1. In 1990 a number of HIV-positive hospital workers were asked to move their support group meetings out of the hospital, lest it create the impression the church was "advocating a homosexual lifestyle." Reported in *Xtra*, February 1992, XS section.

2. The friend in question asked not to be identified. "Church people don't want their names to stand," he said, "because of the sensitivity of the issues involved and the possible repercussions to their careers."

3. Metzger made headlines in 1992 when he parted company with his Anglican church superiors to be in a gay relationship. He left the active priesthood to protest church policy, becoming the third Anglican priest in Canada to come out of the closet.

4. *The Vancouver Sun*, October 28, 1993, pp. A1-2.

5. AIDS Diary 66, December 4, 1991.

6. AIDS Diary 32, March 20, 1991.

Chapter 17: 'No one has ownership of this disease'

1. Letter to Peter, May 29, 1992.

2. Letter to Peter, May 20, 1992.

3. AIDS Diary 71, January 15, 1992.

4. AIDS Diary 98, July 29, 1992. St. Paul's Hospital eventually returned to Burroughs Wellcome as its AZT supplier when the multinational company lowered its price.

5. Interview with the author, *Xtra*, May 1992. Michael Callen remained steadfastly opposed to AZT until his death, more than a year after Peter's, on December 27, 1993. And AZT remained a controversial drug. At the 1993 International AIDS Conference in Berlin, a group of scientists released a clinical trial of 1749 HIV-positive people who had been separated into two "blind" groups: those who started taking AZT early and those who started long after they were diagnosed. The study showed no clinical difference between starting AZT early or late; the progress to AIDS and death rates were the same for both groups. The study was discredited by many in the medical establishment for, among other reasons, failing to include non-AZT users for comparison purposes, but more recent studies have indicated that a high number of PWAs have suffered damaging side effects as a result of taking the drug.

6. Letter to Shirley Young, January 10, 1986.

7. Peter's conversations with Michael Myers, October 1990.

8. AIDS Diary 13, November 7, 1990. Peter had also shared this view with a Simon Fraser University criminology graduate named Russel Ogden. Ogden's thesis, which was completed in early 1994, documented 34 cases of assisted AIDS suicide, 29 of which had taken place in British Columbia. His study received front page coverage in the Vancouver *Sun* on February 12, 1994 — the same day that Sue Rodriguez, a Vancouver Island woman suffering from Lou Gehrig's disease, was assisted in suicide by an unnamed doctor. The death of Rodriguez, whose two-year campaign to legalize euthanasia raised public awareness of the issue, inspired calls for a free vote on the issue in the House of Commons.

Chapter 18: Taking Stock

1. From "AIDS and the Man" by Dan Ferguson, *Vancouver* January 1992.

2. Evans, who has well-groomed black hair and a neatly trimmed moustache, has frequently been described by newsroom insiders and news viewers as "the Mountie." Peter found this amusingly ironic given the post-modern, homoerotic reading of Royal Canadian Mounted Police mythology that "the Mounties always get their man."

3. Audrey Mehler, Paperny's wife, paid $550 for one of the two paintings at an event that raised approximately $20,000 for AIDS Vancouver.

4. AIDS Diary 84, April 15, 1992.

Chapter 19: Long-Term Survivor

1. AIDS Diary 69, January 2, 1992.

2. Peter Jepson-Young letter to Flora Hillier, March 4, 1989. Hillier was surprised by the finality of Peter's decision about Marty, given that the two men had so much in common. "He was just like Marty but he learned to hate him," she said. Perhaps, she said, Peter recognized a side of himself in Marty — a popular A-list party animal — that he didn't want to remember.

3. AIDS Diary 89, May 27, 1992.

4. AIDS Diary 91, June 10, 1992.

5. AIDS Diary 95, July 8, 1992.

Chapter 20: Dying with Dignity

1. Peter was paid about half of the $38,000 budget. Other than a small stipend for a French translation, this was the only time he was paid for any of his work on the diaries. Since it was clear that AIDS Diary would have a life beyond Peter, the CBC wanted to ensure it retained the rights to further broadcasts and licencing, and this payment effectively bought out Peter's rights to the series. However, the CBC has agreed to pass on royalties from future sales to the Dr. Peter AIDS Foundation.

2. AIDS Diary 107, September 30, 1992.

3. AIDS Diary 105, September 16, 1992.

Chapter 21: Border Crossings

1. In the last year of Peter's life, Paperny had grown close enough to his subject that he and his wife, Audrey Mehler, socialized often with him. Toward the end, Audrey joined a small group of Peter's friends who took turns attending to his home care needs.

2. AIDS Diary 110, October 28, 1992.

3. AIDS Diary 111, November 4, 1992.

Chapter 22: 'The energy that is me will not be lost'

1. The Vancouver Sun, February 10, 1994, p. A2. The Oscar went to *I Am a Promise: The Children of Stanton Elementary School*.

2. From Peter's final public statement, November 10, 1992.

Index

262

The Broadcast Tapes of Dr. Peter

The Academy Award nominated video documentary

"A spiritual chronicle" — *New York Times*
"Quietly courageous . . . A remarkable achievement" — *USA Today*
"Unforgettable" — *Daily Variety*

T hrough a series of video diary entries and interviews, this moving documentary chronicles the journey of Dr. Peter Jepson-Young. Known simply as "Dr. Peter," this man of extraordinary courage made public his personal fight against AIDS to become one of Canada's foremost educators in this field.

In this condensed version of the video diaries, Dr. Peter discusses with disarming candour and humour the many issues surrounding his life and illness, including his relationship with his family, his sexuality, and his spirituality. He does not ask for pity, rather for understanding. He explains that his greatest hope in sharing his private battle is to educate the public, to fight misconceptions about the disease and its sufferers, and to mobilize people while sensitizing them to the need for AIDS research.

Producer/Director: David Paperny
Writer: Dr. Peter Jepson-Young
Running Time: 46 minutes (approx.)
A CBC production in association with HBO

Available

In Canada from:
CBC Educational Sales
Box 500, Station A
Toronto, ON
M5W 1E6
416-205-6384

In the U.S. from:
Direct Cinema Ltd.
P.O. Box 10003
Santa Monica, CA 90410
USA
1-800-525-0000
Also available: *The Dr. Peter Diaries*, four cassettes containing the original 111 video diaries, 285 minutes.